**FAIRFAX
COUNTY
CHAMBER
OF
COMMERCE**

On behalf of its large, diverse, and progressive business community, the Fairfax County Chamber of Commerce welcomes you to Fairfax County, Virginia. We are proud of our community, and through the pages of this book you will learn of our many reasons for that affection. We invite you to share with us the pride and sense of community that typifies life in Fairfax County.

When some people think of Fairfax County, they tend to dwell on our past. A rich past it is, with the roots of the American Revolution firmly planted in our soil, soil that would later see much of the terrible fighting of our nation's Civil War. With George Washington's home at Mount Vernon and the Claude Moore Colonial Farm at Turkey Run, visitors can see faithful representations of eighteenth century life for prominent citizens and average residents alike. The Civil War period is also amply represented by battlefield preservations, museums, and exhibits.

The story of Fairfax County does not end with our historical past, however. Indeed, the story of Fairfax County is still being written by modern pioneers, those men and women of commerce who are ensuring our county's success in technological and commercial progress.

The products and services needed by Americans tomorrow are being designed and developed in Fairfax County today. Our county's 800,000 residents have worked to achieve an economy that provides superior jobs, excellent schools, fine government services, and a variety of cultural activities. The over 20,000 businesses of Fairfax County further provide critical financial and volunteer resources to enhance and sustain that economic base.

As the representative of that business community, the Fairfax County Chamber of Commerce plays a vital role in the process by using its influence at both the county and state levels to ensure continued opportunity for business and the maintenance of an excellent quality of life on all levels. The Chamber's primary emphasis is on legislative activities in its program of action, safeguarding companies from unwarranted or burdensome regulations and providing an overall atmosphere conducive to business success. Additional programs include seminars, studies, and activities on important business topics, functions combining networking and formal programs, and monthly luncheons featuring leaders in the political, business, education, and cultural communities.

With fifteen standing committees and over 1200 volunteers, the Chamber offers any number of opportunities for member involvement in the future of business and its success. The Fairfax County Chamber of Commerce is proud to speak for business on issues affecting our total community. In the tradition of George Washington, once a local farmer and businessman, we understand the important role of commerce in the prosperity and vitality of a community. We will continue working to ensure that Fairfax County, building on its noble past, continues its historic march to the future.

Dale Peck
Chairman of the Board
Partner, Beers & Cutler

8391 Old Courthouse Road, Suite 300, Vienna, Virginia 22182
(703) 749-0400   FAX (703) 749-9075

FAIRFAX COUNTY
A CONTEMPORARY PORTRAIT

by Ross and Nan Netherton

Great Falls of the Potamac River
in 1991. Courtesy of the photographer, Scott W. Boatright

THE
DONNING COMPANY
PUBLISHERS

Dust Jacket photo: Tysons Corner.
Endsheet photo: The Skyline Center at Bailey's Crossroads, around 1990. Both photos
courtesy of the photographer, Scott W. Boatright

The Donning Company/Publishers
184 Business Park Drive, Suite 106
Virginia Beach, Virginia 23462

Tony Lillis, Editor
Eliza Midgett, Designer

Library of Congress Cataloging-in Publication Data
Netherton, Ross DeWitt, 1918-
Fairfax County: a contemporary portrait/Ross and Nan Netherton.
     p. cm.
    Includes bibliographical references and index.
    ISBN 0-89865-838-1; $34.95
        1. Fairfax County (Va.)—Pictorial works. 2. Fairfax County (Va.)—
Economic conditions. 4. Fairfax County (Va.)—Industries. I. Netherton,
Nan. II. Title.
F132.F2N38 1992   92-7831
975.5'291043'0222—dc20   CIP
Printed in the United States of America

C O N T E N T S

Foreword — 7
Preface — 8
Acknowledgments — 11

PART ONE
A Contemporary Portrait — 13
CHAPTER 1 — 13
In the Path of History
CHAPTER 2 — 27
In the Stream of Commerce
CHAPTER 3 — 41
Corridors of Commerce; Centers of Growth
CHAPTER 4 — 59
The Power of the Mind
CHAPTER 5 — 71
A Sense of Community
CHAPTER 6 — 83
A Place of Honor
CHAPTER 7 — 95
The Quality of Life

PART TWO
Profiles in Leadership — 118
CHAPTER 8 — 118
Business and Professions
Fairfax County Chamber of Commerce — 120
Fairfax County Economic Development Authority — 122
Freddie Mac — 124
Dickstein, Shapiro & Morin — 126
Dr. Michael Bermel, O.D., Optometrist — 127
Pace Consulting Group, Inc. — 128
Temps & Co. — 129
Vance International, Inc. — 130

CHAPTER 9 — 132
Networks
Inova Health System — 134
Washington Gas — 135
Northern Virginia Community College — 136
Northern Virginia Public Television — 138
CHAPTER 10 — 140
High Technology
BDM International, Inc. — 142
Comprehensive Technologies International, Inc. — 144
DynCorp — 146
EDS Corporation — 148
Ogden Environmental and Energy Services — 150
James Martin & Company — 151
Mandex, Inc. — 152
PRC — 153
SEMA, Inc. — 154
User Technology Associates, Inc. — 156
CHAPTER 11 — 158
Marketplace
Tysons Corner Center — 160
CHAPTER 12 — 162
Building Fairfax County
MRJ, Inc. — 164
West*Group — 165
Scott-Long Construction, Inc. — 166
Appendix — 168
Bibliography — 169
Index — 170
About the Authors — 176

F O R E W O R D

Fairfax County: A Contemporary Portrait—an appropriate title for a book about a very contemporary community. Fairfax County, Virginia, stands as a model of a modern, heterogeneous community. As Chairman of the Fairfax County Board of Supervisors, I welcome you to a place we are all proud to call home.

From modest colonial beginnings 250 years ago to its modern, diversified present, Fairfax County has stood in the front ranks of progress. Fairfax County today is home to over 800,000 residents and more than 20,000 businesses, including some of the nation's largest corporations.

The county enjoys a reputation as a sound place to do business, featuring both proximity to the nation's capital and to a transportation network conducive to regional, national, and international commerce. As one of the nation's centers for technology-related business, Fairfax County is headquarters for numerous high tech firms. Smaller firms call our county home, too, frequently growing into major corporations within the borders of the county.

The superb quality of life and the high standard of living enjoyed by our residents are both directly linked to the condition of our business community. The numerous cultural attractions enjoyed by residents and visitors alike owe much of their funding to the businesses that contribute financial and volunteer assistance. Our schools, known throughout the nation for their quality, also benefit from the revenue generated by the business community, as well as from "Adopt-A-School" programs in which those companies participate.

In this book, you will learn about the history, the people, the businesses, and the future of Fairfax County. You will learn, too, that those four elements are inextricably linked in any discussion of our home. Only when you combine the legacy of its past, the vitality of its people, the dynamism of its business community, and the promise of its future can you truly see the complete picture that is Fairfax County today.

When you put it all together, there are few places in America that can match the quality of life and the opportunity for business growth that are yours for the asking in Fairfax County, Virginia. We are proud to welcome you to our home, and invite you to stay for awhile—or a lifetime.

Thomas M. Davis III, Chairman
Fairfax County Board of Supervisors

P R E F A C E

In Fairfax County approximately a million visitors a year go to see George Washington's Mount Vernon; George Mason's insistence on a Bill of Rights is still firmly set in the nation's memory; and each year thousands of men and women travel great distances to spend a few days dressed in uniforms of blue and gray or in Victorian dresses in order to visit the county's Civil War sites and reenact what went on there in the 1860s. This is the kind of history that Americans love to celebrate; and this is the history for which Fairfax County is famous.

How, then, can one hope to be taken seriously by writing about what has happened in Fairfax County in the 1980s? These are years that many county residents lived through or else knew someone who did. Are things that happened so recently really history?

Assuredly they are, for in the decade of the 1980s Fairfax County was the scene of a social and economic achievement which will alter the life of its residents and of all Northern Virginians until well into the next century. The achievements of the 1980s stand on a unique foundation—or infrastructure—which evolved in the 1950s, 1960s, and 1970s; and which, in turn, was shaped by attitudes and institutions that must be understood in terms of earlier times. One cannot really explain Fairfax County in the 1990s except in an historical perspective.

The persistent theme of the past forty years in Fairfax County is a search for ways to manage population growth and economic development. It affected the way land was developed, resources were used, and capital was raised and invested. It influenced the way the county's work force was recruited, housed, educated, and transported. It became a factor in determining how the county's natural and manmade environments were or were not conserved and used to enhance the quality of life.

Fairfax County in the 1980s was not able to bring the search for ways to manage growth and development to a clear conclusion. Its reputation as being either "pro-business" or "anti-business" continued to swing back and forth as it had for the previous thirty years. Some think that a formula for managing growth may never be fully and finally accepted by the development community and the county government—that it is in the nature of things that the problem of managing growth will never be resolved but merely change its form. If so, success in managing growth depends on dealing with both the merits of the growth issue and certain traits of political human nature. Grace Dawson, in her essay on the county's PLUS program in 1976 cited one lesson learned from that era in this way:

> ... [It] takes more than the best efforts and hopes of planners to accomplish change. It takes the will of the people and the desire of elected officials to provide leadership aimed at affecting change. So long as the objectives of a program remain general—improvement of the quality of life for the existing residents—there may be a consensus among existing residents in its support. When the objectives become more specific, what once appeared to be a constituency for change becomes a collection of interest groups, each pursuing a private interest—the American Way.

Anyone wishing to understand the rise and fall of economic fortunes cannot help being fascinated by the county's efforts to manage the pressures of growth and development in recent years. But preoccupation with the "development community"—whose activities are often presented in popular discussion as being in a perpetual contest with other (residential) elements of the county—is only a part of the story of the total "business community." The larger private commercial/industrial sector, deserves study for other reasons.

In perspective, the institutions on which the social and economic life of Fairfax County rested during the 1950s and 1960s were essentially the same ones that had been felt from the turn of the century. Family businesses of long standing were the leaders of the commercial and industrial community. Capital for economic expansion generally came from local banks and affiliates of Richmond banks, or sometimes from the sale of land that local families had succeeded in holding together in substantial acreage. Legal services were supplied by small and mid-size firms whose members sometimes were third-generation descendants of the founding partners. Insurance, commercial transactions, probate proceedings, personal injury claims and, occasionally, suits against the railroads made up the bulk of their work. Opportunities to start businesses were chiefly in the field of commercial services, and getting a small business started often was aided by networks of family connections.

When the wave of population growth reached Fairfax County in the 1950s and 1960s, homebuilders, construction contractors, and owners of large tracts of land were the main beneficiaries. As newcomers settled in the county at a rate of more than 10,000 each month and sharpened the demand for housing, two types of businessmen prospered particularly well: those who assembled and sold large tracts of land for housing subdivisions or neighborhood commercial facilities, and the construction contractors who reinvested their profits in the purchase of land in the area's major highway corridors. Federal mortgage loan guarantees, intended to encourage home ownership, had a multiplier effect on housing activity and, with it, the accumulation of capital represented by steadily rising land values.

In the years when subdivision and construction led the county's economic growth, the capacity of the workforce to support the new business functions demanded by the economy sometimes became a matter of critical importance. The problem was illustrated by the suddenly increased need of the local legal profession to search and certify land titles on a scale demanded by the flood of real estate transactions. The demand was eventually met, but only as the traditionally conservative local bar made large-scale use of paralegal assistance—some of which was supplied by Cuban attorneys and former judges who had been resettled in Northern Virginia as refugees from Castro's revolution. Similar reactions occurred throughout Fairfax County as similar demands for workers were met by innovative recruiting among groups who previously had not been well represented in the workplace—women, retirees, part-timers, and, later on, refugees from Hispanic and Asian countries.

Other changes began to be visible in the business community. It continued to be predominantly an economy of commercial and professional services, but instead of being concentrated in the county's half-dozen towns and cities it became dispersed throughout the neighborhoods inside the Beltway and in the clusters located in the western parts of the county. Also, as professional office space was put into community commercial and retail centers, it began to be occupied not only by local business but by the regional representatives and occasionally the headquarters of statewide, multistate, and national businesses. This trend accelerated as the Capital Beltway (I-495) and Shirley Memorial Highway (I-95) were completed.

With the increased number of businesses, changes also occurred in the character of the principal professional and commercial services in the business community. As the Economic Development Authority's strategy to attract high-tech business to the county took shape in the 1970s and began to be realized in the corridor of the Capital Beltway, the new Beltway "think tanks" generated new service needs. These were supplied by expansion of the general business community. By 1980, more than 18,000 businesses were active in Fairfax County, with small firms forming a major part of the service sector of the county economy.

In the growth that occurred in the 1970s and 1980s, changes could be seen in the pattern of business ownership. Proximity to the centers of governmental activity and easy access to the world through Dulles International Airport made Fairfax County an attractive location for foreign business organizations and agencies. The county's demonstrated vigor and capacity for growth also made it attractive for investment. As a result, by 1988 Fairfax County led all other Virginia counties in the number of resident foreign businesses and the amount of foreign investment. Fourteen different countries were represented in the county, the largest in volume of business being Great Britain, Japan, France, Canada, Sweden, Switzerland, and Germany.

Another significant and unusual form of foreign investment began to appear in the resettlement of refugees in Northern Virginia. The numbers of newcomers of Asian and Hispanic origin increased notably in the 1970s and 1980s to become a distinct element of the business community. Many of these small commercial and service businesses, operated as family enterprises, came into being first to serve the various ethnic neighborhoods; in other instances they started as elements of the general business community. The new Asian and Hispanic elements also contributed to the region's labor force at all levels and helped meet the demands of the expanded economy for professional, technical, clerical, and manual workers.

These newcomers brought other contributions to the Northern Virginia area which were bound to have long-term effects on the region's economy. They brought their children, strongly motivated to succeed in the new culture and society in which they found themselves; their young people have pursued that goal diligently. As a result, suddenly in the 1970s and 1980s it became noticeable that the lists of high school valedictorians and honor students regularly contained large numbers of Asian and Hispanic names.

Among recent developments that are changing the business community is an effort to develop a tourism component in the county's economy. In 1985, the county Board of Supervisors appointed a group to study ways of marketing tourism and business travel in Fairfax County. In neighboring Arlington and Alexandria, tourism has been successfully cultivated; there seemed to be no reason why Fairfax County could not do so. And initial efforts seemed to verify this: in 1984, travel dollars spent in Fairfax County amounted to $240 million; three years later this had risen to almost $540 million. Easy access to the national capital—called by some "the world's largest theme park"—a comfortable suburban setting with agreeable environmental qualities, and a number of historic landmarks of its own, were emphasized as Fairfax County's particular advantages for tourism.

These are among the many signs that Fairfax County's business community in the 1990s will differ in several ways from what it was in the 1960s. The business community will reflect the striking achievement of the county government and its Economic Development Authority in aggressively marketing the county as an attractive place for large high-tech businesses to locate. In this respect the strategic goal of bringing the tax burdens of the residential community and the commercial-industrial community into better balance was accomplished. In 1980, the commercial-industrial portion of the county's real property tax base was 12 percent; by 1990 it was 28 percent. When all taxes were considered business accounted for almost 36 percent of the county's revenue.

This was accomplished by inviting growth and development, and it succeeded to the point that the momentum now built up will carry through the 1990s and beyond. Without doubt the question of how this momentum is to be managed will continue to be a central theme in county affairs. And for reasons suggested in earlier descriptions of changes that are occurring in the infrastructure for growth and the general business community, the context of growth management policy in the 1990s and beyond will differ from that of other periods, even the recent past. In this continuing evolution, Fairfax County's corporate experience of over 250 years is likely to serve it well to avoid extremes and stick to basic values. Such a view of Fairfax County and its setting in Northern Virginia was reflected in a 1988 interview of Sidney Dewberry, a senior statesman of the region's business community. *New Dominion* magazine asked: "In terms of planning and development, what is the smartest thing Northern Virginia has done in the past 15 years?" Dewberry answered: ". . . I think it has been to provide an atmosphere conducive to business . . . . the formation of business, the growth of business, the development of business."

And then: "What was our biggest mistake?" Dewberry responded: "Not having the statesmanship to stick to a master, comprehensive plan."

And finally: "Where do you see Northern Virginia in the next 15 years?" Dewberry's answer: "I think it's going to improve."

ACKNOWLEDGMENTS

The authors appreciate the assistance of the staffs of the Donning Company, the Fairfax County Chamber of Commerce, the Fairfax County Economic Development Authority, the Office of Comprehensive Planning, and the Virginia Room at the Fairfax County Public Library for supplying counsel and reference materials for the writing of this book. Historical information and graphics were also supplied by Fairfax County Public Schools, the Park Authority, the Regional Park Authority, the Council of the Arts, the Police Department, Fire and Rescue Service and others.

Seven insightful Fairfax Countians read and made helpful comments on the book's manuscript. They were Gerald Gordon, Executive Director of the Economic Development Authority; Philip M. Reilly, Vice President for Finance of Kol Bio-Medical Instruments and former Chairman of the Chamber of Commerce; Florence Townsend, Chief Executive of the Northern Virginia Community Foundation; Earle Williams, Chief Executive Officer of BDM International, Inc., and former Chairman of the Economic Development Authority; Edith Moore Sprouse, former Chairman and current member of the Fairfax County History Commission; Stephen Lopez, Senior Planner, Office of Comprehensive Planning; and Suzanne Levy, Librarian of the Virginia Room collection.

Numerous other individuals took an interest in the project as well, and helped in various ways. They were: Helen Ackerman, William L. Allen, Stephen Anderson, Scott Boatright, Dolores Bohen, Stephanie Bolick, Robert Boughton, Kellie Boyle, James Bradley, Carol Brown, Diane Cabe, Warren Carmichael, Lynne Caswell, Donna Caudill, Bert Chamberlain, James Chido, James Cleveland, Carol Ann Cohen, Brian Conley, Nancy Cook, Nancy Corrigall, Lea Coryell, Carol Crouse, Elizabeth Dahlin, Debra Deustch, Carol and David Dunlap, Gary Erewich, Merni Fitzgerald, Judith Forehand, Caroline Frankil, Naomi Frenkel, Kenneth Gardner, Paula Grundset, Linda Hale, Jean Hall, Sandra Hartman, Ed Hoole, Peter T. Johnson, Suzanne Kelly, Marie Kisner, George Kranda, Beth Lehman-Marzullo, John Lord, Ahmad Malek-Mohamadi, Linda Mays, Mildred Monahan, Barbara Naef, Wayne Nickum, Ursula Nogic, Luther Nossett, Beth O'Connor, Nancy Overbey, Theda Parrish, Lindsay Petersen, Peggy Pillar, Anita Ramos, Betty Reed, Paul Regnier, Tricia Reneau, Gene Sands, Marjorie Schonenberg, Thomas Schudel, Sheng-Jieh Leu, Claudia Smith, Lisa Smith, Don Sweeney, Paul Torpey, Ruth Walker, James Warfield, Jane Welch, Harry E. Wells, Charlotte Wilhelme, and Carl Zitzman.

Nan & Ross Netherton

CHAPTER

1

In the Path of History

For two and a half centuries Fairfax County has stood squarely in the path of history, associated with people and events that have shaped the fortunes of Virginia and the nation. Proximity to the national capital has contributed to this, but a far more consistent factor has been that the county has always been in the path of commerce. Long before man-made influences were felt, geography was a determining force. Along the Potomac River from the Occoquan River up to the head of navigation at the Little Falls (just upstream from Chain Bridge) numerous tributary streams enabled residents to have wharfs for ships that sailed the Chesapeake Bay, the coastal waters, and even the Atlantic.

The early European settlers came to look for mineral wealth and did in fact find a little gold and copper. But mainly they became planters whose fortunes rose and fell with the price of tobacco on the London market. The tobacco era lasted until the American Revolution and by the time it ended it had set in motion several trends that were to influence Fairfax County's development for more than a century. One of these was a movement westward as tobacco exhausted the tidewater soil and forced planters to clear new areas for cultivation in western Fairfax and present Loudoun counties. A network of roads was created to connect the new inland areas with the tobacco warehouses and Potomac landings. These were the famous "rolling roads" over which hogsheads filled with tobacco leaf were rolled. Some of these later became interregional arteries radiating from Alexandria west across the Blue Ridge to Winchester, south to Fredericksburg, and southwest to Warrenton and Culpeper.

Following creation of Fairfax County by carving it from Prince William County in 1742, its first courthouse was built at a site

The Great Falls of the Potomac were a barrier to using the river as a commercial route to the mines and rich farmlands of western Virginia and the Shenandoah Valley. Although bypassed briefly by a canal in the early nineteenth century, the falls thwarted Fairfax County's hopes to navigate the river's full length. Drawing by G. Beck, Philadelphia; engraving by J. Cartwright, London, 1802

This Potomac River front view of Mount Vernon was painted in 1792, during George Washington's lifetime, by an unknown artist. Courtesy of Mount Vernon Ladies' Association of the Union

Fairfax County's economy in the eighteenth century was based on the tobacco trade and local roads connecting inland plantations to wharfs and riverside warehouses were essential. Many of these so called "rolling roads"—named because tobacco hogsheads were rolled over them—survived to be improved and serve wagon traffic in later years as the farm economy changed. Painting by Carl Rakeman. Courtesy of Federal Highway Administration

near present Tysons Corner. But in 1752 the courthouse was relocated in Alexandria, which then was a new port with high expectations. The courthouse remained there until 1800 when it became necessary to remove it because Alexandria was included in the federal district formed as the seat of the new national government.

A new courthouse was built where the turnpike from Alexandria to the Little River at Aldie crossed the road from Chain Bridge to the Occoquan. For the next seventy-five years it was known as Fairfax Court House, although after 1805 the village that grew up there was officially named Providence by the General Assembly.

Relocating the courthouse nearer the geographical center of the county was symbolic of other socioeconomic changes that occurred in the first half of the nineteenth century. In the previous century's tobacco-based economy, its planter and merchant class presided over a well-defined social structure. As tobacco gave way to grains, vegetables, flax and livestock, the old family estates broke up, replaced by small farms that could be intensively cultivated without reliance on the slave labor associated with plantations. Also, hard times and a wave of migration into the Kentucky and Ohio country took population from Northern Virginia, especially labor with technical skills needed for a diversified economy.

These trends, plus the turmoil and trade embargoes of the American and French revolutions and the second war with England (1812-1815), brought changes in the old ways. The decennial censuses from 1790 to 1840 showed a decline in Fairfax County's population. For the first time since its settlement, Northern Virginia ceased to be oriented to transatlantic connections and turned inland to domestic markets and manufacturing. Alexandria's promising prospects as a port declined; Colchester all but disappeared. At the same time Falls Church, Centreville and

Fairfax Court House—all located on turnpikes to the Shenandoah Valley—began to grow. Overland travel south to Fredericksburg by the "Old Potomac Path" was replaced by water passage, especially after 1815 when steamboats came into use.

Northern Virginia's turnpike era lasted from 1795 to the early 1850s, and resulted in building a trunk network of roads for the region. In this period also, the principal Potomac bridges were built—Chain Bridge (originally in 1797 and several times rebuilt); the "Long Bridge" (1809, presently the Fourteenth Street Bridge); and the Aqueduct Bridge (1843, replaced by Key Bridge in 1923). These roads and bridges influenced the direction and pace of development in Northern Virginia until the 1950s.

In this period Northern Virginia made an unsuccessful bid to develop the Potomac Route to the West—a dream that started with George Washington. The most formidable obstacle to river commerce was the Great Falls, and in 1802 a canal was completed around the falls on the Virginia side. Although rightly hailed as the foremost engineering achievement in North America at that time, the Patowmack Canal did not assure navigation to the west or ultimate financial success. Due to extremely high or low water most of the year on the Potomac River, boat traffic did not move well. Its end came in 1828 when the Chesapeake & Ohio Canal Company was organized to build a canal on the Maryland shore capable of operating in all seasons.

By 1840 Northern Virginia also was losing the race to establish links with areas in the west and south because of its slow start in railroad building. In Maryland the Baltimore & Ohio Railroad was chartered in 1828, and by 1836 rails connected Winchester with Baltimore via the B&O line at Harper's Ferry. Alexandria did not react to this threat until 1852 when the Alexandria, Loudoun & Hampshire Railroad was chartered intending to link Alexandria and the national capital area with western Virginia's coal fields. By 1861, however, service was provided only as far as Leesburg. Meanwhile a connection between Alexandria and central Virginia was established by the Orange & Alexandria Railroad, with a connection to the Valley via the Manassas Gap Railroad.

Organization of the Orange & Alexandria Railroad in 1848 pointed Fairfax County's growth toward the south and west, leading eventually to establishment of new communities around stations at Seminary, Edsall's, Springfield, Ravensworth, Burke's, Sideburn, Fairfax Station, and Clifton. Courtesy of the artist, Robert Clay, Virginia State Library and Archives

As the 1850s ended, Fairfax County farmers and merchants had reason to be optimistic, notwithstanding that Baltimore had seized a large share of traffic from the Winchester area. A rail network reaching out from Alexandria was in operation and farmers in Centreville and western Fairfax County had three railroads passing within a few miles of them, all leading to markets for their produce. In little more than a decade an economic transformation had occurred. In the 1840s travelers described Fairfax County in terms of scrub pine overgrowing abandoned tobacco fields, deserted houses on small farms that could neither keep nor sustain their occupants, and poor conditions of overland travel. The lingering effects of the Panic of 1837 made capital scarce. What cash income the county's nine thousand plus residents had came from catching or curing fish, selling firewood and garden produce in Alexandria and Georgetown, and renting or selling slaves.

By 1860 this had changed and Fairfax County was being described as a garden spot, prosperous and with an apparently stable future. The population decline had been reversed due in large part to purchase and settlement of land by newcomers from New York, New Jersey and New England. In addition to their numbers they brought new capital, new vigor, and new methods of farming. Quakers from the Hudson Valley were particularly successful in restoring soil fertility and introducing dairy farming. Building on practices of earlier "scientific farmers" like George Washington and his foster grandson George Washington Parke Custis, others

Fishing for subsistence and for export from Alexandria and Georgetown was carried on widely in the Potomac, especially during the springtime runs of shad and herring. In the 1830s, large seines up to seven thousand feet long were introduced into this activity and drove many small fishermen out of business. Courtesy of Virginia State Library and Archives

In colonial times and the early nineteenth century mills powered by water wheels were essential parts of Northern Virginia's economy, and the complex design of their machinery was a notable engineering achievement. The huge handmade wooden gears shown here are in the grist and flour mill which the Fairfax County Park Authority has reconstructed as the Colvin Run Mill. Photograph by Marcie Fram, Courtesy of Fairfax County Park Authority

St. Mary's Church at Fairfax Station, built in 1858 by Irish immigrants recruited to build the Orange & Alexandria Railroad, became a symbol of humanity in the Civil War as the site of Clara Barton's work to help wounded soldiers from the Second Battle of Manassas and Battle of Chantilly. Painting by Gerald Hennessy. Courtesy of the artist

joined in rebuilding Northern Virginia's agricultural economy.

Productive farms needed ready access to substantial markets before prosperity could be enjoyed. By 1860, such a market was present for Fairfax County in the District of Columbia and Alexandria, which had a combined population of 90,000. A market of this size only a few miles away made it feasible for Fairfax County farmers to improve their land, invest in new equipment, and experiment with innovative ideas that otherwise would have been unaffordable.

More than that, it became possible for Northern Virginia's economy to increase its diversification. Census returns for 1860 showed that among the county's eight thousand white residents, 650 classified themselves as farmers, 120 listed themselves as mechanics (e.g. blacksmiths, coopers, wheelwrights), about 100 were professionals (doctors, lawyers, surveyors, teachers, clergy), 53 were carpenters, 32 merchants, 11 millers, along with a scattering of other occupations. There was expansive talk about building a manufacturing center at Great Falls, using water power to run flour, paper, and wooden mills, and for rolling copper and iron. More realistic investors concentrated on grist mills, sawmills, and stone quarries, relying on steam as well as water power.

The 1850s were a time of confidence, reflected in the county's middle-of-the-road politics. Although extremists on both sides of the slavery-secession issues were active in state and national debates, this was not reflected in Fairfax County, possibly because of the mix of natives and newcomers who had come to comprise the county's residents. When the question was forced to a vote, Fairfax residents generally supported a platform of "Liberty and Union", trusting that all issues could be resolved by compromise. When Virginia seceded, however, the county ratified the action—though several districts voted against secession. The following day federal troops entered Northern Virginia.

Few places in the nation suffered as much as Fairfax County did during the Civil War. From the day it was occupied it was fought over by both North and South, and parts of it were ruthlessly ravaged and robbed by each side in turn as opportunities arose. The parts of Fairfax County that felt these impacts most were probably stripped as clean as those elsewhere that felt the wrath of Sherman and Sheridan, but in Fairfax this went on for almost four years. Many of the county's residents—some estimate about one-third—left their homes to go further north or south to escape life in this no-man's land atmosphere.

Descriptions of Fairfax County at the end of the Civil War depict tasks of rebuilding the economy, repairing the physical damage and restoring human resources that exceed imagination. Yet rebuilding began wherever tools could be found. Some came from stockpiles of military supplies in Northern Virginia that were salvaged or auctioned off to save costs of removal. These became sources of emergency supplies, tools, building materials, and horses and mules. Steps were begun to get the region's railroads back into private hands and operating. And there was an influx of new residents from the North and Midwest, bringing new energy, capital and enterprise, just as had occurred in the 1840s and 1850s. Fortunately, these contributed to healthy growth and not "carpetbagger" regimes as elsewhere. The same mixture of population that had dictated the county's middle-of-the-road politics before the war worked again to prevent the worst forms of extremism from taking over the county's reconstruction.

By 1870, Fairfax County's economy had improved substantially. Its population was just under 13,000—an increase of nine percent since 1860. Schools and churches were being built or restored, and a new railroad from Alexandria south to Fredericksburg was started. Telegraph lines, post offices and post roads were being extended. Postal villages (Falls Church, Vienna, Herndon) were growing, and new ones were coming into being at Accotink, Chantilly, Clifton, Merrifield, Lewinsville and Thornton Station (near present Reston). In 1870, the county reported having ninety-four milling and manufacturing enterprises, utilizing nineteen waterwheels and ten steam engines for their power. The list of businesses included carriage and cabinetmakers, brick and lumber yards, grist and flour mills, sawmills, and other works typically associated with serving an agricultural economy.

As an agricultural economy, Fairfax County was also beginning to excel. By 1870 it ranked twenty-ninth among Virginia counties in size and twenty-sixth in acres of improved land; but it was first in milk production; eighth in butter production; second in potatoes; fourth in hay; fifth in fruit; thirteenth in corn; fifth in market products; and in total value of farms, Fairfax County was sixth highest in the Commonwealth.

Organizations to promote agriculture first made their appearance in George Washington's day with groups that exchanged correspondence on scientific farming. A century later Fairfax County farmers established local chapters of the Patrons of Husbandry, better known as The Grange. In the 1870s and 1880s the largest private farm organization was the Potomac Fruit Growers Association, a forerunner of the twentieth century trade association. But the organization that helped Fairfax County lead the list of dairy counties was the Piedmont Milk and Produce Association. From its creation in 1873, its purpose was to promote dairying and improve the worn-out lands. It helped members' marketing efforts by renting a warehouse for them in Washington and by the 1890s Fairfax County farmers successfully operated several milk routes in Washington and Georgetown. The main factor limiting further expansion was the inefficient transportation system which required use of wagons, steam trains and ferryboats to move products from farm to market.

This limitation was greatly reduced when the electric railway—the trolley car—was introduced into Northern Virginia, drawing communities closer together and increasing their access to Washington and Georgetown. The first successful electric trolley line was built in Richmond in 1884. Four years later the *Fairfax Herald* announced that "a syndicate of Western capitalists" had received the right to build and operate an electric railway in Alexandria and to Mount Vernon. A new era of growth began.

Steam trains and horse-drawn wagons were not replaced overnight, but between 1890 and 1896 a handfull of electric railway companies was formed in Northern Virginia. Many failed, but two managed to survive to become prime movers in restarting the momentum of growth in the area. The Washington, Alexandria & Mt. Vernon Railway Company (WA&MtV) began serving eastern Fairfax County in 1892. In the same year, the Washington & Arlington Railway Company (W&A) began operations to the west, and in 1895, reorganized as the Washington, Arlington & Falls Church Railway Company (WA&FC), it entered Fairfax County in Falls Church. By 1906, it went on to Vienna and Fairfax.

The effects of these improvements were far-reaching. Residents of Falls Church, Vienna and Fairfax, and all along the trolley line could ride into Washington, Georgetown or Alexandria at a breathtaking average of twenty-one miles per hour. Fresh dairy and garden produce could be sent into the city markets in a few hours. Commuters from the county seat, previously resigned to long, dusty horse-and-

The Fairfax Court House, built in 1800 on a design by James Wren, who also designed Pohick Church, the Falls Church, and Alexandria's Christ Church, became the style-model for Virginia county courthouses until displaced in that role by Thomas Jefferson's design for the state Capitol building. From the 1740s until the 1860s, the meetings of the county court were the focal point of local government in Fairfax County. Courtesy of Fairfax County Economic Development Authority

From the 1880s to the 1940s, the organization known as the Patrons of Husbandry, or "The Grange," served as a forum for farmers to exchange information about improved equipment and methods of cultivation. Their meetings and other activities also provided a social outlet for farm families that otherwise were isolated by poor roads. Both functions helped Fairfax County's agricultural economy gain a position of leadership among Virginia counties in the 1920s and 1930s. Shown here is a meeting of the Fairfax County Chapter of the Grange in 1940. Photograph by Arthur Rothstein, Courtesy of the Library of Congress

NEW LINE
AND
LOW FARE!!

THE NEW, LARGE AND ELEGANT STEAMER
MARY WASHINGTON,
M. E. GREGG, COMMANDER,
Will, until further notice, run as follows:

FARMERS' ACCOMMODATION

Will leave Accotink daily, Sundays excepted, at 6 a. m., precisely, for Alexandria and Washington, stopping at Gunston Hall, Whitehouse, Marshall Hall, Mount Vernon, Fort Washington and Collingwood.

MOUNT VERNON TRIP

For the accommodation of Excursionists, Pleasure Parties, Parents and Children, will leave Washington at 10 a. m., precisely, (city time) for Mount Vernon, giving the passengers ample time, not only to visit the Mansion and the Tomb, but all the classic grounds surrounding.

Fare from Washington and Alexandria to the new landing called "Mount Vernon Springs" and return. ONLY FIFTY CENTS; children under 12 years, half price. Parties visiting the Mount Vernon Mansion will be charged 25 cents extra for stage fare—one mile over an excellent and delightful road—and 25 cents, the admittance fee charged by the Mount Vernon Association.

Parents, Teachers and Guardians, bring out the little ones, and give them a safe and delightful trip on the new and commodious steamer to Mount Vernon Springs and the Tomb of Washington.

Returning to Accotink will leave Washington at 4 p. m., touching at all the intermediate landings.

buggy trips, could catch trolleys to Washington every half-hour from 7:00 to 9:00 a.m. and 1:00 till 4:30 p.m. Real estate development surged. Falls Church, which had three real estate agencies in 1890, had eight in 1911. Permanent residences were interlaced with homes for summer retreat from the humid heat of Washington.

Daily contact with the national capital became a way of life for a substantial number of county residents. They commuted to work and school, received Washington and Baltimore newspapers the same·day they were printed, and enjoyed entertainment in Washington knowing that the Washington & Old Dominion Railroad trains departed downtown at 12:05 and 12:50 a.m. for theatergoers returning to Northern Virginia.

During the years 1890 to 1920, a reciprocal relationship grew up between Fairfax County and Washington. It was not correct to call the county merely a bedroom community for the city. A broader reciprocity began to emerge. Fairfax County helped feed Washington; it was a nearby place to escape the city's summer heat; and it offered a variety of options to relax and refresh the spirit on trolley car excursions to Great Falls or Mount Vernon. In turn, Washington helped the county by providing jobs, schools, and commercial and cultural benefits otherwise unavailable to those who resided beyond the reach of the trolley lines.

Poor roads and shortages of horses and wagons hampered rebuilding Fairfax County's farm economy after the Civil War, but along the Potomac from the Occoquan River to Great Hunting Creek farm-to-market transport was offered by river steamers. The Mary Washington was popular in the 1870s for its excursions and pleasure trips as well as transporting farm produce. Courtesy of Fred Tilp

Completion of the trolley line from Washington to East Falls Church brought Fairfax County within an hour's travel time of the national capital. The traffic jam at East Falls Church, shown here, consists mainly of horse-drawn taxis waiting to take passengers to Camp Russell Alger, a training camp for the Army in the Spanish-American War in the summer of 1898, but it reflects the close connection between transportation and population growth. Courtesy of Falls Church Historical Commission

J.W. Brown opened his general merchandise and hardware store in 1885 at the corner of Leesburg Pike and Lee Highway in Falls Church. Brown's Hardware has been operated at this same location by J.W. Brown's descendants continuously since that time, and is one of the oldest family businesses in Northern Virginia. Courtesy of Falls Church Historical Commission

The Clifton Hotel was built about 1877 by Harrison G. Otis of Ontario County, New York. The little postal village of Clifton was a resort for decades as people arrived by train from Washington and other cities in order to escape the summer heat. Altered several times in its 100-year-plus existence, it was totally rehabilitated in 1987 by James Swing and Serge Barbe. It is now called "The Hermitage" and is a restaurant and banquet facility. It is on the Virginia Landmarks Register. Courtesy of the photographer, Tom Schudel

Established in 1882, the Fairfax Herald was printed on a hand-operated press in the building shown here. During the next ninety years the Herald was an influential factor in the political, economic, and cultural life of Fairfax County. Shown in back of the Herald's office building is the old Town Hall, built in 1900. Courtesy of the photographer, William Edmund Barrett

In the 1870s, Anderson Freeman kept a general store in the town of Vienna. Subsequently, it also housed the post office, an insurance office, and the garage for the town's first fire engine. In 1969, the Town of Vienna purchased and restored the building as shown here, to be a museum house and store. Photograph by Marie Kisner, Courtesy of the Town of Vienna

In the 1910s, Herndon was a thriving railroad town and market center for the farmers of western Fairfax County. With a population of 1,100, Herndon listed twenty-seven "milk shippers" among its businesses. Schneider's store sold hardware, tools, shown in the background here, and farm implements to residents of the town and surrounding area. Travel from farm to market (or railroad station) was often by mule team over dusty dirt roads. Courtesy of J. Berkeley Green

At the same time, all trolley trips did not lead into Washington. As steam train and trolley travel became easier and cheaper, communities like Falls Church, Vienna, Fairfax, Herndon, Burke, Accotink, Clifton and Wiehle were transformed into local centers for supplies and services. Their marketing areas became defined in relation to the railroads. The country doctor who previously made house calls with horse and buggy now settled down in an office beside the trolley line. Tradesmen with shops in town could put goods on the train or trolley for delivery to customers along the way. Churches, civic groups and all types of social organizations widened their reach along the tracks. And shortly before the turn of the century this community-building process was aided by introduction of the telephone. The first commercial line in the county ran from downtown Washington to Merton Church's pharmacy in Falls Church in 1888. In short order telephone exchanges were opened in Falls Church, Fairfax, Vienna, Herndon and Leesburg, and in Prince William and Fauquier counties. These served the area until they were sold to the Chesapeake & Potomac Telephone Company in 1916.

Development of a sense of community in Fairfax County was aided by transportation and communication that pulled the parts of the county together physically. The county community matured in other ways as a result of lessons learned in the First World War and after. Wartime expansion of the federal government brought more newcomers to Northern Virginia, but the period 1910-1930 showed a population growth of only about five thousand residents. Significant lessons came from the experience of sharing shortages of food, fuel and rail service, in dealing with questions about the civil rights of aliens and dissenters against the war, in supporting the war effort by volunteer work or enlisting to fight, and in coping with the worldwide influenza epidemic of 1918-1919. The latter experience resulted in the creation of a county public health department. Consisting first of a doctor and

a public health nurse, it concentrated on teaching the public to deal with home sanitation, childhood diseases, dental problems and parasitic ailments.

Other experiences of the 1920s forced residents to examine the kind of community they were and the kind they wanted to be. One of these was the Noble Experiment of Prohibition. Virginia had approved statewide prohibition in 1916, so it quickly ratified the Eighteenth Amendment. But expectations were too high, and eventually turned to disillusionment. Another problem for which no clear-cut solution was found in the 1920s concerned the changing role of women in the socio-economic system. During the war years, women had been welcomed in the work force, in government service, in trade and industry, and on the farm. A wartime slogan had boasted that each woman in war work released a man for active duty. After the war many tried to continue in these roles or open up new ones, with less success.

Even those who stayed home found that their roles were changing. Commercial ice, canned and packaged foods, sewing machines, washing machines and electricity changed the historic routine of the home. Women had leisure time and used it to pursue new interests—suffrage, temperance, civic projects. In Northern Virginia one cause that this new energy focused on was public education. Although education had become a public responsibility in Virginia in 1870, the first compulsory school attendance law was not passed until 1918. In the 1920s and 1930s, it remained for the public—mainly women's groups—to insist that the patchwork of

Stalled in the mud near the town of Fairfax in 1911, this car illustrates the condition of Northern Virginia roads during the years when Fairfax County's agricultural economy was growing to serve the markets in the national capital area. It was not until the county roads were taken into the statewide system under the Byrd Road Act in 1928 that paving was started to make them all-weather highways. Courtesy of Virginia Department of Transportation

Fairfax County's neighborhood schools be consolidated into districts and become a truly countywide system, efficiently managed and adequately funded. Gradually such a system took form—even though initially it meant inaugurating truck transportation for students to reach schools in some places.

There were other problems, such as matching the school programs with the prevailing needs of the economy. In his 1923-1924 report, the Virginia Agricultural Extension Service's county agent complained that Fairfax County's schools "give absolutely no assistance in agricultural education . . . [and are] absolutely unfair to the 90 percent of our farm children who do not go beyond the grades." Recognizing the dependence of the economy on a trained work force, Floris Vocational Agricultural High School was established to serve the needs of the county's farm youth. Another gap in the county's regular school system was filled by a newcomer from Ohio, Mattie Gundry, who settled in the town of Falls Church and established a school for retarded children in 1893. It grew to be the largest of its kind in the South, and Mattie Gundry received national recognition for her methods. These examples of progressive education were, however, well in advance of Virginia's typical educational system at the time.

The success of Fairfax County's dairy farm and garden economy of the 1920s depended on the closeness of the Washington-Georgetown-Alexandria markets and being able to deliver to these markets rapidly and reliably by train and trolley. In other respects though, transportation problems restricted the economy's prospects drastically. Any thought of serving wider markets foundered on the deplorable condition of the roads statewide. Interregional travel was difficult and costly—to such an extent that Virginius Dabney recalls how in 1921 the Automobile Club of America urged motorists to bypass the state.

In the early 1920s, Fairfax County led all other Virginia counties in dairy products. In the Maryland and Virginia Milk Producers Association, Fairfax County had 121 members with herds of over 15,000 cows. Symbolic of the county's supremacy in milk production is "Sadie", a Holstein judged the world's best milk producer for several years in succession. Courtesy of Fairfax County Library Photographic Archive

This situation began to change when Harry Byrd was elected governor in 1926. In the four years that followed, programs were launched to provide a new infrastructure for the state's economy and a new framework for conducting the state's business. By creating the Virginia Department of Highways in 1927 and establishing the road building program on a pay-as-you-go basis with gas taxes and license fees, Byrd literally paved the way to a statewide system of efficient and economical highways. Under the Byrd Road Act in 1932 counties were invited to put their local roads on the state's secondary road system in return for giving up a one-cent county gas tax. Fairfax County elected to accept this invitation, and was still sufficiently rural to get back more in state road building expenditures than it gave up to the state. Moreover, it already had begun to ask the state to take responsibility for certain of its roads. In 1926 the Board of Supervisors had requested that the road from Gum Springs to Mount Vernon be put on the state system "as this road is heavily traveled by a tremendous number of high-class tourists each year and the necessity for its proper maintenance is great."

During the decade of the 1920s, this accelerated road building activity continued, rehabilitating and extending the arterial highways and hard-surfacing the rural roads. A county Chamber of Commerce publication in 1928 noted with satisfaction that "of the 34 communities shown on county maps, 25 are connected by improved, hard-surfaced roads with Washington . . . .'Railroads serve 22 of the

Delivery of daily papers and goods like this bicycle from Washington to local stations along the W&OD Railroad tracks symbolizes how the electric railway changed the social and economic life of Fairfax County. The impacts of closer connection with Washington were felt in educational, cultural, and social benefits as well as in commerce, agriculture, and industry. Courtesy of E.E. Edwards

34 points . . . [and] 8 have both railroads and hard-surfaced highways. Buses run through 18 of the 34 points on regular schedules, and in most cases affording frequent service."

The shift toward reliance on highways and automobiles was increased by the decline of rail services. Railroads and trolley companies had postponed maintenance and replacement of equipment during the First World War and the Depression years, and were at a disadvantage. By 1935, bus lines had taken over much of the trolleys' commuter patronage, and many other Northern Virginians became motorists for travel to work and local trips of all sorts. At the end of the decade the state roads commissioner, Henry Shirley, reported: "Practically all horse-drawn equipment has vanished from the highways and motor equipment has taken its place, requiring a road that can be travelled the year-round." He might well have added that the passenger traffic of trains and trolleys also appeared to be going the way of the horse.

As this process went on, two bus lines emerged to provide service in and out of Washington: the Alexandria, Barcroft & Washington (AB&W) line, serving eastern Fairfax County, and the Washington & Virginia (W&V)—"The Arnold Line"—serving the western part. Unlike the train and trolley that carried passengers, mail and freight, the buses were solely people-movers, and they rearranged their schedules and routes periodically to serve changing residential patterns. Truck traffic, with even more flexibility to pick up and deliver goods, took over much of the freight

In its early years the Fairfax County Chamber of Commerce brought together representatives of all parts of the county's agricultural economy, plus the main professions and businesses, to generate support for economic development. It also worked for improved public health services, libraries, roads, and water systems. Shown here are some of the Chamber's members in front of the Court Clerk's office about 1934. Courtesy of Fairfax County Library Photographic Archive

Although the Washington & Old Dominion Railroad ceased passenger operations in 1951, it handled freight on a diminishing network of tracks until the entire system was abandoned in 1965. Courtesy of H.H. Harwood, Jr.

business that previously had gone by rail.

More of the infrastructure for growth was provided during the 1930s. Electricity originally was supplied by the Alexandria Light & Power Company, which extended its lines into Fairfax County toward Falls Church, Vienna and Fairfax. Elsewhere in the county electric power was provided by Virginia Public Service, the Bull Run Power Company and others. During the Depression years, the Rural Electrification Administration's programs achieved notable results so that in 1935 Fairfax County led all other parts of Virginia in electrification, with 270 miles of lines in operation for almost 2,400 customers. Subsequent consolidation of these and other companies led to creation of the Virginia Electric & Power Company.

In the 1920s Fairfax County's population increased only by about three thousand, yet some of the land-use planning tools that would be needed in later times of faster growth were being put in place. Specifically, in 1928 ordinances were passed that required subdivision plats to be approved by the county engineer before they were recorded; that prescribed minimum street widths; and that mandated connections with adjacent subdivisions and the general road system. A sewage disposal ordinance was adopted, but it was many years before an integrated sewer system for the county could be undertaken.

Development of subdivisions in Fairfax County slowed down in the Depression years, although disastrous waves of home mortgage foreclosures were averted by federal housing legislation in 1934. Moreover, the national capital area proved to be less vulnerable to the Depression's impacts than were other places heavily dependent on commerce or industry. Nevertheless, in 1933 one out of every five heads of Fairfax County families was out of work, and the county welcomed allocation of a number of federal and state-funded public works projects to improve the county's streets, the jail and the schools.

As the New Deal extended the activities of the federal government and added employees to its agencies in Washington and vicinity, Fairfax County received its share of these new residents. From 1930 to 1940 the county's population grew as much as it had from 1870 to 1930. New businesses also were started, almost entirely in the services sphere for local residents or government agencies. As the decade ended Fairfax County appeared to be on the way to fulfilling the prediction made in a Chamber of Commerce publication in 1928, as follows:

> [T]o a great extent the future of Fairfax County is written in the future of the United States and its National Capital . . . There is no question that the Nation's Capital will grow in population and size as the United States increases in wealth, population and world importance. As the southwestern arc of Greater Washington, Fairfax County is destined to develop into one of Washington's most charming environs.

As the rural character of Fairfax County gradually was replaced by suburban residential, commercial, and industrial development, farming became an exceptional activity which was successful only when it was carried out on a large enough scale to justify use of labor-saving machinery. Shown here is a plowing scene at Sunset Hills farm near present Reston about 1959. Courtesy of A. Smith Bowman Distillery

2

In the Stream of Commerce

O n the eve of the Second World War there were some who foresaw that Fairfax County was to become more than "one of Washington's most charming environs." To them it was clear that most of the new growth of the national capital area would be in Fairfax County. Geography indicated this because the District of Columbia and Virginia's Arlington County had too little space left. The nearby parts of Maryland's Montgomery County were committed to long-settled residential development; and Prince George's County lacked good access. Fairfax County in the 1940s was in the path of commerce.

But Fairfax County in 1940 lacked much of the infrastructure needed to handle large or rapid growth. Thus, the era of 1940-1980 was a time of preparation for accepting and managing the growth that would transform its economy from being a satellite of Washington to a separate economy of independent means, with an agenda based on its own goals and capabilities, its own national and international connections, and its own leaders in local government, business, education, science and the arts. It would be a complete community, and, indeed, have satellites of its own.

To accommodate and manage a transformation of this sort and magnitude Fairfax County had to develop an infrastructure consisting of four types of elements: (1) physical facilities, both public and private; (2) an adequate workforce; (3) a system of rapid and reliable communications; and (4) a framework of supporting policies and procedures administered efficiently by local government.

These elements were not developed in a series. They evolved

The Seven Corners Market beside Route 50 at Seven Corners illustrates one trend of retail business in the 1950s as Fairfax County felt the impact of rapid suburban growth. Suburban residents, spread over wide areas, depended on automobiles for travel to work, shopping, and recreation. Retailers sought locations alongside arterial routes, catering to customers by providing parking in front of their stores and posting large legible signs in their storefronts. Photograph by Quentin Porter, Courtesy of Fairfax County Library Photographic Archive

together, often in combination with each other. In the war years of the 1940s, Fairfax County began acquiring the human resources that eventually made up the critical mass to sustain its independent high-tech economy of the 1980s. This population growth was closely associated with a change in the form of county government and with homebuilding on an unprecedented scale. These, in turn, became factors in showing the county's planning approach to land development and growth management.

The expansion of the federal government in Washington and its environs in the 1930s, continued at an even faster rate in the 1940s to meet the manpower demands of the Second World War. When fighting stopped a great deal of the workforce stayed on, making the area a permanent home. As a result, Fairfax County's population more than doubled between 1940 and 1950—from 40,900 to 98,500.

Most of this population settled in newly-built subdivisions and promptly started asking for paved streets, schools, libraries, storm sewers, police and fire protection, and reliable water supplies. They were willing to pay their share of the cost, but these were services of a type and scale that the county was unprepared to provide.

Two groups took the lead in searching for ways to increase the capacity and responsiveness of county government. One was the Fairfax County Federation of Citizens Associations, organized in 1940; the other was the League of Women

In 1922, volunteers formed the McLean Community Fire Association, later designated Volunteer Fire Company No. 1, the first fire company in Fairfax County to become incorporated. Within a year, the organization owned an acre of land, a fire house, several pieces of fire fighting equipment, and an alarm bell mounted on the firehouse roof. This photograph shows the company's equipment on display in the 1940s. Courtesy of McLean Volunteer Fire Department

In 1916, local telephone companies serving Falls Church, Fairfax, Vienna, Herndon, and their nearby areas were consolidated in the Chesapeake & Potomac Telephone Company which subsequently expanded to cover all of Northern Virginia. One of the manually-operated switchboards that served Fairfax County in the 1940s is shown here. Today, telephone service in Fairfax County is provided by Bell Atlantic (C&P) Continental Telephone, MCI, AT&T, and Sprint. Courtesy of Falls Church Historical Commission

Voters of Fairfax County, organized in 1946. In 1949, the Federation and the League joined in petitioning for a referendum on a proposed county manager form of government. Opinion tended to split along suburban-rural lines, and eventually a compromise was reached in favor of a more moderate change to the county executive form of government. This was approved in a referendum in November 1950, to be effective in January 1952. The new structure required creating departments for such matters as public works and tax assessments, regular examination of every office's books and papers, and regular reports from department heads and County Executive to the Board of Supervisors. A research task force was formed, headed by David Lawrence, publisher of U.S. *News & World Report* and a county resident, to plan the transition to the new form of government.

On January 1, 1952, the first meeting of the new government was held. The new County Executive was Carlton Massey, who had previously served eight years as manager of Henrico County, Virginia. The principal constitutional officers were the clerk of the circuit court, sheriff, and supervisor of assessments. To provide a proper home for the new government, a major addition was constructed in the style of the historic 150-year-old courthouse, which was incorporated as one wing of the new building.

Army engineers at Fort Belvoir train in construction of bridges for use of heavy military equipment. During the 1970s and 1980s, Fort Belvoir's role in training engineer officers was replaced by emphasis on specialized missions, research, and development. It became the Army's Engineer Research and Development Laboratory, providing testing facilities for many important innovations in engineer equipment. Other notable activities located at Fort Belvoir in recent years were the Humphreys Engineer Support Center and the Defense Systems Management College (formerly the U.S. Army Management School). Courtesy of the Engineer Museum and U.S. Army Public Affairs Office, USAFB

The work of the new board quickly became preoccupied with land development problems. A steady flow of applications for rezoning to accommodate new residential subdivisions and local commercial space made up an increasing proportion of the board's business. Most cases brought with them problems of access control, septic tank standards and water supply. But in 1953 a new type of commercial development occurred when 32 acres at Seven Corners were rezoned from suburban residence to general business to accommodate Fairfax County's first regional shopping mall. Designed to serve up to 50,000 people, it invited visitors to shop at branches of two major Washington department stores (Woodward & Lothrop and Garfinkel's), stores of several national chains (Woolworth's, Brentano's), and a variety of specialty shops. An innovative multi-level highway design sorted out the tangle of seven arterial and local roads which intersected at that point, and parking space for approximately 2600 cars was provided.

The impact of this new type of shopping center was soon seen in the marketing strategies of business, in the shopping habits of the public, in social life, youth culture, political campaigning, and, indeed, in the basic relationship of county residents to downtown Washington. By the example of Seven Corners, one important facet of Fairfax County's role as a "suburban bedroom" satellite of Washington began to change. The full extent of that reorientation was not realized for years to come, but at the opening ceremonies in 1953 it was clear that Kass-Berger, Inc., the developers of Seven Corners, had given Fairfax County new momentum for change as well as growth.

New residential development along arterial roads westward past Falls Church and south past Annandale continued. But problems associated with these new subdivisions and local employment centers appeared in a broader context of sewer and water services, schools, public health service, fire and police protection, a broader financial base, an integrated area road system, and a rational method of naming and numbering streets. How to organize county government's response to all these needs was the problem given to planning consultant Francis Dodd McHugh, who had previously done a master plan for Westchester County, New York.

The McHugh Master Plan appeared to adopt the premise that Fairfax County's future would run parallel to Westchester County and so it would remain an

Opened in 1944 as a wartime measure to relieve traffic, the limited-access road between the Pentagon and Leesburg Pike (Route 7) was named Shirley Memorial Highway, and it ushered in an era of expressway construction in Northern Virginia. Shirley Highway was extended southward through Fairfax County to the Occoquan River and later became Interstate Route I-95. Courtesy of Virginia Department of Transportation

attractive residential suburb of an adjacent metropolis. One of its studies, by planner Homer Hoyt, asserted that ninety percent of the county's workers were federal employees and its population growth would level off by 1980 at about 320,000. Accordingly, McHugh's plan was aimed at slowing down random development in western parts of the county until the close-in areas which already had sewers and other services could be filled up. Ultimately, the plan foresaw Fairfax County absorbing this growth in concentric belts of suburbs of the national capital.

Not everyone adopted this agenda. The Fairfax County Chamber of Commerce continued to seek the relocation of light industry and laboratories along the county's arterial road system, claiming that it could offer more suitable sites within thirty minutes' drive from downtown Washington than all the rest of the metropolitan area combined. The tempo of public debate over the master plan reached the point where it turned the Board of Supervisors election of 1956. Five of seven members, with a combined total of fifty-four years of service, were replaced.

A majority of the incoming members favored adopting a master plan and getting on to implement the county's 1950 reorganization. They adopted a version of McHugh's plan which included a six-month zoning moratorium and a two-acre minimum lot size for development of the western part of the county. This had the effect of stabilizing the pace of development for about two years, which was the period needed for owners of western county farms to successfully challenge its validity in the courts.

As the 1950s decade closed, construction of subdivisions and the facilities to serve them remained the most active part of Fairfax County's economy. The county continued to attract newcomers; and they continued to expect to receive county services even though the leap-frogging pattern of growth into the county's open parts meant higher taxes to provide duplicate services in those areas.

Interstate Route I-66 provides a radial expressway from Washington southwesterly through Fairfax County, and since being opened to traffic in December 1982, it has become the axis for some of the most dynamic development planned for the 1990s. The right-of-way provides space for the Metro System's transit tracks in the highway median strip. The aerial photo here looks east from the vicinity of the West Falls Church Metro station. Courtesy of the photographer, Scott W. Boatright

Those remnants of the McHugh Master Plan which survived the decade became practically unrecognizable in the 1960s as the practice of rezoning and permitting spot commercial development on request or "as of right" became the rule. With no strong comprehensive plan, the planning staff, Planning Commission, Board of Supervisors, and the courts found they had to spend an inordinate amount of time on a backlog of zoning matters while delivery of services to residents countywide lost ground.

Although the county's record in managing its growth may not have pleased everyone, it stood as an achievement in that the county had survived a population increase of more than 150 percent—from 98,500 to 248,800—and managed to remain attractive enough to almost double its numbers in the 1960s—from 248,800 to 454, 300. And as part of this survival process, the county had created several of the essential elements of the physical infrastructure that would be needed for continued growth.

One of these elements was an adequate countywide water and sewer system. In 1950, the Alexandria Water Company supplied residents adjacent to Alexandria with water, and the Falls Church Water Company to its adjacent area. The rest of the county was supplied by private wells of individual landowners or wells of developers who operated them for their subdivisions. A 1955 study showed that fifteen private and four publicly-owned water companies supplied 45 percent of the county's population. This had serious implications for the rapidly growing county since three years of drought (1951-1954) had made Northern Virginia's water resources unreliable. Prospects of a solution suffered set-backs when voters defeated sewer and water bond issues in 1955, and the town of Fairfax opened negotiations to bring its own water line from the Goose Creek reservoir in Loudoun County. With deliberate speed the Board of Supervisors approved the establishment of the Fairfax County Water Authority and appointed its first governing board. Various separate water companies were acquired by the Authority and planning was started to secure water from the Potomac River in the event of need.

Recourse to the Potomac River for water supplies was possible in part because Fairfax County and others along the river had succeeded in dealing with at least the worst of their sewage problems. Prior to 1950 Fairfax County had been lax in enforcing its 1928 ordinance against dumping sewage into the Potomac. After 1950 creation of sewage treatment facilities in a series of sanitary districts and extension of sewer lines led to a countywide system which substantially reduced threats to the quality of water in the Potomac.

Tysons Corner, shown here in 1957, was a commercial crossroads from earliest times, located at the intersection of the Alexandria-Leesburg Turnpike (Route 7) and Chain Bridge Road (Route 123). Within a decade after this picture was taken, Tysons Corner began its transformation into the dynamic urban center it became in the 1980s. Photograph by S.R. Pearson in Donie Rieger Collection. Courtesy of Fairfax County Library Photographic Archive

Related to development of adequate countywide sewer and water systems was the need to dispose of the solid waste generated by the the county's residential, commercial and industrial sectors. As Fairfax County changed from a rural to a suburban community, waste disposal was at first handled for individual neighborhoods by contract services that picked up trash and hauled it to county-owned sanitary landfills. By the end of the 1950s, however, these arrangements began to be inadequate. In 1962 the county leased a 104-acre landfill on West Ox Road south of Interstate Route 66 and here, using the most advanced sanitary engineering technology, a central facility was established. It proved adequate for the next twenty years, during which more than three million tons of solid waste were deposited to an elevation of 575 feet—the highest landmass in the county, named "Mount Murtagh" for its designer. In 1982, a new landfill was opened at Lorton.

In the decades of most rapid population increase, one of the most basic infrastructure needs was the development of transportation facilities serving the county and the region efficiently. This system had to be based on highways since regional passenger and commuter service on railroads had ended in 1951. And it had to be based on the premise that Fairfax County would be the strategic center of this regional network. Studies were made to integrate the county's needs with regional and interregional transportation needs and to classify the county's 2,300 miles of roads by the various functions performed. The system which emerged was anchored by four expressways: I-95, the main north-south route along the Atlantic seaboard; I-66, an east-west expressway to the Shenandoah Valley; I-495, the Capital Beltway; and the Dulles Access Road, connecting western Fairfax County with the Beltway. These roads form a hub-and-spokes pattern crossed by a circumferential route that allows easy access to all parts of the county.

The first of these expressways was opened in 1944 in a two-and-one-half mile section from the Pentagon road system to Leesburg Pike (Route 7) as a wartime measure to relieve the heavy traffic of workers commuting to and from Washington through Arlington and Fairfax counties. It was named Henry G. Shirley Memorial Highway to honor the Highway Commissioner who presided over construction of Virginia's statewide highway system in the 1930s. Steadily Shirley Highway was extended south until in 1951 it reached Prince William County at Woodbridge and was carrying traffic of 35,000 vehicles per day. This capacity was quickly exceeded by the demands of the 1950s and 1960s, and had to be increased by repeated road widenings. In the 1970s, renamed Interstate Route 95, this highway became the main north-south route through eastern Virginia. Within Fairfax County it also

This aerial view shows the Tysons Corner area as it was being developed in the mid 1960s. The vertical road (left center) is Route 123; Route 7 is horizontal in the upper fourth of the picture; the Capital Beltway and its interchange are horizontal-center; and the Dulles Access Road is vertical and angled to the right. *Courtesy of Fairfax County Public Library Photographic Archive*

Robert E. Simon, Jr. pioneered the "New Town" concept of developing commercial, industrial, and professional areas close enough to residential areas to eliminate commuting. His concept was realized in the unincorporated community of Reston, which celebrated its twenty-fifth anniversary in 1989, and welcomed the arrival of its 50,000th resident family in 1987. *Courtesy of Hunter's Woods Community Library, Fairfax County Public Library*

served a heavy volume of commuter and local travel generated by high-density development around the interchanges at Newington and Springfield.

Within the available right-of-way, efforts to improve traffic-carrying capacity were made on Fairfax County's other arterials and parkways. Because they often used alignments of nineteenth century turnpikes, there were serious restrictions on what could be done. A major step toward making these radial arteries work better was taken with construction of the Capital Beltway beginning in 1958. Designated I-495, this circumferential expressway was designed to be a bypass around Washington for interregional traffic. Inside Fairfax County it also served as a distributor for local and commuter traffic. In a 22-mile arc, from the American Legion Bridge on the north end to the Woodrow Wilson Bridge in Alexandria at the south end, this highway had twelve interchanges with radial routes which included the George Washington Memorial Parkway, Interstates 66 and 95, and US 7, 29, 50 and 236.

Construction of the Capital Beltway went on until 1966 as successive sections were completed and opened to traffic. From its earliest stages the Beltway was a central element of Fairfax County's foundations for growth. When fully opened in 1966 it carried 44,000 vehicles per day and went far toward integrating the local highway system which, like the sewer system of the 1950s, had suffered because of the random pattern of residential development that had occurred. The Beltway's influence was not limited to reduction of commuting time and diversion of through traffic from local roads. Very quickly it was possible to see changes in land use, property values, travel and shopping habits, commercial services, and residential and recreational patterns. The concept grew that transportation planning should be more concerned with moving people than with moving vehicles. Planners found themselves dealing with issues of social impacts, environmental pollution, mass transit, and special transportation facilities.

Those who foresaw that Fairfax County would someday have a population approaching a million and an economy more dynamic than any other in Northern Virginia recognized that the transportation infrastructure of the economy would have to include a mass transportation element. Although the AB&W and WV&M bus lines were obvious choices to grow into this role, they could not do so for two reasons: First, in the 1950s and 1960s the county's population grew too fast, and second, the pattern of suburban development thwarted efforts to establish bus service to many neighborhoods that were separated from the centers of employment by substantial undeveloped areas. Outside the Beltway these conditions dictated that cars and carpooling were the accepted method of travel.

Throughout the 1950s and 1960s, however, the mass transit option was kept alive when circumstances favored it. In 1951 when congestion at rush hours on Shirley Highway (I-95) became extreme, certain lanes were reserved for buses and commuters were encouraged to leave their cars in fringe parking lots and ride express buses. The experiment succeeded, and Fairfax County became the first place in the nation to use this method of persuading more rush hour commuters to ride buses than drive their cars. Similar arrangements for express bus service on older arterial routes also enjoyed success.

The mass transit initiative which eventually succeeded on a regionwide basis came in 1972 when construction began on Metro, the national capital area's subway/surface transportation system. When completed—estimated to occur in 1993—Metro would have 101 miles of track and eighty-six stations in Washington, Maryland and Virginia. The system was constructed and operated by the Washington Metropolitan Area Transit Authority (WMATA), and the authority was responsible for the bus as well as the rail components.

Metro commenced operations in 1976, and as the rail component grew the bus component was shifted to more remote areas to provide connections to Metro rail stations. In the corridor running from Rosslyn to Falls Church and Vienna, Metro rail surfaces in Arlington and travels above ground in the median area of I-66. In the corridor from Rosslyn to Alexandria it uses a combination of public land and industrial area with the result that its impact on neighborhood integrity and amenities is kept to a minimum.

The planning and construction of Metro was an experience in regional cooperation on a scale not before attempted in the national capital region. It had the effect of tying the areas which it served more closely together, just as the electric trolley had done in its era of 1890-1930. In the case of Metro, however, history did not fully repeat itself. Whereas the trolley had contributed greatly to making Fairfax County the national capital's suburban bedroom, other influences that strengthened Fairfax County's independent role in the region were at work in the era of Metro.

Nothing represented these other influences better than Dulles International Airport, located on Fairfax County's western boundary. First called Chantilly after a nearby nineteenth century community, this airport was built by the Federal Aviation Administration in 1962 on 17,500 acres of land. Its present site was chosen after years of opposition from local residents forced the airport to move from the site first selected near the Burke community. In its present location the airport's control tower, terminal building and mobile lounges for passengers were designed by the noted architect Eero Saarinen. They have been praised for their beauty and efficiency, and in Saarinen's own opinion were his best work. During the 1960s and 1970s airlines serving Washington were slow to close out established use of other airports and move to Dulles. The potential importance of this large and modern airport, with domestic and international service, was not diminished by this slow start, and its importance was realized in the 1980s. In 1980, approximately 2,622,000 passengers were enplaned and deplaned at Dulles International Airport; in 1990, the number was 10,424,444.

By the mid-1970s much of the physical infrastructure needed to sustain an independent regional economy centered in Fairfax County was in place or clearly in view. The county's population was approaching the critical mass needed to provide both a workforce for national and world-class businesses and a market of consumers for comparable commercial and professional enterprises. Major concentrations of retail business had grown up at Tysons Corner and Springfield, and had passed Seven Corners in size. Moreover, this population and its support service industries were housed without excessive crowding, with reasonable care for environmental values and often with space devoted to amenities that enhanced the quality of life. There were no critical or recurring shortages of water, power, sewer or waste disposal; no glaring examples of slums; and both the crime rate and tax rate stayed within acceptable limits. Schools were performing well; university and community college-level education was available in the county; and the crises of the 1950s over expansion and integration of the school system were past. Even in the development of a transpor-

Fairfax County's first regional shopping mall, Seven Corners, opened for business in 1956 on a thirty-four acre tract of land crossed by major regional highways. It was an immediate success and became a prototype for others that followed in the 1960s and 1970s at key crossroad locations. It was enclosed as a climate-controlled mall in the 1970s. Kass-Berger was the original developer. With 500,000 square feet of space in the complex, the anchor store is Woodward & Lothrop, one of seventy stores and businesses in all. Courtesy of the photographer, Scott W. Boatright

Once a confusing tangle where seven roads met, Seven Corners was redesigned with over-and under-passes for the thoroughfares when the regional shopping center was built in 1956. The twin buildings shown in the background, built in 1972 and 1988, are the headquarters, on Route 50, of First Virginia Bank. It was founded in 1952 by Virginia-born and educated civil engineer Edwin T. Holland. The first bank holding company in Virginia, First Virginia presently has more branches—thirty-two—than any other bank doing business in Fairfax County. Courtesy of the photographer, Scott W. Boatright

Sidney O. Dewberry is principal partner of Dewberry & Davis. He is shown here with an antique level and transit which surveyors used in the 1850s to draw the path of the Alexandria, Loudoun & Hampshire Railroad (later called the Washington & Old Dominion) through Northern Virginia. Photograph by Joe Grimes, Courtesy of Dewberry & Davis

tation system—probably the part of the infrastructure where shortcomings were most visible—Fairfax County had made impressive progress with an international airport, Metro, and a trunk highway system. All in all, not a bad record.

Looking at the county's institutional infrastructure, other accomplishments could be cited. One was defensive in character, but nevertheless essential to secure the county's future. In the 1950s Alexandria, Vienna and Fairfax literally nibbled away parts of Fairfax County by annexing adjacent areas. In a period of rapid and random development, it was tempting for these municipalities to annex areas of high-density development—and high taxpaying potential—adjacent to their boundaries. Efforts to protect the county from this practice led to formation of a committee in 1958 to devise a plan for the General Assembly to incorporate the county. In 1961, this resulted in a proposal that Fairfax County and the town of Clifton consolidate into a new metropolitan county with a charter that would protect present borders. Existing towns would either cease to exist or become cities. Pending annexation suits were either dropped or dismissed, and Fairfax obtained court permission to become a second class city. Robert E. Simon's "new town" development in Sunset Hills, called Reston, proceeded without expectation of incorporation. In the General Assembly the legislation to create a chartered metropolitan county was never passed, but the point was clearly made that annexations of the county's best revenue-producing areas would not be allowed to succeed in the future.

Another important part of Fairfax County's foundation for growth was supplied by establishing its credit in the municipal bond market. The county's first experience with borrowing came in the 1950s when money was needed to acquire land for parks and water companies, and to build schools, libraries, and other government facilities. Voter approval for these things by bond referendum was not always automatic in the 1950s and '60s, but the referenda forced the issues to undergo public debate and the successful issues turned out to have the necessary support when revenue for repayment had to be raised. As a result, since 1975 the county's general obligation bonds have carried an Aaa rating from Moody's Investors Service, the highest rating given municipal bonds by that company. In 1978, Standard & Poor also gave Fairfax County an AAA rating. Of the nation's more than 3,000 counties, only twelve have such triple-A ratings from both rating services, and this achievement has given Fairfax County an important positive force for its future growth.

The most difficult part of the county's institutional infrastructure for growth, and one that never was fully fashioned in the 1970s, was settlement on a policy and procedure for planning and managing land development. Following its experience with the McHugh Master Plan and subsequent zoning ordinances, the county went through what has been called "the Soaring Sixties" with only a piecemeal approach to planning and zoning in the western two-thirds of its territory. Land prices were rising in the vicinity of the Beltway and other employment centers, but uncertainty prevailed about undeveloped

The county office building, named in honor of the first County Executive Carlton Massey, was opened in September 1969 behind the old Fairfax County Courthouse on Chain Bridge Road in Fairfax City. Here, the regular meetings of the Fairfax County Board of Supervisors were held for more than twenty-three years. Courtesy of the photographer, Tom Schudel

A Concorde takes on passengers from a mobile lounge at Dulles International Airport. Air France and British Airways began flying their supersonic planes in and out of Dulles on a regular basis in May 1976. Courtesy of Fairfax County Economic Development Authority

A 1991 aerial photograph of the Annandale campus of Northern Virginia Community College shows Route 236, the Little River Turnpike in the foreground, then the pond, and, behind it, the college buildings and parking lot. This was the first of five campuses developed by the regional educational institution. Courtesy of the photographer, Scott Boatright

First opened as an extension of the University of Virginia in 1950, and later named George Mason College, George Mason University was elevated to independent status in 1966. George Mason University's central campus library, shown here, was named after Senator Charles Fenwick of Arlington who was an early leader in working for establishment of the university. Photograph by Carl Zitzman, Courtesy of George Mason University

The permanent headquarters home of the Central Intelligence Agency in Fairfax County was completed and occupied in 1961. Currently the CIA is a major employer in the county and houses a wide range of activities concerned with gathering and evaluating information from more than 150 countries worldwide to be used by the Federal government in carrying on its functions. Courtesy of Office of Public Affairs, Central Intelligence Agency

land because much of it lacked public facilities (water, sewer, roads) and the county's policy on providing them was not yet settled. Experiments were carried out with special tax districts to finance sewer construction, but few proved economically feasible. These efforts ceased when, in the early 1970s, a sewer moratorium was declared allegedly because additional sewage treatment capacity was not available.

Meanwhile the county planning staff addressed the problem of managing growth in the western lands by proposals to avoid the concentric rings of urban sprawl that had grown up in the eastern part. Rather, they proposed, the western parts should be developed in "satellite clusters" surrounded by low density conservation zones and open spaces. County zoning became more flexible through use of "planned development communities," reflecting the success of developers in persuading the county to allow denser development patterns where needed to cope with rising land costs. Whereas single-family, low-density housing had been the style of the 1950s and 1960s, the trend of the 1970s was multi-family units, townhouse developments and flexible planned communities. These gave county government more leeway in negotiating with developers for dedication of school and park land and other amenities; but the county's planning process took little initiative in channeling growth, except in the case of Reston.

The decade of the 1970s opened with a national concern for environmental quality and national legislation which encouraged closer scrutiny of the environmental consequences of development practices at all levels. The 1971 Board of Supervisors election reflected this in a campaign that linked unplanned land development with traffic congestion, air and water pollution, strip development, drainage problems, and higher costs of government. The Board that took office in January 1972 was committed to controlling growth more effectively, but the question of how to do so was not clearly answered at the polls. Experiments with regulating allocation of sewer taps and zoning moratoria failed to relieve pressure to develop the western part of the county. Then, in 1973, the Board created a Task Force on Comprehensive Planning and Land Use Control to develop an agenda for preparing a bold and highly visible comprehensive program for managing growth, with firmer legal footing and acceptance by the development community than previous efforts had enjoyed.

The United States Geological Survey occupied its new national headquarters building at Reston in 1973. It moved out of Washington, D.C., as part of the federal government's effort to decentralize many of its agencies. Within the million square foot building are housed the world's largest earth science library, modern geological and hydrological laboratories, and a topographical mapping plant. Courtesy of Fairfax County Economic Development Authority

The result of this effort was the county's Planned Land Use System, popularly called PLUS. This did not disturb the Board of Supervisors' decision-making function in the management of growth, but aimed at improving the amount and quality of information that the Board had to perform that function. Instead of basing decisions on the litmus tests of access to sewer and water, the PLUS program sought to provide data on air and water quality, traffic congestion, school enrollments, and a wide range of other consequences of a proposed development. It would identify and compare options of density control for the Board's consideration. After extensive public debate the Board approved the system in principle and ordered an agenda to be prepared for implementing it. The timetable called for the necessary studies and plans to be completed by 1975.

Throughout 1973 and 1974 public debate focused on proposals for an Interim Development Control Ordinance, regarded by developers as another moratorium, and adoption of the ordinance was followed by the filing of over one hundred lawsuits challenging its validity. They succeeded in nullifying the moratorium and any other chance of directly influencing the timing of development in western Fairfax County.

While the county's attorneys tried unsuccessfully to find an acceptable method for timing development, its planners were gathering the data for new land-use plans throughout the county, district by district. Such a compilation of data had not occurred since the McHugh Master Plan of 1959. Emphasis was put on building a basis for planning comprehensively with a unified approach to the analysis of growth problems. Detailed applications of the countywide plan would be worked out in four designated "planning areas" and a procedure was established for increasing cooperative participation of officials, staff and the public. A massive remapping and rezoning review was undertaken based on the expanded and updated body of planning information.

Adoption of the PLUS program in September 1975 put in place a critically important part of the foundation needed to receive and manage the pressure for development that could be seen in every part of Fairfax County. Throughout the steps taken in adopting the four Area Plans and the Countywide Plan, the Board of Supervisors had insisted that the planning process must involve the public; PLUS was not to be solely the product of professional planners in ivory towers. Remarkably, also, the entire county had been replanned in a year and a half, and from this new plateau the board would have a better chance than ever before to avoid the consequences of uncontrolled growth. The work of implementing this new perspective was hampered by continuing land-use litigation. In addition, county elections

The Skyline Center at Baileys Crossroads provided an urban center at the eastern end of the county with mixed-use residential and commercial highrise buildings when it was constructed in the early 1970s. The Washington Monument can be seen in the distance. Courtesy of the photographer, Scott W. Boatright

held two months after adoption of the PLUS program, highlighted issues of growth, environment, housing, and the backlog of zoning business accumulated during the "Pause for Planning" that had occurred. In the 1975 election the chief proponents of PLUS were defeated. The new board approached the problems of development with the premise that the county's management objective should be to emphasize the quality rather than the quantity of growth. This was echoed in the report of a special committee—The Committee to Study the Means of Encouraging Industrial Development in Fairfax County—appointed by the Board of Supervisors in June 1976. The committee, popularly called "The Blue Ribbon Committee," was composed of sixteen leading members of the business and development communities. Its charge was to find out why the county was not able to attract major business investment to it and recommend what should be done to improve that situation. The critical need was to relieve residential taxpayers of the growing burden of their property taxes by increasing the share of taxes paid by business and industry. With news of the recent California taxpayers' revolt clearly in mind, and with nearly 65 percent of Fairfax County's workforce traveling daily into Arlington and Washington, the task force foresaw that unless it realigned its tax base the county would continue to be a bedroom community and would eventually lose its ability to finance the high quality of public service it desired.

In its report The Blue Ribbon Committee singled out three basic factors impeding attraction of new business and five secondary problem areas. Basic factors included (1) a general perception that the county government was "anti-business"; (2) a finding that substantial inefficiency prevailed in parts of the county's administrative process for approving business development proposals; and (3) the county's economic development program lacked sufficient support from the Board of Supervisors to enable it to assure that the county's economic growth goals would be achieved.

The Committee's advice was equally direct and forceful: change the county's reputation to a pro-business attitude; do whatever was needed to achieve greater productivity and efficiency in handling approval of development proposals; and support the Economic Development Authority in "an aggressive marketing and sales campaign" to increase the commercial-industrial portion of the county's tax base. The Committee also cited five problem areas that were secondary to the basic issue of the county's image in the business world. These were a tax structure that discouraged business, unrealistically high costs of housing for moderate income residents, unrealistic wage rates that discouraged local recruiting of needed labor, transportation and utility deficiencies, and a school system that needed strengthening.

The Blue Ribbon Committee's report became a blueprint for the county's economic development strategy from 1976 to 1987. In varying degrees all of its recommendations were accepted and acted upon. Several of its members went on to become members of the new Fiscal Policy Advisory Commission, formed to assist in developing details of a new tax structure. Its report in March 1979 emphasized The Blue Ribbon Committee's call for increasing the commercial-industrial share of the tax base, from fourteen percent to twenty-five percent in ten years, but it also recognized the larger context of this task. Philip M. Reilly, a former Chairman of the Fairfax County Chamber of Commerce and member of the Fiscal Policy Advisory Commission, remembered the group's role this way:

[We recognized] we can't just have wild cancerous growth. But . . .the population was going to come here, and if we didn't want wall-to-wall subdivisions we had to do something to grow the business infrastructure . . . The trick is to make it manageable, and liveable, and to make sure the facilities are there so we can enjoy what's going to happen here. This is, after all, a great place.

Shown at the 1991 Fairfax County Chamber of Commerce Annual Turkey Roast are, left to right, former Chairman of the Chamber Philip Reilly; Northern Virginia Congressman Frank Wolf; and Chairman of the Chamber Burwell Gunn. Courtesy of Fairfax County Chamber of Commerce

CHAPTER

3

Corridors of Commerce; Centers of Growth

At the opening of the 1980s, Charles Gulledge, Chairman of the Fairfax County Economic Development Authority, described the authority's aim for the county as follows:

We did not want to be the bedroom community for Washington. Our objectives were to control the quality of growth, to attract corporate headquarters and high technology organizations rather than heavy industry, and also to attract the supporting infrastructure—small businesses, shopping centers, and the like.

The EDA pursued this objective through advertising the county's quality environment, its first-rate schools, educated workforce, AAA bond rating, and, most important, its available office-industrial sites close to Washington. Although many observers believed it impossible to achieve, EDA commissioners announced a goal of raising the commercial-industrial portion of the county's tax base from 14 percent (the 1976 level) to 25 percent in ten years. The new Board of Supervisors, under Chairman John Herrity, endorsed the objective and set about expanding the inventory of land available for business development. It was nothing short of astonishing that the goal was surpassed; by 1987, the commercial-industrial share reached 25.5 percent; in 1989, the commercial-industrial portion of the county's real estate tax base rose to 26.76 percent.

Hard work was involved in changing Fairfax County's image to the one projected in the ads, and prospects wavered before they turned in favor of the county. Many thought the upturn came in 1980 when Mobil Corporation moved its U.S. Marketing and Refining Divisions to Fairfax, to be followed by the company's world-wide headquarters. In any event, the campaign to make Fairfax County a high-technology center gradually began to show results. The EDA's definition of "high-tech" business was

Flowering trees and shrubs enhance the Mobil Corporation headquarters building entrance in spring and summer, making it an attractive neighbor in the area and a pleasant place in which to work. Mobil is one of three Fortune 500 companies in Fairfax County. Courtesy of Mobil Corporation

The Mobil Corporation opened a branch of the company on Gallows Road and I-495 in 1980. The relocation of the entire corporate headquarters from New York to the county was completed in 1990. About four thousand employees in all work for Mobil in Northern Virginia. Courtesy of the photographer, Tom Schudel

deliberately put in general terms—"organizations using technological innovation as a basis for providing services or products by technically oriented disciplines involving skilled technical and professional labor and reflecting the existing state of the discipline's art." The EDA concentrated on five categories of such business:

Operations Research, providing research and development services in highly specialized fields relating to defense and other federal programs dealing with complex telecommunications and logistical problems. By 1983, the county had more than 120 of these "think tanks" including Advanced Technology, BDM International, Matrek Division of MITRE, Planning Research Corporation (PRC), and TRW's Defense Systems Group.

Electronic Research and Development firms producing electronic hardware and software components—computers, computer programming, radar, communications systems—testing and fabrication of prototypes and limited numbers of models. Almost one hundred such firms were in the county by 1983, including Melpar Division of E Systems, Pulsecom Division of Harvey Hubbell, Inc., and various divisions of Sperry Corporation.

Computer Programming and Data Processing firms specializing in processing information, computer sale and service, systems analysis and programming. About 90 firms of this type were in Fairfax County in 1983, including Tandem Computer Corporation, Computer Sciences Corporation and Boeing Computer Services.

Biological/Environmental Research and Development firms working in biological, chemical, medical, environmental and related fields to develop vaccines, protein-rich foods, synthetic human skin, kidney filters and pharmaceutical products. Among the leaders in this category in 1983 were Hazleton Laboratories, Meloy Laboratories and National Health Laboratories.

Telecommunications firms offering information transmission by a variety of carriers with highly sophisticated electronic components and systems using computers and satellites. Some of the major members of this category in 1983 were Satellite Business Systems, Comsat Telesystems, GTE Telenet Communications, and AT&T Long Lines.

Better than one out of every four firms in Fairfax County in 1981 were classified as high technology according to the Economic Development Authority, and this number grew as the economic recession of 1981-1982 gave way to a period of optimistic expansion. By 1990 these benchmark figures of the early '80s had boosted the number of high-tech firms to 660. Other types of supporting services also were drawn to the centers where the high-tech industries were located—consulting services, financial, accounting and legal services, printing, temporary help and delivery services, restaurants, hotels and the like. In addition, a growing number of corporate headquarters and administrative offices, associations, and foundations were attracted to the county. In particular they settled in the Tysons Corner area, mostly in buildings of modern design in campus-like settings.

The new businesses locating in the Tysons Corner area joined a concentration of earlier retail development that by the early 1980s already commanded a regional market. In the mid-1960s Leesburg Pike (Route 7) west of Tysons Corner had become the "automobile row" of western Fairfax County as rising land values in Arlington County forced the automobile retail district there to move. As this occurred, in 1968, construction of Tysons Corner Center—one of the first covered shopping malls in the country—drew national attention to the area. As of 1987, Tysons Corner, with 1.8 million square feet, consisted of five major department stores (Hecht's, Woodward & Lothrop, Bloomingdales, Lord & Taylor, Nordstrom), 140 shops, 18 restaurants and 12 movie theaters. After a renovation and expansion costing $150 million–the most expensive in retail history—the mall had 2.2 million

BDM was a pioneer in integrating Command/Control/Communications/Intelligence (C3I) systems by combining BDM-developed software and interfaces with off-the-shelf hardware components. Systems to forecast and manage large-scale resource requirements need complex development and integration skills. Photo by Kay Chernush, Courtesy of BDM International, Inc.

When Melpar, a subsidiary of Westinghouse Airbrake Company, now E Systems, constructed their brick office building on Route 50 in 1952, it changed the perception of how development should be done. Set back from the busy highway next to what in the 1960s became the Capital Beltway, the sweeping lawns, elaborate foundation plantings, numerous mature trees, and small pond provided a splendid example of how a workplace should look. The campus-like appearance has been emulated in Fairfax County and Northern Virginia business and industrial development ever since. Courtesy of E Systems

The regional headquarters for AT&T Communications was built in Oakton in 1980. A "crystal palace" of glass, it stands as a constant reminder of the growing importance of sophisticated electronic communications in the computer-oriented network of present-day industry and government. Courtesy of the photographer, Tom Schudel

The present intersection of Route 7 and Route 123, shown here, gives no hint of the small stores which once occupied the corners of this former country crossroads shortly before Tysons Corner I, now Tysons Corner Center, opened in 1968. Courtesy of the photographer, Scott W. Boatright

43

Route 7, the Leesburg Pike, is shown in the lower left corner of this view of Tysons Corner taken in 1991. The first major Tysons Corner development was undertaken by Theodore N. Lerner and completed in 1968 as Tysons Corner I, (foreground). Major additions to the lower level and new parking garages were added in 1988, and Nordstrom and Lord & Taylor opened in 1990. The total number of stores and businesses is 230. Other anchors are Bloomingdales, Hecht's, and Woodward & Lothrop, with a total of 2,082,877 square feet of space. Tysons II, the Galleria (upper center) was developed by H-L Mall Venture—the Homart Development Corporation and Lerner Development Company. It opened in 1988 with 120 stores in 800,000 square feet of space. Anchor stores are Macy's, Saks Fifth Avenue, and Nieman Marcus. Courtesy of the photographer, Scott W. Boatright

This 1991 aerial view of part of the Tysons Corner complex shows Tycon Tower and the Marriott Hotel in the middle foreground. Tysons Corner Center is to the right of center. Leesburg Pike, Route 7, runs diagonally to the top right corner. The three buildings which form Fairfax Square, left of center, include such businesses as AT&T, Merrill Lynch, Tiffany & Company, Gucci, Hermes, Morton's, la cicogna, Louis Vuitton, Primi Piatti, and Fendi. Courtesy of the photographer, Scott W. Boatright

This poster was used to promote Fairfax County's Tourism and Convention Bureau at a Philadelphia conference in 1989. Leisure travelers come to Fairfax County to shop as well as to visit cultural and historic sites and recreational facilities and to attend conferences. Tourism figures have risen dramatically in recent years. Courtesy of Fairfax County Economic Development Authority

square feet of retail space, making it one of the largest shopping centers in the United States. In 1988, also, a companion development, Tysons II, was opened adjacent to Tysons Corner Center and began a fifteen year project intended to add a 375,000 square foot corporate office center and a retail mall which would bring the area's retail space to 3.3 million square feet. By 1989, this new space was rapidly being occupied, paced by such legendary stores as Macy's, Nieman Marcus and Saks Fifth Avenue.

Impressive as this record of retail accomplishments was, the reputation of Tysons Corner as "Virginia's largest downtown" is based equally on success in attracting and accommodating a broadly-based spectrum of business—corporate headquarters, banks, technical and business services, research and development firms, and precision technical manufacturing. The Fairfax County EDA's *Directory of Business and Industry* for 1988 listed Tysons Corner as having 463 businesses (or 725 with the McLean and Vienna area included), occupying 16.6 million square feet of office space and over 5 million square feet of retail, hotel, and other commercial uses, and employing 70,000 to 80,000 people.

A more spectacular success in promoting economic growth could scarcely be imagined; certainly it exceeded the goal set by the county's Fiscal Policy Advisory Commission in 1979. But, similar to the experience in other rapidly-growing urban centers, there were certain tradeoffs. Among these tradeoff areas were the quality of the environment and the convenience of transportation. Although the businesses that Fairfax County attracted were "clean" industries that did not produce unusual amounts of hazardous wastes or byproducts, there was an inevitable increase in commuting and other traffic with all the impacts found to be associated with such activity.

In contrast to Tysons Corner where the planning process had to be reactive to development pressure, the other two centers of growth at the beginning of the 1980s had had the benefit of advanced community planning and proceeded to grow more consistently in accordance with planned objectives. Springfield, located in the Shirley Highway/I-95 corridor where it intersects the Capital Beltway, was the first place in Fairfax County to implement a large-scale development plan. Washington Realtor Edward R. Carr conceived his own master plan for the Springfield area in 1946, acquiring for it the last sizeable tract of accessible undeveloped land within a twelve-mile ring around Washington. When sewer and water became available in 1952 residential development was commenced, followed by shopping centers, schools, churches and parks. In the 1960s, as I-95 was expanded and the Beltway was added, these advantages, plus access to the lines of the Southern Railway and the Richmond, Fredericksburg & Potomac Railroad, gave Springfield the capacity to develop a mix of industrial, business and retail uses along with a residential component.

In 1982 Edward R. Carr Associates was Northern Virginia's largest local builder and had brought national recognition to both Carr and Fairfax County for success-

The interchange of Routes I-395, I-495, and I-95 near Springfield is the busiest and most congested in Fairfax County. The Capital Beltway overpasses Route I-395 at this point. Utilization of nearby space includes three ballfields and several community parks adjacent to the busy highways. Courtesy of the photographer, Scott W. Boatright

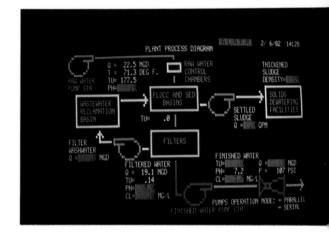

At the Fairfax County Water Authority's filtration plant near Herndon, the water treatment process is controlled, monitored, and recorded through computerized equipment located in an operational control center which also houses supervisory personnel and laboratory facilities. Serving 900,000 people, the Authority also supplies water to Alexandria, part of Prince William County, and will eventually supply Loudoun County. Its purification facility can process 186 million gallons a day. Courtesy of Fairfax County Water Authority

ful planning and development. It also had prepared the way to expand with the county's business boom. Around the unique combination of transportation facilities Springfield developed a central business district (offices, hotels, banks, restaurants, commercial services), one of the county's four shopping malls (Springfield Mall), and, running south from the core area, a strip of automotive dealers and service businesses.

Springfield's central business district is flanked by two industrial parks north of the Capital Beltway and by the U.S. General Services Administration's 70-acre Storage Depot on the south side. Further south in the I-95 corridor the concentration of industrial and commercial use continues with warehouses, storage tank compounds, lumber yards, and automotive services. Springfield's industrial and commercial areas are the oldest such areas in the county, and in the 1990s will be the first to be ripe for redevelopment. The timing of such redevelopment hinges on completion of the so-called Springfield Bypass, now known as the Fairfax County Parkway, a projected outer circumferential expressway through the western parts of Fairfax County from the Leesburg Pike (Route 7) past Herndon, Reston, Centreville, and Burke Centre to I-95 at West Springfield. By the summer of 1990 construction was completed from the Dulles Access Road to I-66 with completion of the remainder pending availability of funding.

The third center of growth going into the 1980s was the "new town" of Reston, planned and commenced by Robert E. Simon in 1962. Later taken over by Gulf Reston (1967) and then by Reston Land Corporation (1978), it had grown to a population of 35,000 in 1980. Facing the new decade, Reston looked both to its past and to its future. In 1981, the Fairfax County Board of Supervisors designated Washington Plaza in Reston's Lake Anne Village Center as a historic district and nominated it for listing on the National Register of Historic Places for its successful application of the New Town planning and design concepts.

Looking forward, as the national economic downturn of 1980-1981 subsided, Reston was positioned extremely well to become a center of high-tech research and development, business services and administrative headquarters. A sampling of the businesses moving to Reston in the 1980s included Sperry Systems Management's research and development facility; Centec, an energy and environmental consultant; the headquarters of the American Alliance for Health, Physical Education, Recreation and Dance; the American Press Institute, and Sky Courier, an international delivery firm. In 1981, Tandem Computers, at that time the fastest growing computer manufacturer in the United States, built its eastern regional headquarters in Reston's industrial park, explaining its choice by the geographical location plus the strong sense of community and environmental values. Two years later, GTE Business Communications made similar statements as it opened Reston's Tech Park. No better proof of this high-tech advantage could be asked than when in 1986 the National Aeronautics and Space Administration (NASA) chose Reston as the site of its space station program headquarters and prepared to communicate by space satellite with the U.S. Geological Survey, located at the opposite end of Reston's Sunrise Valley Drive. As the 1980s ended, Reston clearly was on the leading edge of both the wave of high-tech development and the desire to have residential and business development and amenities in well-planned proximity.

As favorable economic conditions returned in 1982, Reston's total community concept and environmental design attracted increased development and its fourth village center was opened. Prospects for its future were strengthened in 1984 by construction of toll lanes parallel to the Dulles Access Road from Reston to the Beltway at Tysons Corner. The toll lanes were named after their Virginia legislative sponsors in July 1991; the road is now called the Omer L. Hirst-Adelard Brault Expressway. At about the same time, route alignment for the Fairfax County Parkway through Reston was agreed on with construction to begin in 1986. This also was the year when plans were completed for Reston's Town Center, a 460-acre district designed to serve as "Downtown Reston," with an 85-acre urban core

Developed by Franconia Associates, Springfield Mall, near Route I-95 on Franconia Road, first opened in 1973 with 230 stores and Penney's and Montgomery Ward as anchors. In 1991, a new anchor, Macy's (foreground) was added as well as 45 new stores with a total of 1,700,000 square feet in area. Courtesy of the photographer, Scott W. Boatright

One of the largest and best-known such companies in the eastern United States, Virginia Concrete was founded in 1941 by C.J. Shepherdson, Sr., who still serves as a vice president and director of the now parent company, Florida Rock Industries. The first plant was at the Alexandria-Fairfax boundary line on Telegraph Road. There are now twelve plants in Northern Virginia, four of them in Fairfax County. This photograph was taken at the Springfield plant in the 1980s. Vulcan Materials Company nearby is Virginia Concrete's main aggregate supplier. Courtesy of Fairfax County Economic Development Authority

The eliptical plaza at Lake Anne Village Center was designed in part as a "people place" where groups could gather for numerous cultural and recreational activities. It has accomplished this purpose in addition to functioning as a business and residential center. Courtesy of Reston Land Corporation

Washington Gas Light Company provides natural gas service throughout Fairfax County. Additional gas mains are being laid as shown here for new customers, but strong conservation measures have actually decreased consumption. Courtesy of Northern Virginia Natural Gas

Robert Simon's original master plan for Reston called for a Town Center to provide a highly urban landscape in the heart of a rural setting. As opened in the fall of 1990, the Town Center consisted of a 12 story Hyatt Regency Hotel, twin office buildings, commercial and residential components, and a cultural center. The architects for this project were RTKL Associates. Courtesy of the photographer, Scott W. Boatright

Westfields International Conference Center opened in 1989 at an 1,100-acre campus office park off Route 28 near Dulles International Airport. Like a number of other new conference centers in Northern Virginia, its main business is generated by continuing education programs and corporate executive retreats. State-of-the-art media centers are among many specialized service functions, along with lodging, dining, and recreational facilities. The meetings market has more than tripled in the past ten years. Courtesy of the photographer, Scott W. Boatright

Fair Lakes One houses the Hazel/Peterson Companies headquarters. Tall specimen hardwoods were retained on the site. Water resources engineering resulted in an adjacent manmade lake which, with its fountains and surrounding forest, helps to create an aesthetically pleasing environment. Courtesy of Fairfax County Economic Development Authority

accommodating office and retail space, a hotel, restaurants, theaters, structured parking, and pedestrian streetscapes. Adjacent to the center was located the county's regional government center. Reston's Town Center had its grand opening in September 1990 as *The New York Times* commented that it might well "be setting a new national pattern for what would be called a new city"—an urban place in a rural setting.

While achievement of an independent economy based on high-tech industries and their associated services was progressing in the three major centers in Fairfax County coming into the 1980s, foresighted developers were preparing the way for others like them. One of the most successful of these developers was Hazel/Peterson Companies, which acquired tracts of land near the crossing of I-66, US 50 and West Ox Road. This area became known as Fair Lakes, a center for commercial and residential development. Nearby, Taubmann Construction built the Fair Oaks shopping mall and office complex. Adjacent to these developments is the site of the new county government office complex, completed in 1992. This location at the center of western Fairfax County will rely on the presence of the county government to make it a major growth center in the future.

Fairfax County Parkway near Route 66 was a Dewberry & Davis transportation project in the late 1980s. The Fair Lakes complex built there consists of 660 acres of a mixed-use business park whose companies include firms such as Aetna, Mohasco, TRW Federal Systems, a Hyatt Hotel, and Hazel/Peterson. Photograph by Maxwell MacKenzie. Courtesy of Dewberry & Davis

Another area identified for development was the corridor running south from Dulles Airport along Route 28 to Centreville. On the west side of Route 28 the Dulles South Industrial Area of seventy-five acres is zoned for industrial and commercial uses by a variety of airport-oriented businesses. On the east side of Route 28 the Dulles East Suburban Center is zoned for a mix of retail, industrial and commercial uses. Here developers foresaw the potential for new industrial parks developed to serve retail, office, warehouse, manufacturing, and business service needs. As 1984 ended, the Fairfax County Economic Development Authority reported that half of the industrial and hybrid development going on in the county was taking place along Route 28 and its total industrial/hybrid development was fast overtaking the total of the Springfield/Newington area—the county's long-standing industrial center. As the decade of the 1990s began, the Dulles/Route 28 corridor looked forward to growing into an urban center in fact if not in name.

The critical question in the decade of the 1980s was managing the timing of growth at Fair Oaks, along Route 28, and at a handful of other sites in the county. In some instances, this timing depended on extending or improving transportation facilities, but this was a period when the Virginia Department of Transportation (VDOT) and Fairfax County could not increase road building appropriations. In such circumstances, innovative measures by private sector groups appeared. In the case of Route 28, the need for increasing local highway capacity was approached through formation of a "transportation management association." Created in 1988 and representing a wide range of public agencies and private interests concerned with transportation, the group made traffic congestion its first target. Its efforts ranged from promoting employer-sponsored van pools to persuading developers to donate additional right-of-way for road widenings.

Efforts to speed up timing of development in the Route 28 corridor took the form of creating a special tax district under enabling legislation by the Virginia General Assembly. All the land in the Dulles South Industrial Area and East Suburban Center lies within the Route 28 Tax District and use of the special tax district will accelerate completion of the highway infrastructure of the corridor without waiting for governmental roadbuilding programs. Use of a special tax district was also proposed in 1988 to finance construction of a rapid transit rail line in the median strip of the Dulles Access Road from the airport to the West Falls Church Metro station and to extend the Dulles Toll Road westward from the airport to Leesburg. Meanwhile, a bond issue was passed to fund express bus service to Dulles Airport, and to build necessary parking lots for users.

The former Northern Virginia Building Industry Association headquarters, now the Fair Lakes Office Building, won a merit award from the National Association of Industrial Office Parks. Courtesy of Dewberry & Davis

Parsons Brinckerhoff has specialized in transportation planning and design since 1885 and has been active in projects related to Fairfax County's infrastructure for over twenty years. Shown here is a bridge which provides access to the new Fairfax County government center and the Fair Oaks Mall and office and hotel complex. It crosses over Route I-66, and opened to traffic in 1990. Courtesy of The Artery Organization

The Fairfax County Government Center opened in 1992 replacing the Massey Building, which has opened in 1969 in Fairfax City. The new center is located across route I-66 from Fair Oaks Mall and contains 675,000 square feet of floor space. The architects of the U-shaped building were RTKL Associates, Inc. of Baltimore; the builders were Charles E. Smith Company/ The Artery Organization Partnership. It is made of reinforced and precast concrete, has tinted glass windows, and natural stone and wood veneer interior trim. Courtesy of the photographer, Scott W. Boatright

Another important method of accelerating the timing of development, known in the 1970s but used increasingly throughout the 1980s, was the so-called "proffer system." Under legislation passed in 1978, the county was authorized to accept the donation of property or improvements by landowners or developers in order to remove "development issues" arising in processing zoning applications. Thus, when Mobil Corporation elected to build its headquarters on Gallows Road near the Beltway, it made generous contributions of property and money to help promptly provide the additional roads to solve traffic problems at that location. And Canadian developers of land at US Route 50 and the Beltway agreed to similar contributions so they could go forward with development at that site. Proffers also have been used to bring project plans into compliance with various environmental protection standards or residents' concerns about impacts of development. Enhancement of neighborhood amenities and preservation of natural or historic landmarks also have benefitted from the use of proffers.

The continuing development of Tysons Corner in the 1980s tested the proffer system severely as the costs of land and road construction there soared. One example in 1982 involved negotiations over contribution of land for three interchanges and $25 million toward their construction costs. In this case, VDOT's position that these needed improvements could only be provided if the owner proffered them was criticized as too great an expectation. One observer summed up the matter thus: "There just are so many Mobils . . . The idea that Fairfax is such a great place that developers will pay any price is an idea that will have to be dispelled." This case notwithstanding, the proffer system generally worked well in the 1980s to ease development proposals past many of the prerequisites that determined the timing of growth.

Not all problems of opening new areas to dense development could be solved by proffers, however, and no case in the decade demonstrated this more dramatically than the efforts to preserve water quality and supply in the watershed of the Occoquan River, covering much of the southwestern sector of Fairfax County. Acting on the premise that the water resources in this area would be threatened if dense development was allowed, the Board of Supervisors in June 1982 downzoned much of the Occoquan Basin to maintain its prevailing sparse residential pattern. Henceforth, rights to develop it to greater density, even with proffers aimed at reducing adverse environmental impacts, could be granted only by special approval of the Supervisors.

Suits challenging both the county's power to downzone and its application in this case were promptly started, but in 1984 the merits of the county's action were upheld by the courts. Subsequently similar holdings sustained downzoning in other places where conservation needs were established, until, in 1988, the Northern Virginia Chapter of the Associated Builders and Contractors protested them as being piecemeal action and called for the issue to be faced on a countywide basis.

This call was part of a larger public discussion over the county's policy on the pace of growth which had gone on at varying levels of intensity since the 1950s. As it was carried on in the 1980s, the case for a slow growth policy was made by Supervisor Audrey Moore who argued in 1982 that rapid residential growth had driven up costs, especially of schools, and was keeping taxes high and services thin. Other members of the Board were more cautious, feeling that the county's efforts to stimulate commercial-industrial development were gradually achieving the desired balance in the tax base, and that more aggressive growth-control measures would stigmatize the county as "anti-business and anti-growth". Moreover, many in the county agreed with Board Chairman John Herrity's view that it was too late to check residential growth and so priority should be given to conserving the remaining supply of commercial and industrial land.

The debate over growth policy also touched the matter of incentives to postpone development. As early as 1980 the Board of Supervisors ordered a study of the pros and cons of assessing land according to its actual use rather than its market value. State law authorized assessment for agricultural, horticultural, forest and open space uses as ways of helping farmers who wished to keep their land intact rather than sell it because of high taxes. This incentive became more realistic in 1981 when the General Assembly authorized creation of miniature agricultural and forest districts as small as 25 acres. Fairfax County's first such district was established in 1981 for 638 acres of dairy farm and open space near Dranesville.

The time required to review and approve development proposals for compliance with planning and zoning procedures had been a major target of criticism by the Blue Ribbon Committee in 1976. Since then processing by the Department of Environmental Management and other county agencies had become more time-consuming as requirements for analysis and evaluation of environmental, socio-economic and other impacts were added to the normal schedule of zoning reviews. Private sector resourcefulness, however, reacted to this problem. Conceived by Sidney Dewberry, head of Dewberry & Davis, one of Northern Virginia's most successful engineering and planning firms, the Engineers and Surveyors Institute (ESI) was established in the fall of 1987 as a nonprofit group representing nineteen of the area's land development and engineering firms. Their first target was reduction of the time consumed by the county's approval procedures. Cooperative dialogue with the concerned county staff produced a number of improvements both in preparation of private architectural and engineering plans and in state and county processing of project applications. In another instance VDOT agreed to complete work on sixth high-priority intersections during the 1988 construction season if the time usually needed to draft design and engineering plans could be saved. ESI arranged for its members to donate $150,000 worth of design services to produce the necessary plans and so expedited elimination of some of the county's worst traffic bottlenecks.

Dewberry and the ESI have stressed the critical need for education of both public and private sector players in the development process. Fairfax County's land use regulations had become complex, and an understanding of them as well as sound engineering was necessary if high quality work was to be expected.

Fairfax County's business community has also recognized its stake in education by supporting strongly the creation of a school of engineering at George Mason University in 1985, and in the secondary school system it has provided money and in kind help for the Thomas Jefferson School for Science and Technology. Business people have served on school committees and chaired school bond referenda committees. The keynote for efforts to strengthen this part of the infrastructure of growth may well have been expressed by Earle C. Williams, President and Chief Executive Officer of BDM International, Inc., addressing a meeting of academic administrators in 1982:

There is no question but that the new technologies will profoundly alter our economy and society in future years and that the colleges and universities must prepare their students for this changing world. Industry and business need to develop a new relationship with the higher education community and to begin a serious and meaningful dialogue to see how each can help the other . . . Meeting the technical needs alone will not be adequate. Our educational response should be comprehensive and should provide a place for the liberal arts and sciences and the humanities in the technical curriculum. Our community will not benefit from narrow, socially and culturally illiterate technocrats as citizens and neighbors.

Earle C. Williams, President and Chief Executive Officer of BDM. Courtesy of BDM International, Inc.

The Fair Oaks Shopping Center, which opened in 1980, with an addition completed in 1987, was originally developed by Fair Oaks Associates of Troy, Michigan. The complex contains 1,400,000 square feet of space. Two flyover bridges, designed by Dewberry & Davis, facilitate control of vehicular access from Route 50. There are 210 stores and five anchors—Woodward & Lothrop, the Hecht Company, Sears Roebuck, Penney's, and Lord & Taylor. Courtesy of the photographer, Scott W. Boatright

Fairview Park, located at the Capital Beltway and Route 50, was planned and the initial phase was built in 1988 as a high quality mixed-use development appropriate to the prime location and the county's objective of economic development and compatible infill. Dewberry & Davis designed the main road, the lake, and stormwater management design and site engineering for each of the office buildings. The complex was recognized for excellence in design by both the Northern Virginia Community Appearance Alliance and the Fairfax County Exceptional Design Awards Program. Photograph by Joe Romeo, Courtesy of Dewberry & Davis

Work for the Washington Metropolitan Area Transit Authority included design components by Dewberry & Davis of the H-1 section of Metro's line to Springfield-Franconia in the 1980s. The Washington, D.C., skyline can be seen across the Potomac River in this view. Courtesy of Dewberry & Davis

Fairfax County in the 1980s learned a great deal about managing the dynamics of growth. Although this generally had been accomplished without destroying the very socio-economic and environmental values that made the county attractive, it was apparent to many that the debate over growth had not been entirely resolved. Despite the spectacular success to be seen in its urban centers, the impressive evidence of prosperity reflected in the development activity going on, and the pride derived from knowing that the county had more commercial office space than Baltimore, Philadelphia, Houston and Cleveland combined, a clash of attitudes toward growth surfaced in the Board of Supervisors elections of 1987, and swung the composition of the board to a decidedly more cautious approach.

It was, however, possible to see a change in the context as it carried into the 1990s. Specifically, the alignment of the board members was changing from a division along lines of Democrats and Republicans to a division of developed versus developing areas of the county. The developed areas—close-in, older, thoroughly urbanized and less wealthy than the developing districts of the western part of the county—now began to see concerns focusing on assigning priorities. It was not an issue limited to the context of land subdivision; it would be reflected in such things as proposals for emergency housing shelters and funding of special language programs to teach Vietnamese and Hispanic residents to read English well enough to become part of the labor force and understand the American marketplace.

In this context the human resources for growth are becoming a focal point. Looking ahead to the labor force needed to support the high-tech economy of the county's urban centers, several things were becoming clear in the 1980s. The number of entry level and low-wage jobs grew faster than the traditional local sources of supply grew. The pool of young workers was shrinking because the Baby Boomers were aging. Also it was not easy to build up a new pool when the region's supply of moderate and low-cost housing was disappearing. Throughout the 1980s little was done to control the trend to convert to condominiums the older garden apartments built in the 1950s and 1960s, or to assure that such conversions did not leave the new owners with serious basic improvement needs beneath the cosmetics applied by the converters. This trend went on in the older developed areas while new housing developments moved further west into the county's open spaces to become accessible only by automobile.

As the decade of the 1990s began employers in the "urban centers" of Tysons Corner, Springfield, Reston and Fair Oaks began to experiment with sources of labor such as retirees, military spouses and immigrants. Success in using these sources often turns on the availability of child care, elder care, and educational programs to help reentry into the workforce. In many personnel offices of the county's business community the marching orders for the 1990s were: "Recruit, Retrain, Retain."

The most visible aspect of the growth issue as it was faced in the mature and the new developing parts of the county was, of course, the priority given to redevelopment efforts. The earliest recognition of this need was in the US Route 1 corridor—an eight-mile strip from Alexandria south to Fort Belvoir and Woodlawn Plantation, characterized by uncoordinated local retail commercial enterprises. Housing developed in the same uncoordinated pattern behind the roadside commercial strip, and ranged from high-rise apartments and condominiums near the Huntington Metro station at the north and through townhouse and single family residential neighborhoods and mobile home parks further south. Little new development was started along US Route 1 in the 1970s, but significant interest in some of the open space at the south end of the corridor appeared in the late 1980s. Redevelopment was difficult because land ownership along US Route 1 was fragmented into hundreds of individual holdings. Accordingly in 1981, when redevelopment was seriously considered, it was proposed that a non-stock, nonprofit corporation be

Dewberry & Davis provided architectural and engineering services to the Marriott Corporation for development of The Fairfax, a 37-acre campus-like lifecare facility for elderly and retired military personnel near Fort Belvoir, the old Fairfax family estate. Photograph by Joe Romeo, Courtesy of Dewberry & Davis

formed to manage a large urban-style redevelopment project. The first step toward making the project attractive for investment would have to be to consolidate ownership of the land to be redeveloped in one party. Such an approach would require the support of county government, business and residents, but eventually would result in re-arranging the existing strip development into a series of four Community Business Centers separated by suburban residential neighborhoods.

Any future redevelopment of the US Route 1 corridor will necessarily be strongly influenced by the future development of Fort Belvoir, located at the corridor's southern end. This federal military reservation contains approximately 8,300 acres divided between Fort Belvoir's military post and the Humphreys Engineer Center. Originating in the First World War to train military engineers, it was retained as the Army's principal school for engineer officers and one of its active engineering research and development centers. In the 1940s and 1950s, its hospital and fire department served the nearby civilian community, and presently these activities, plus police support, are still carried out under mutual aid agreements. The tradition of service continues. In 1991, Fort Belvoir received the Pentagon's "Communities of Excellence" Award as the best medium-sized post in the Army in terms of the services it provided. In recent years, Fort Belvoir has been one of Fairfax County's largest employers with a military and civilian workforce of approximately 12,000. Military personnel living on the post number about five thousand of which some are employed at other military installations in the area. Fort Belvoir is a major traffic generator in the area and has attracted satellite commercial strip development along US Route 1 and Telegraph Road in the vicinity of the post.

In 1988, as a result of federal legislation ordering the closure or relocation of many military bases and activities, Fort Belvoir began the transition from an active training base to an administrative and support center for Army activities in the national capital area. The Engineers School was relocated and replaced by a number of smaller headquarters of activities involving intelligence and security, logistics, mapping, management systems, research and development, and community and family support. Currently the county Comprehensive Plan envisions the development of Fort Belvoir as a Large Institutional Area. The county would also have an opportunity to add significantly to its park and recreation resources. Fort Belvoir now already includes wildlife reserves of some 1,250 acres, plus wetland wildfowl refuges and numerous locally and nationally significant historic and archaeological resources.

Other areas that in 1990 were candidates for redevelopment included Seven Corners, the Bailey's Crossroads-Annandale area, Merrifield, parts of Springfield, Herndon, and Centreville. All were areas with commercial histories from at least the mid-nineteenth century, and all qualified as suburban centers or community business centers. Commercial and industrial development was a mix of retail, personal and technical services, construction and improvement firms, professional, light manufacturing, branch banking, and wholesale distribution. New business locating in these areas during the 1980s introduced professional services, technology-oriented business and research and development firms.

Recognizing in 1984 that these and similar mature developed areas needed continued reinvestment if they were to remain economically competitive, the Board of Supervisors authorized a revitalization program. In 1987, refurbishing of neighborhoods, streets and streetscapes was begun. A year later county voters approved a $42 million bond issue for major public improvements to streets and utilities.

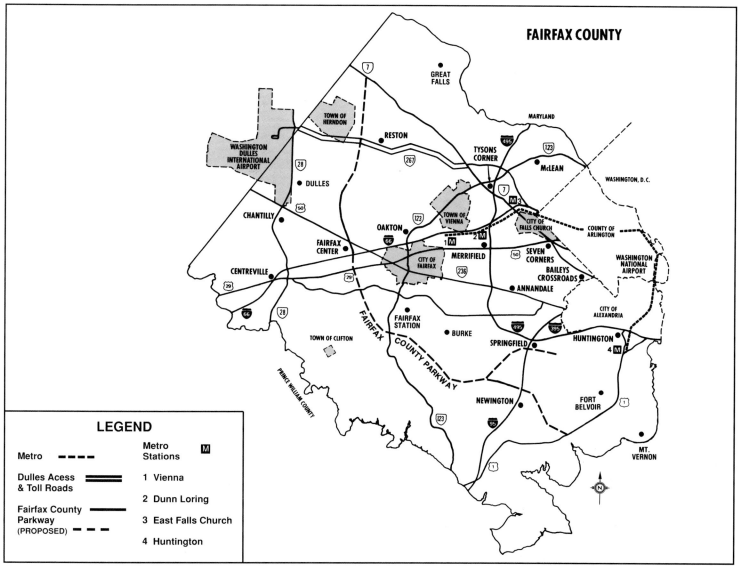

FAIRFAX COUNTY

LEGEND

Metro - - - -	Metro Stations [M]
Dulles Acess & Toll Roads ═══	1 Vienna
	2 Dunn Loring
Fairfax County Parkway ────	3 East Falls Church
(PROPOSED) - - -	4 Huntington

Revitalization aided efforts to bring new business into these areas but in addition the Economic Development Authority could offer qualifying small businesses the opportunity of financing through Industrial Development Bonds (IDBs) issued in conjunction with a federal Small Business program. During the high-interest years of the early 1980s such bonds appeared as an attractive alternative to bank financing. Changes in the federal tax code during the mid-1980s, however, eliminated the applicability of IDBs, resulting in substantially fewer applications being submitted to the EDA. Better news for small businesses was the creation of the Northern Virginia Local Development Company, a cooperative program of private financing plus the Small Business Administration guaranteed funding for acquisition of land, buildings, heavy machinery, equipment and the like.

Redevelopment was not always an easy task, however. By 1988, county officials were discovering challenges not usually found in new development. Projects in which the owners replaced small buildings with larger, more modern structures (as allowed by the zoning) changed the neighborhood's character — sometimes subtly, sometimes dramatically. Frequently, redevelopment also necessitated new infrastructure to meet the needs of increased density. Reston and Merrifield in particular were two areas facing this challenge.

As a response to the need for strengthening the planning process, the Board in 1987 initiated "Fairfax Planning Horizons," a complete review and re-writing of the county's Comprehensive Plan. Extensive study followed to produce a revised

A 1990 map of arterial highways, the Metro, and Washington Dulles International Airport shows major transportation systems. The Norfolk Southern and Richmond, Fredericksburg and Potomac rail lines (not shown) operate on tracks which cross the southern half of the county. Copyright 1990, courtesy of Fairfax County Economic Development Authority

The Lafarge Corporation, one of Fairfax County's three Fortune 500 companies, occupies the white rectangular building on Sunrise Valley Drive in Reston shown in the center of this aerial photograph. It is the American component of a French corporation whose primary business is cement manufacturing around the world. Shown clockwise from Lafarge are Software AG, Lucas Aerospace, Lake View Plaza, and the American College of Radiology. Courtesy of the photographer, Scott W. Boatright

statement of policies, goals and guidelines and, eventually, detailed plans for each of the county's four Planning Areas. The new Comprehensive Plan's Concept and Land Classification System was adopted by the Board of Supervisors in August 1990.

The plan carried forward without revision existing plans applicable to Tysons Corner, the Route 28 District, and Fort Belvoir's Engineering Proving Ground, all subjects of special planning studies. For the rest of the county, however, it provided a means of achieving more consistency in dealing with decisions on county growth over the next twenty years. Based on a massive countywide effort to involve officials, business, organizations and the public, the new Comprehensive Plan is meant to provide a framework for continuing public-private participation and to serve as the institutional framework needed for accommodating county growth in the 1990s.

The goal of Fairfax Planning Horizons is to reach a balance between the needs of the residential and business communities while preserving the factors that are key to the area's environmental well being. As part of that preservation effort, and to comply with a Chesapeake Bay Preservation Act passed by the Virginia General Assembly, the county is working on a compliance ordinance. The ordinance will serve to protect environmentally-sensitive areas where inappropriate development could pose a threat to the county's water quality and to the Chesapeake Bay itself — a natural and economic resource for the entire region.

These two events in their way express the focus that shapes Fairfax County's debate on growth policy in the future. Their implications may well have been summed up best by BDM International's Earle Williams in May 1991 when he said:

Fairfax County is entering a new stage in its life cycle. It faces many challenges which are associated with those of a "mature" county. As a community, we now have to make hard choices about our priorities and how to find them—how will we continue to provide the quality services that our citizens have grown accustomed to, while at the same time maintaining a reasonable tax burden—and addressing the many crucial issues that confront the county, most notably transportation. Everything can't be a priority.

There are no easy solutions, but I believe the answer lies in bringing together all parts of the community to work to solve our problems. We need strong, enlightened leadership to bring people together and develop creative solutions to today's challenges. A vibrant business community is a vital part of the solution. Cooperation by the county's private sector employers and strong support from the local government are essential elements in the development of a healthy economic climate which is key to a bright future for Fairfax County.

Mohasco Corporation, a producer of home furnishings, relocated its corporate headquarters from New York to Fair Lakes Office Park in Fairfax Center in 1986. Other companies located on Fairlakes Court include Datatel and AFCEA. Courtesy of the photographer, Scott W. Boatright

This view not only emphasized the importance of a supportive local government in the county economy's infrastructure, but it forecast the theme of local elections in November 1991. Political debate highlighted charges of "pro-growth" and "anti-growth" bias among the candidates, with growth-oriented organizations vigorously backing candidates who challenged the policy of growth controls. The outcome was election of a Board of Supervisors pledged to consistently seek economic prosperity through growth and a favorable business climate.

Whether the Board of Supervisors elected in 1991 will be able to stabilize Fairfax County's attitude toward economic development and growth during the 1990s cannot be known yet. But, as the economic recession of 1990-1991 is replaced by another period of good times, it seems certain that this element of the infrastructure of Fairfax County's economic system will be tested again.

McLean facilities of BDM include this architectural award-winning complex at 1501 BDM Way. Courtesy of BDM International, Inc.

The Power of the Mind

Few areas in the United States offer the scope and quality of educational opportunities that are found in Northern Virginia; and few communities in the nation have demonstrated as deep a commitment to education or participated as fully in these programs as Fairfax County has. The county's educational resources, many of which are unique to the national capital area, are major attractions for businesses locating here and for newcomers taking up residence.

Nationally recognized institutions of higher education in the metropolitan region offer a multitude of academic programs at undergraduate and graduate levels, all of which are available to Fairfax County residents either within the county or in easy commuting distance. American, Catholic, Georgetown, George Mason, George Washington, and Howard universities, plus the nearby University of Maryland, comprise this group of distinguished institutions with campuses in the national capital area and regularly attract students and visiting faculty from across the nation and abroad.

Innovative Academic Programs

George Mason University, located in Fairfax County, is known for its innovative academic programs, particularly in economics and information sciences. "Fast-rising," "innovative," "ambitious", "tough academics"—these are some of the words which have been used to describe George Mason University over the past few years. The *Wall Street Journal* describes it as "a giant growing just outside Washington, D.C.," while *New York Times* education writer Edward Fiske selected it as "A Best Buy in Education." Most recently, U.S. *News and World Report* listed George Mason's School of Law as the top up-and-coming law school in the nation.

George Mason's Center for the Arts was opened in 1990. Internationally known artists have appeared there including pianist Emanuel Ax, violinist Itzhak Perlman, flutist James Galway, the Alvin Ailey Dancers, and the Vienna Choir Boys, among others. Photograph by L. Hoang, Courtesy of George Mason University

George Mason began in 1957 as an extension center of the University of Virginia. Leading Northern Virginians were eager to see a strong institution of higher education in the region to match the growth and potential of the area. By 1963, they had organized the purchase of land for a campus centrally located on the border of Fairfax City. The following year, the new campus opened with 357 students. In 1972, the Governor and the General Assembly signed legislation authorizing the establishment of George Mason University. The then-enrollment of approximately four thousand has grown to over 20,000 students, with ninety-nine degree programs offered through eight schools and colleges.

George Mason's reputation rests on its outstanding faculty and innovative programs. The faculty includes 1986 Nobel Laureate in economics James Buchanan, leading creator of public choice theory. It also includes the Robinson Professors, sixteen scholars distinguished in their fields and their interest in undergraduate education. Other faculty members are notable for their work as biographers and novelists, leading researchers in high technology, in business and in law.

Innovative programs include the nation's first Ph.D. degrees in conflict resolution and in information technology, and the award-winning PAGE program, designed to give students in their first two years an integrated and comprehensive approach to their studies.

The top choice for major has been business administration, with a total of 2,725 out of 25,148 undergraduate alumni. Nursing is second, with 2,189, followed by third place psychology, with 1,667, which is followed by English at 1,503, and accounting at 1,266.

Graduate students have been remarkably consistent with their choices since 1980, even though the number of enrollments has almost tripled over the last ten years. Business administration tops the list, with 1,049 graduates. Psychology is the second most popular discipline, with 624 graduates.

One of the changes in the profile of George Mason's alumni reflects the growing cultural and ethnic diversity of the population of the Northern Virginia region. There were no minority graduates in 1968, but in 1990, twenty-two years later, seventy-eight African-Americans and 281 other minorities were graduated.

Executives of high technology companies in Fairfax County have had a growing concern over the shortage of engineers, scientists, mathematicians, and qualified technicians needed in the high-tech field. Businesses have realized the importance of preparing students for the work place and are playing an increasingly important role in the education of elementary, high school, and college students.

In an effort to strengthen their position of academic leadership in technology, local universities have joined with the business community to explore new areas of commercial interest. The George Mason Institute for Science and Technology (GMI) and the Center for Innovative Technology (CIT) epitomize this cooperative spirit. GMI was established to spearhead liaison activities between the university and Northern Virginia's growing high technology industry. Created by the Commonwealth of Virginia, CIT enhances technology transfer to the private sector by making available the technical resources and research facilities of the state university system. Such cooperative ventures between the business and academic communities expand the educational opportunities for Fairfax County residents and help keep local industry vital and competitive.

George Mason's new Center for the Arts opened in 1990. The Center includes a two thousand seat concert hall, an experimental theater, dance and music studios, a choral studio, and gallery space. It has attracted such internationally renowned artists as Itzhak Perlman, Yo Yo Ma, Roberta Flack, and Wynton Marsalis. Some arts critics are of the opinion that the Center will be strong competition for the nineteen year old Kennedy Center in Washington. The new building has excellent acoustics, is computerized, offers free parking, lower rental costs, cheaper tickets, and an easier commute to its location just outside the Capital Beltway. But the general consensus of the metropolitan area arts community seems to be that rather than being a strong competitor to existing arts facilities, George Mason's Center for the

A recent aerial of part of the George Mason University campus shows the Finley Administration Building in the foreground, classroom buildings, center, Student Union I, center right, and the Fenwick Library and its twin brick towers, center left. Courtesy of the photographer, Scott W. Boatright

Arts will create new audiences and a new pool of theater-goers for the future.

Situated on the outskirts of the nation's capital, just thirty minutes from downtown Washington, the university has access to a profusion of intellectual and cultural riches. Resources like the Library of Congress, the Smithsonian Institution, the National Institutes of Health, the National Archives, and many other internationally respected libraries, museums, galleries, and other cultural institutions give students and faculty broad research and learning opportunities.

The support of a highly educated public and successful businesses, many involved in state-of-the-art high tech research, enables the university to achieve a level of excellence difficult to attain in a more usual setting. In 1991, George Mason University launched the Northern Virginia Institute, an initiative designed to advance the economic and educational interests of Northern Virginia. The institute combines a new magazine, *Mason*, a research resource center, a series of regional networks, and a public policy forum to provide Northern Virginia's leadership with the research, analysis, and exchange opportunities needed for informed decision-making regarding Northern Virginia's future.

Through its efforts to meet the needs of its region and its emphasis on excellence, George Mason University has attracted the attention of both the educational world and the general public. Under the leadership of Dr. George W. Johnson, who became president of the university in 1978, George Mason has developed into a major state institution, and has added a law school to its programming.

Dr. Johnson plays an active role in the Northern Virginia Community, serving on a number of boards and committees. These include the boards of the Center for Innovative Technology, the Fairfax County Chamber of Commerce, the First American Bank of Virginia, and the Washington Airports Task Force. In 1984, he was named Washingtonian of the Year, and has received a number of other community awards.

Major donors ($100,000 or more) to the George Mason University Foundation from the Northern Virginia community in recent years have been: A VA Limited Partnership, AT&T, BDM International, Inc., James M. Buchanan, Mr. and Mrs. Joseph Cantone, Carthage Foundation, Charles G. Koth Charitable Foundation, Clarence Robinson Trust, Claude R. Lambe Charitable Foundation, County of Fairfax, Stephen M. Cumbie, Danforth Foundation, Inc., David H. Koch Charitable Foundation, Bernard J. Dunn, Foundation for Research in Economics and Education, Arthur F. Furman, Alan B. Furman, Annetta Hyde Gibson, Harris Charitable Foundation, William A. Hazel, John T. Hazel, Jr., Omer L. Hirst, John M. Olin Foundation, Inc., Lilly Endowment, Inc., Edwin Lynch, Mark and Catherine Winkler Foundation, Mr. and Mrs. Sonny Mathy, Media General Cable of Fairfax, Mitre Corporation, Mobil Foundation, Inc., Mobil Oil Corporation, Planning Research Corporation, Sarah Scaife Foundation, Inc., Smith Richardson Foundation, TRW Foundation, The Lynde & Harry Bradley Foundation, The Proctor & Gamble Company, The Starr Foundation, The William & Flora Hewlett Foundation, Vernon K. Krieble Foundation, Xerox Corporation, and Earle C. Williams.

Dr. George W. Johnson became president of George Mason University in 1978. Under his leadership, George Mason has developed into a major state educational institution of over twenty thousand students. A law school component has been added during his administration. Courtesy of George Mason University

A Multitude of Offerings

Two of Virginia's other state universities have branches in Fairfax County. The University of Virginia's Division of Continuing Education has since the late 1940s operated a Northern Virginia Center which offers four master's degree programs and has over ten thousand credit and non-credit students currently enrolled. The Virginia Polytechnic Institute and State University first opened a branch in Fairfax County in 1969. In 1980, the program became an official part of Virginia Tech's graduate school. As the Northern Virginia Graduate Center of Virginia Tech, the institution conferred more than 275 graduate degrees in 1989-1990. It offers eight graduate programs with a current enrollment of about 1,600 students each semester.

The Community Cultural Center on the Annandale Campus of Northern Virginia Community College was completed in 1991. It is already being heavily scheduled for college and community workshops, meetings, classes, and cultural events. NOVA is the largest institution of higher learning in the Commonwealth of Virginia. Courtesy of Northern Virginia Community College

Northern Virginia Community College opened its first branch in 1965 as a technical college in a warehouse at Baileys Crossroads. In 1968, the same year the first building was completed on the Annandale Campus, Dr. Richard J. Ernst, shown here, was appointed president of the complex which now includes five branches in the region. Courtesy of Northern Virginia Community College

Many other colleges and universities, as well as scores of training centers and private institutions in the county and region, offer programs in the trades and professional fields.

A National Leader in Innovative Programs

There are also institutions that prepare university-bound students and provide special training. Northern Virginia Community College (NOVA), with five campuses, offers vocational training and ongoing professional development through degree and certificate programs.

The Annandale campus, on Little River Turnpike, is the branch of NOVA within Fairfax County's borders. The first building was completed there in 1968, the year Dr. Richard J. Ernst succeeded the first president of the college, Herbert McKee. As the development of campuses at Alexandria, Woodbridge, Manassas, and Loudoun proceeded, NOVA achieved the largest student population in Virginia's higher education system in 1973 with 17,260 students.

By the 1980-1981 school year, there were five active campuses serving almost 55,000 different students in credit courses, and 15,910 students in continuing education courses. In the 1990-1991 academic year, NOVA was still the largest institution of higher learning in the Commonwealth of Virginia and the second largest multi-campus community college in the United States. It remains a national leader in providing innovative programs and services to students and to the community.

The Extended Learning Institute (ELI) of the college began offering home study courses in 1975. ELI has to date served more than 100,000 students. It provides courses for those who prefer not to attend regular classes on campus. Instruction for ELI courses utilizes television, audio and video cassette tapes, and printed materials designed specially for independent study. Most courses are self-paced, and the maximum time allowed for completing ELI courses is usually longer than for on-campus courses.

NOVA established a Center for Business and Government Services in 1985 to respond to the demand of employee training and upgrading. It conducts seminars and other programs designed to meet the specific educational/training needs of public and private sectors. Another new addition made in 1985 is the NOVA Telecommunications Center which has the capacity to receive and transmit local, national, and international broadcasts. The Center's fully equipped studio for telecourse production and community service programming provides flexibility in meeting the educational needs of students and businesses.

In response to demonstrated needs over the years, a community and cultural center building was completed on the Annandale campus in 1991 to serve both the community and the college with a centrally located facility for fine arts, performing arts, training programs, meetings, and an additional auditorium/theater and physical education facility. Similar centers are planned for the other four campuses in the future. In a representative week during April 1991, gatherings were scheduled for drama, art exhibits, poetry reading, a Fairfax Fair Corporate Board meeting, a drug and alcohol abuse committee meeting, and an Annandale Festival of the Arts meeting, among others, indicating a wide diversity of interests.

Funding for the operation of the college comes from the state, the nine political jurisdictions served by NOVA, from government agencies, from tuition, and from gifts. In order to supplement state and local monies, the college established the Northern Virginia Community College Educational Foundation, Inc., in 1979, as a non-profit, tax-exempt charitable organization. Its purpose is to raise money to support the college's programs, students and activities. Some of the largest gifts and grants to the college foundation have come from the Chesapeake & Potomac Telephone Company, Suzanne H. Paciulli Conrad, the Planning Research Corporation (PRC), the George and Carol Olmsted Foundation, the West* Group of McLean, Virginia Power, the Mobil Corporation, Media General Cable, IBM, Control Data Corporation, U.S. Corps of Engineers, Earle C. Williams, The U.S. Department of

Education, and Arabian Data Systems, Inc.

In keeping with the mission of the Virginia Community College System, the mission of NOVA is to respond to the educational needs of a changing community and its institutions, ensuring that all individuals in the Northern Virginia area have an opportunity to develop and enhance their values, skills, and knowledge. The programs and courses of instruction, up to the associate degree level, encompass occupational-technical education, college transfer education, general education, developmental education, training for business and government, continuing education and community services, and experience in the work environment. They are designed to enhance economic, cultural and educational partnerships between the college and the community. The overall goal is to provide a diversity of education to a diverse student population, stressing educational excellence and providing full accountability to its constituents.

In 1988, Dr. Ernst, president of NOVA, was presented the National Marie Y. Martin Chief Executive Officer award by the Association of Community College Trustees for outstanding leadership in 1986-1987.

Hilly, 399-square-mile Fairfax County, much of it served by narrow, winding roads, has one of the nation's largest school bus fleets to transport public school students from kindergarten through high school. Courtesy of Fairfax County Public Schools

Among the Top Ten Systems in the Nation

The Fairfax County Public Schools (FCPS) system ranks among the top ten school systems in the nation with respect to enrollment. This is to be expected in a county whose total 1990 population census figure is 818,584, greater than the total population of each of seven states—Alaska, Delaware, Montana, North Dakota, South Dakota, Vermont, and Wyoming, and the District of Columbia. Fairfax County's is also one of the nation's outstanding school systems with the quality of its teachers and the excellent programs of study at primary and secondary age levels, as well as special curricula for students requiring additional assistance or challenge. With its work force of professionals and support staff totalling 20,000, the Fairfax County Public Schools system is the second largest employer in the Commonwealth of Virginia, surpassed only by the Norfolk shipyards. The School Board of ten members and a student member is appointed by the Board of Supervisors and sets general school policy.

Mathematics teacher Vern S. Williams is shown here in his classroom at Longfellow Intermediate School. He was chosen Fairfax County Public Schools Teacher of the Year in 1990. He received the Washington Post Agnes Meyer Outstanding Teacher Award for educational excellence in showing initiative, creativity, and an exceptional degree of professionalism in teaching. Photograph by Tom Schudel, Courtesy of Fairfax County Public Schools

Not only is Fairfax the largest school system in Virginia, it also has a tremendous fleet of school buses to serve the students in the 399-square-mile county, which transports 87,000 of the students, about as many per day as the Long Island Railroad's daily passenger figures. School enrollment rose from 127,000 in 1981 to about 130,000 in 1990. In addition, Fairfax operates an unusually large and comprehensive program for adults covering many areas of knowledge and skills development, including preparation for the GED examinations. The National Merit Semi-finalists in Fairfax numbered 150 in 1980-1981; in 1990-1991, 147, representing 41 percent of the state's total. In addition, students averaged 974 on the SATs, well above the national average of 904. About 91 percent of the graduates of the county's high schools in 1990-1991 continued their education in some post-secondary institution. This is virtually a private school record in a public school setting.

Assisting the professional teaching staff are volunteer parents and other members of the community who contributed more than one million hours of assistance to the public school system in 1990.

The influx of foreign-born students has encouraged the establishment of a widely acclaimed "English as a Second Language" program which enrolls about four thousand students. They include international students from over 126 coun-

The Thomas Jefferson High School for Science and Technology was established in 1984. Photograph by James Corrie. Courtesy of Fairfax County Public Schools

Dr. Robert R. Spillane, superintendent of Fairfax County Public Schools, is shown here with Dolores Bohen, assistant superintendent of communications. Photograph by Randy Wyant, Courtesy of Fairfax County Public Schools

Students explore playground equipment at an elementary school. Courtesy of Fairfax County Public Schools

tries and students born in the United States and its territories whose native language is not English.

Special school and community programs were begun in the 1980s to further encourage both the high quality and appropriateness of education in the public schools of Fairfax County. In the fall of 1985, Fairfax County opened the Thomas Jefferson High School for Science and Technology, which is designed to meet the needs of students with interests and aptitudes in science, mathematics, and engineering. The high school, during its short tenure, has become recognized as one of the nation's premier science and mathematics centers for high school students.

The school's ten state-of-the-art laboratories, developed and supported by local business and industry, are what make Thomas Jefferson so distinctive. These laboratory facilities allow students the unique opportunity to experience first-hand the challenges of experimentation and investigation using the latest technology. In 1988, Jefferson students won a super computer for their school in a national competition.

Thomas Jefferson offers standard four-year and special one-year programs of study for high school seniors. The high school is designed to provide students with a solid background to continue their studies or to enter the work force immediately after graduation.

Fairfax County's high quality academic instruction and facilities could not be maintained without the support of the community. Realizing this, the school system has actively sought to include the community in all phases of program development. In fact, the strong commitment of Fairfax County's highly educated populace has turned rather tenuous projects into rousing successes. The Thomas Jefferson High School is one such project. Many of the school's special laboratories and equipment did not qualify for public funding. The superintendent of schools turned to local business executives for support. As a result, the Business/Industry Advisory Council (BIAC) was founded in November 1982, representing the business/industry perspective. It continues to serve as a nucleus for initiating, promoting, and supporting partnership efforts within the school system. The BIAC established the Fairfax County

Group participation is experienced in a kindergarten class. Courtesy of Fairfax County Public Schools

Terraset Elementary is an underground school built in Reston. Solar panels for heating are mounted on the roof. Courtesy of Fairfax County Public Schools

Elementary students are given opportunities to familiarize themselves with computers early in their school experience. Courtesy of Fairfax County Public Schools

An intermediate school student learns to use a sewing machine during a home economics class. Courtesy of Fairfax County Public Schools

An intermediate school student learns to use a jigsaw during shop class. Note the safety glasses. Courtesy of Fairfax County Public Schools

A touch football team plays a game at Langston Hughes Intermediate athletic field. Courtesy of Fairfax County Public Schools

Public Schools Education Foundation, Inc., to fund innovative projects from private sources. Since 1983, the Foundation has raised more than $2 million in equipment and cash for the high school. It is unique among school foundations because it is located in a suburban setting, not urban, and is funded by corporate trustees, not by public funds. It provides an organized means for businesses, community groups, and individuals to support the school system.

The Foundation has expanded its role and assisted FCPS with other programs. This cooperative relationship between FCPS and the Foundation was recently cited by the U.S. Department of Education as an outstanding example of a business/education partnership. The interaction creates a dynamic and enriching educational environment and makes FCPS one of the finest school systems in the nation.

High school band students play trombones and French horns in a practice and a special program. Courtesy of Fairfax County Public Schools

Major donors who have supported the Foundation's programs in excess of $20,000 include: Advanced Technology, Incorporated, Atlantic Research Corporation, AT&T, BDM International, Inc., C&P Telephone Company, Computer Sciences Corporation, Digital Equipment Corporation, A.J. Dwoskin Associates, Inc., Dyncorp, Electronic Data Systems, John T. Hazel, Hazleton Laboratories, Inc., Hekimian Laboratories, Inc., Honeywell, IBM Corporation, The Irving Group, Koons of Manassas, Martin Marietta Corporation, Mid-Atlantic Coca-Cola, NEC America, Sallie Mae, Sony Corporation, Strong Foundation, Systems Center, Inc., TRW, Tautron Corporation, Versar, Inc., and Virginia Power. Two major fund raising events are held by the Foundation each year: a luncheon and a golf tournament.

The Fairfax County Public School system has also initiated an Adopt-A-School program which enables businesses or organizations to "adopt" specific schools and share their time, skills, resources, and expertise. In 1989, there were over sixty Adopt-A-School partnerships; 57,900 students were involved in the program, and 6,400 business employees donated 13,000 hours of their time and expertise.

One example of the success of this program is illustrated by the Governor's Award made on behalf of the Northern Virginia Community College Education Foundation by Virginia's Governor L. Douglas Wilder in March 1991. It was given to Media General Cable, which had "adopted" Centreville High School and provided students with programs designed to give them added incentives to do well in school and out. It was conferred on Media General as an "outstanding leader in business and educational partnerships in support of Northern Virginia."

In summing up the significance of public education in Fairfax County for now and the future, Dr. Harold L.Hodgkinson of the American Council on Education wrote in 1987:

> Fairfax represents a new kind of development some call a Penturb. It will not become just another suburb of a major city—indeed, Fairfax *now* has as many jobs as households, and more people will commute *to* Fairfax to go to work. It also has "non-cities" like McLean which baffle demographers. Jobs, businesses, housing, shopping centers, symphony orchestras, colleges and universities, airports, cows, small farms, medium and high tech, world class traffic jams—all are part of the present and future of Fairfax County. It is already a self-contained urban area although it is a county.

Some of its inhabitants make one trip to Washington, D.C. each year, just to make sure it's still there, as one would visit a museum. As one considers the kind of infrastructure needed in Fairfax in the future, education will clearly be at or near the top, but is likely to be chased strenuously by other services—roads, health care, communication, arts centers and elderly services to name just a few. The only constant in Fairfax's future is change, most of it quite predictable. The schools must continue to provide leadership in the development of this extraordinary county, both in education and in most other areas of county development.

The Fairfax County Public Schools Superintendent's Business/Industry Advisory Council sponsored a special conference in April 1990 called "Forging the Future of Education in Fairfax County, 2010," to examine some of the anticipated problems and possible solutions. To quote the perceived needs for the year 2010 which were summarized in a booklet published after the conference:

The work force needs of 2010 will be shaped by a technology-driven economy that is even more complex and fast moving than the economy of today. To keep pace with the changes, the need for scientific and mathematical skills will be crucial. Beginning today, tomorrow's new work force—which will include many more minorities and young women—must be persuaded to pursue careers in those fields. A global perspective in the curriculum will be another critical need as we compete with technologically superb industrialized societies worldwide. Finally, the employees of 2010 must be capable of adapting to change.

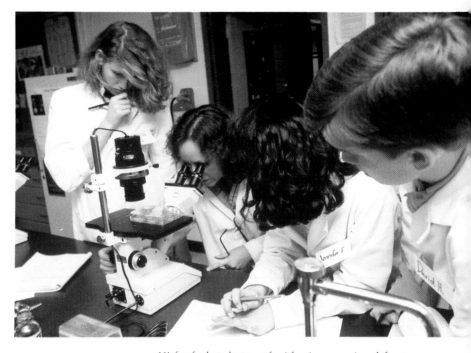

High school students work with microscopes in a laboratory class. Courtesy of Fairfax County Public Schools

Virginia's Largest Free Library System

On an average day, approximately 14,000 people and 24,000 books and other materials move through the twenty-two public libraries in Fairfax County. And more than eight hundred employees, from reference librarians and circulation aides to behind-the-scenes managers, catalogers, book selectors, and computer operators, work to bring the best service and resources to patrons. They include students researching school assignments, preschoolers attending story time programs, business executives reviewing financial reports, retirees checking out the latest do-it-yourself guides, families borrowing movies on video cassettes—people of all ages and interests who depend on the library to educate, inform, entertain and inspire.

People with special needs and interests also are library users. Visually-impaired readers use the library's "talking books" and editions with oversize print. Deaf patrons with special attachments for their telephones can communicate directly with some branch libraries. Outreach became a major program in the mid-1970s. Within its scope are included bookmobiles, visits to nursing homes, home-bound readers and senior citizens, the county jail and juvenile detention centers, low-income housing, and drug abuse centers. Sculpture, framed reproduction prints, and music scores may also be borrowed from circulating collections.

From its beginnings in 1939, Fairfax County Public Library has grown into Virginia's largest free library system and one of the busiest in the nation, considering its size. During an average year, people borrow more items, more often, from Fairfax County Public Library than from public libraries in major cities like St. Louis, Cleveland, Denver, San Francisco, Boston, and Atlanta. According to a recent survey by the American Library Association, Fairfax County Public Library's per capita circulation ranks eighth in the nation for public libraries serving comparable

A high school class rehearses a science project presentation for a video taping session. Courtesy of Fairfax County Public Schools

At the first open house held at the Pohick Regional Library in June 1987, ten thousand people came to see the new library with its award-winning building design by Cross and Adreon, and contemporary book and audio-visual materials collections. This branch consistently leads the county library system in circulation figures. Courtesy of Fairfax County Public Library

population areas. It also tops seventeen public libraries serving a million or more people, including the giant library systems in New York, Los Angeles, Miami-Dade, and Chicago.

Excellence in library service, however, is not a simple matter of numbers. To strengthen its commitment to provide high quality services, materials and convenient access to these resources, Fairfax County Public Library recently embarked on a five-year, $39.1 million capital improvement program.

Approved by voters in a 1989 bond referendum, the program provides for construction of four new libraries in Great Falls, Centreville, Chantilly, and Herndon and three kiosk libraries along major transportation routes. Four existing libraries—Sherwood Regional Library, Mount Vernon area; King's Park Library, Burke; Patrick Henry Library, Vienna; and George Mason Regional Library, Annandale—will be expanded and modernized to ensure attractive, efficient facilities for a growing population.

Computerized information retrieval services provide a unique resource available on a fee basis at the six regional branches. They offer access to over two hundred businesses and scientific databases such as Newsearch, International Software, Medline, VU/TEXT, BRS, DIALOG, PsychoINFO, and ABI/INFO. Also available when the legislature is in session in Richmond is the Legislative Information Services (LIS), which allows individuals and businesses to follow bills through the General Assembly. Periodicals, reference works, and business or technical information reports are available at all of the regional branches.

Regularly scheduled story hours like this one are part of the extensive children's program planning done throughout the county's library system. They are not only entertaining for the children but they also stimulate an interest in reading. Courtesy of Fairfax County Public Library

In addition to professional library staff, an active corps of citizens contributed 22,686 volunteer hours in Fiscal Year 1981 and 46,635 in Fiscal Year 1990 assisting at local branches. Friends of the Library, an organization of volunteers, lends support to FCPL through book sales and other projects.

In the near future, the Fairfax County Public Library also plans to enhance its role as an information resource and will explore development of a Fairfax County Government and Information Center (GLIC) in the new county governmental center, primarily as a resource for county agencies and employees. Edwin S. Clay, III is the director of libraries.

The Most Comprehensive Channel Line-Up in the Country

Media General Cable, whose parent company is Media General, Inc., based in Richmond, Virginia, is one of the largest cable television systems in the nation and the largest system in Virginia. It serves most of Fairfax County. Media General offers over ninety channels of programming, the largest and most comprehensive channel line-up in the country. Its program choices offer entertainment—movies, arts, family fare and sports; information—science, news, nature, and health; and educational, financial, political, and ethnic programs.

In an upscale county whose population is well-educated and possesses the highest effective buying income in the United States, Media General has attracted more than 184,000 subscribers; 65 percent of the total households able to subscribe to cable do so. This figure is substantially above the national average of 58.9 percent.

Media General has been recognized by the television industry with repeated national honors for excellence in programming, marketing, and public relations. The company began operations in Fairfax County in 1982. Since that time, it has invested over $300 million in property, plant, and equipment. It currently employs approximately six hundred people, most of whom live in the service area. Some of the local programming includes televising Board of Supervisors and School Board meetings.

Medianet, Media General's business communications service, offers video, voice and data transmission for public offices and commercial firms. Special applications such as point-to-point or point-to-multi-point video conferencing, shared-use video, digitized video, and links to satellite carriers augment the business communications networks.

Within the Reston community, cable service is provided by Warner-Amex Communications. Over nine thousand Reston subscribers have access to twenty-seven channels.

Media General Cable, one of whose linemen is shown here, has a system with more channel capacity —120— than any other cable television system in the nation. Since 1983, its service has been available in Fairfax County, Fairfax City, Falls Church, Vienna, Herndon, and Clifton. In 1991 Cable TV reached more than 184,000 homes throughout Media General's system. Over 3,598 miles of cable have been wired —approximately the distance between Fairfax and London.

The Reston area is served by another cable company, Warner Amex. Photograph in 1987 by Gary D. Landsman, Courtesy of Media General Cable

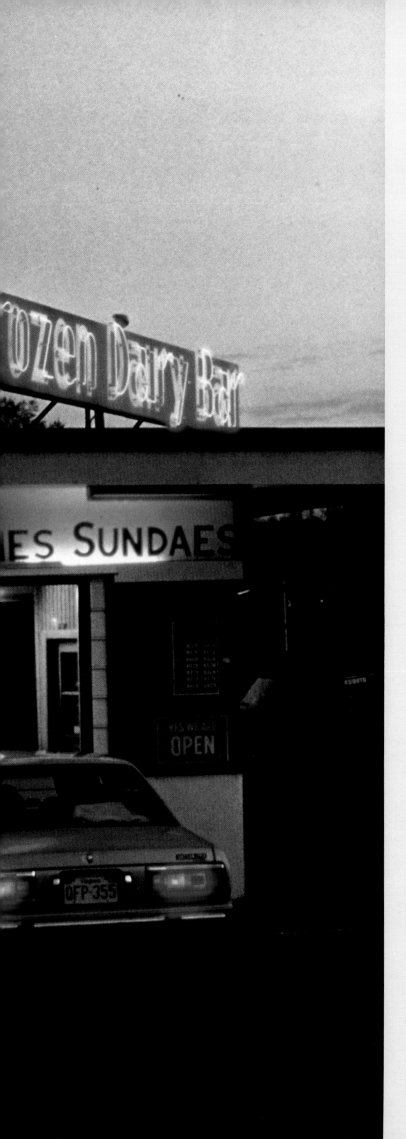

A Sense of Community

T he "sense of community" can be experienced on several levels and in several ways. In a county like Fairfax, fast approaching a population of one million, it is easy for individuals to get lost in vast numbers of people. The population in the 1980 U.S. Census for Fairfax County was 596,901, greater than the populations of Alaska, Delaware, Vermont, and Wyoming. The figures for 1990 in Fairfax were 818,584, still greater than the first four states mentioned, plus Montana, North Dakota, South Dakota, and the District of Columbia. But there are many options available in Fairfax County, provided by public agencies, private organizations, and individuals for assistance, for participation and involvement, and for the constructive use of leisure time, all activities which foster the feeling of individual identity and belonging to a community.

An information explosion has been necessary to assist the public in knowing what is expected, what is happening, and what is available. This can be seen in a variety of periodical publications. An increasing ethnic diversity in the county is recognized in the *Fairfax County Citizens Handbook*, published every two years by the Office of Public Affairs. Starting in 1988, the back of the title page carried information on where to get explanations of information, or assistance in translation of the Handbook in four languages besides English—Vietnamese, Spanish, Cambodian, and Farsi. The pamphlet which the county mails out with the tax bills each year, FYI, contains an informative paragraph in Spanish. Other special publications are issued by the Recreation Department in appropriate languages when the need is indi-

The Frozen Dairy Bar first opened its doors in 1950, near the corner of Route 50, Arlington Boulevard, and Annandale Road just outside of Falls Church. The old-fashioned soft ice cream in chocolate or vanilla flavors is made from scratch out of butterfat, milk, sugar and cream in Electro-Freeze machines built in the 1940s. The Fletcher brothers, Bob, Ray, and Carl, are not certain of the future of their neighborhood neon-lit art deco emporium, shown here in 1991. An historical landmark of sentimental local significance, it may soon become a victim of rising commercial property values in the vicinity. Courtesy of the photographer, Donald M. Sweig

Knowing that the future of Fairfax County is in the hands of its children, the police department frequently involves itself in outreach efforts such as "kids 'n cops" gatherings, school programs, and fairs. Here, officers demonstrate some fine points to interested youths and adults at the annual Fairfax Fair. Courtesy of the photographer, Scott W. Boatright

In addition to the seats inside the amphitheater at Wolf Trap, there is space for three thousand more people on the gently sloping lawns surrounding, where performing arts aficianodos can bring blankets and picnic baskets and enjoy an entertaining evening under the stars. Courtesy of Fairfax County Economic Development Authority

cated in a particular community. The Board of Supervisors publishes their *Weekly Agenda* for distribution, and the Economic Development Authority produces frequent publications of interest of the business community.

Fairfax County has itself become a global community, with 150 languages represented in its public school enrollment in 1990-1991, an increase of one hundred over the fifty languages counted in the 1980-1981 school year.

The printed word is an important stimulus to a sense of community, and local and area newspapers and newsletters are numerous in Fairfax County. There are thirty-nine local newspapers, including the daily *Fairfax Journal*. Publications by various public agencies and private organizations are meant to keep the county citizenry informed. The Fairfax County Public Schools publish periodicals focused on special audiences: parents, teachers, administrators, and the award-winning *Partners in Education*, a newsletter for the business and professional communities interested in the schools. The Fairfax County Park Authority has published *Parktakes* since 1985, which includes descriptions of programs and public facilities managed by the agency. It is mailed to every household in the county on a quarterly basis, as is *Classes, Etc.*, by the Department of Recreation. *This Month*, a free calendar of public library concerts, exhibits, and other events, first published in 1988, is available at all branch libraries. The Fairfax Area Agency on Aging publishes the monthly newsletter, *The Golden Gazette*, for senior citizens.

The League of Women Voters of the Fairfax Area publishes *Facts for Voters* each year. It is mailed by the League on request, and in 1991 was funded by nineteen corporations doing business in the county, the principal contributors being AAA Disposal Service, BDM International, Inc., and Virginia Power. The League also publishes a monthly *Bulletin* with issue papers. It is a nonpartisan civic organization of women and men that encourages the informed and active participation of citizens in government and political issues. It influences public policy through education and advocacy.

A sense of community can be experienced in many of the county's special gatherings. Two countywide celebrations are held each year. The Fairfax Fair of recent times began in 1982. It is held the second weekend of June at George Mason University to feature the best of Fairfax County. The only such annual event, the celebration welcomed more than 120,000 visitors in 1991. It is produced by the nonprofit Faxfair Corporation and includes county and regional agencies, health and trade exhibits, demonstrations, competitions, a variety of foods, a carnival, children's games, arts and science activities, and three stages of live entertainment.

Another annual program is given at Wolf Trap Farm Park for the Performing Arts outside of Vienna and was presented for the twentieth year in 1991. On an evening in May, the Recreation Department opens its outdoor summer concert series with the admission-free Fairfax County Family Night at the Filene Center, held in cooperation with the Wolf Trap Foundation and the National Park Service. Music and dancing entertain the whole family, performed by local artists and groups. Approximately three thousand people attend each year.

The Fairfax County Federation of Citizens' Associations is a volunteer, nonprofit, nonpartisan umbrella for the organized citizenry of the county. It has represented the interests of hundreds of civic, homeowners, condominium, and townhouse associations for over fifty years by working together with the magisterial district councils of citizens associations and the county government. Through its committee structure and its monthly *Bulletin*, the Federation considers a broad scope of countywide concerns in the transportation, education, budget and finance, health and human services, public safety, land use, environment, and related functions. Its resolutions and the positions taken by the Federation are actively promoted with county policy makers, both elected and appointed.

In addition to encouraging interest and participation in neighborhood, community, magisterial district and county issues and activities, the Federation, in cooperation with the Fairfax County Council of the Arts, the Committee of 100, United Community Ministries, the County Council of PTAs, the Fairfax/Falls Church

United Way, and the League of Women Voters of the Fairfax Area, selects the recipient of the *Washington Post* Fairfax County Citizen-of-the-Year Cup. The forty-two awardees, sometimes couples, so honored since 1950 reflect the unusually deep and sustained interest of numerous county residents, not only in the operation of their local government, but in public schools, community services and programs, environmental issues, and human rights.

Business support for community organizations manifests itself in another way which contributes to Fairfax County's strong sense of community. Each fall and spring, Fairfax County's social calendar is crowded with festive black tie balls and galas which are attended by thousands and raise millions of dollars for organizations like the George Mason University arts program, the Cancer Society, the American Heart Association, the Fairfax

In the 1890s the town of Clifton, population under 150, had two general stores. One of these was Buckley Brothers, who offered "everything from a pin to a plow." Their store, shown here, was typical of the town's businesses, which served the area's farmers and was a stop on the railroad line. Courtesy of the photographer, Tom Schudel

Symphony, the Hospice of Northern Virginia, Fairfax Hospital, and many other organizations. These worthwhile events, so heavily subsidized by business, have become increasingly important in cementing the diverse elements that comprise the community of Fairfax County.

Volunteerism in the form of time and talent donated results in the gift of hours numbering in the hundreds of thousands annually. Boards, commissions, and committees, community programs to help the less fortunate and elderly many sponsored by churches, service clubs, musical and drama organizations, interest groups and volunteers in libraries, hospitals, nursing homes and schools, extended programs and enrich the lives of both givers and receivers. There is a Voluntary Action Center in the county which refers citizens to agencies where they can serve others and at the same time develop their own talents and learn new skills.

Three towns and two cities are within the county's borders. But there are also a large number of unincorporated communities which, like the old post villages or hamlets, retain parts of their earlier identity. Most of them have a strong community spirit, some a community center, a separate historical society, or even a formal homeowners association like Reston, Burke, Burke Centre and others.

All three towns—Clifton, Herndon, and Vienna—and the cities of Fairfax and Falls Church hold elections every two years on the first Tuesday in May for the mayor and a town council of six, with the exception of Clifton, which has five.

Clifton was established as a postal village in 1869 and was incorporated as a town in 1902. Its early industries were farming, lumber and firewood, and crushed soapstone. It is now a quarter-mile square of residences, shops, and restaurants, one of which, the "Heart in Hand," enjoys the patronage of celebrities from Washington as well as neighbors from Northern Virginia who come for its home-cooked meals and its unique setting. Clifton's Main Street was featured in the opening scene of the acclaimed film, *Broadcast News* in the 1980s. The town's historic district was placed on the state and national registers of historic places in 1985. Community celebrations each year include a July 4 celebration and Clifton Day, held in October with from 12,000-15,000 visitors annually.

Clifton's mayor, Wayne Nickum, may hold the nation's record for the smallest amount of campaign expenditures. He walks from door to door, talking about his candidacy to his neighbors in the tiny town. His only out-of-pocket expenses in all five successful elections for mayor since 1982 have been the cost of two stamps and

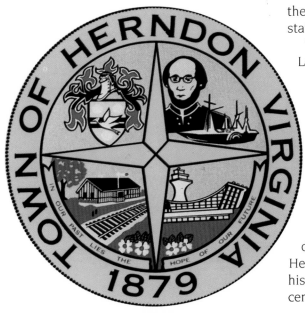

The Herndon town seal has four symbols representing the past, present, and future of the municipality. Clockwise from the upper left quadrant are the Herndon family coat of arms; Captain William Lewis Herndon and his ill-fated ship, the Central America; the terminal and tower of nearby Dulles International Airport; and the old railroad station and Washington & Old Dominion right-of-way, now a bike/hike recreation trail. Courtesy of Town of Herndon

The sense of community is fostered by symbols that reinforce commonly-held values. Thus, Vienna's centennial caboose, standing beside the right-of-way which comprises the present Washington & Old Dominion Railroad Regional Park, is a reminder that from the 1850s to the 1960s railroads were a major force in sustaining and shaping the life of the town and its place in the region. Photograph by Ross Netherton

the envelopes in which to mail his declarations of candidacy to the county and the state. Clifton's 1980 census population figure was 170; in 1990, it was 176.

The post office was established at Herndon in 1858 beside the Alexandria, Loudoun and Hampshire Railroad. It was named after Captain William Lewis Herndon, a Virginia-born sea captain who had heroically gone down in his ship, the Central America, in a hurricane off the US coast near Charleston, South Carolina, in 1857. The town received its charter in 1879.

The Central America was found by shipwreck salvagers in 1988, with three tons of gold aboard, but in eight thousand feet of water. The crew is using robots to bring the salvage from the ocean bottom, and have been in touch with the Herndon Historical Society on several occasions. Members of the Society and the Herndon High School Marching Band were invited to celebrate the discovery, at Norfolk in 1989.

Symbolic of its railroad heritage, a railroad caboose was obtained for the depot museum from Norfolk Southern in 1989, the same year that the Downtown Heritage Preservation District was placed on the state and national registers of historic places. Herndon holds a festival in early June each year at their community center. The town's 1980 census figures were 13,524; in 1990, 16,139.

Once known as Ayr Hill, the Vienna post office was established in 1862. The town received its corporate charter from the General Assembly in 1890. Like Herndon, Vienna was a railroad town, and in anticipation of the centennial year, Historic Vienna, Inc., requested a surplus caboose for the town's historic area. It was given to the town by Norfolk Southern in 1989, permanently placed on a short section of track between the Freeman Store and the old Vienna railroad station. The Town of Vienna leases the station to the Northern Virginia Model Railroaders.

Vienna has two major celebrations each year. The Halloween parade, held the Wednesday evening before that holiday, usually attracts about 20,000 people and entries of floats, marching bands, and other ceremonial groups. Sponsored by the Greater Vienna Chamber of Commerce, the forty-fifth parade was held in 1991. The second event is Viva! Vienna! which began in 1984 with about four thousand people in attendance. In 1990, about 30,000 people came to see the flags, band concerts, performers, crafts, and country fair features displayed on Church Street, which is blocked off for the purpose between Park Street and Lawyers Road on Memorial Day weekend. Vienna's 1980 population was 14,999; in 1990, it was 14,852.

Fairfax City was incorporated as Providence in 1805, but was generally called Fairfax Court House until incorporated as the Town of Fairfax in 1875. The county's courthouse has been located in Fairfax town (later city) since 1800; the Board of Supervisors has had its administrative offices there, also, since 1870. The city charter was granted in 1961. The municipality contracts with Fairfax County for a number of services, including social and health, schools, judicial, and library. There are two community celebrations each year, the July 4 parade and the Fall Festival, which is held the second Saturday in October. The attendance figures for the latter in 1990 were estimated at 90,000. Fairfax City's 1980 population was 19,390; in 1990, it was 19,622.

Falls Church became a post village in 1849 and was incorporated as a town in 1875. The town applied to the state legislature in 1948 and was granted city status separating it from Fairfax County. Being a small city of about ten thousand residents, a number of services are purchased from adjacent counties. Under contract, Fairfax County provides most social services; Arlington provides for the administration of judicial services and Community Development Block Grants (CDBG). The Falls Church Volunteer Fire Company provides fire services, and the Fairfax/Falls Church Community Services Board provides mental health services.

Although it is not chartered as a separate municipal government, Reston is a distinct community designed as a "new town" by developer Robert E. Simon in 1961 for seven thousand acres of land on the Dulles Airport road near Herndon. Gulf Reston took over development in 1967 and the Reston Land Corporation (Mobil) acquired Gulf's interest in 1978.

Restonians have a strong sense of their community where the live-work-play lifestyle is possible without tediously long daily commutes to the work place. They have worked over the years with their homeowners' association and through committees and boards in their civic organizations with the developers and county officials. They have financed and built a large community center, worked for improved roads and bridges, and resolved many other issues of local importance. Reston Land Corporation's population count in 1980 was 34,500; it was 53,791 in 1900.

The community has an annual Halloween parade and it also has a triathlon on the Sunday after Labor Day. Begun in 1984 with 165 triathletes, the registration for 1991 reached a maximum level of five hundred participants. Each registrant must swim one mile, run ten kilometers, and bicycle twenty-four miles in order to complete the course. The Reston Triathlon is rated as one of the top ten events on the East Coast by *Triathlon Today* magazine.

The Burke Centre community, built by Hazel/Peterson Companies and Giuseppe Cecchi of International Developers, Inc., in the 1970s and 1980s, was patterned after the new town concept of having major amenities and employment centers in place when residents moved into their new houses. It occupies part of the land the U.S. government planned for a major airport in the 1950s. But the Burke community fought the idea and eventually the Chantilly site was chosen for what became Dulles International Airport. Burke Centre has five community centers with outdoor swimming pools, shopping centers, office buildings, a trails system, and an underground elementary school, Terra Centre, patterned after Reston's Terraset. Burke Centre's 1990 census figures were 17,242.

Other unincorporated communities with distinctive history and character within the county's borders include Annandale, Bailey's Crossroads, Burke, Centreville, Chantilly, Dranesville, Fairfax Station, Great Falls, Gum Springs, Lincolnia, McLean, Rose Hill, Springfield, and Tysons Corner. Some have recreation centers or community buildings, and/or libraries which serve as gathering places and centers for community activities.

The Fairfax City Hall was built in this colonial style in 1962, a year after the town became an independent city. A small brick outdoor amphitheatre next to the building provides a place for summer band concerts and other community celebrations. Courtesy of the photographer, Tom Schudel

The central business district in the city of Falls Church spreads out in all directions from the crossing of Route 7, the Leesburg Pike (Broad Street), and Routes 29 and 211, Lee Highway (Washington Street). The triple building on the southwest corner is George Mason Square. The small building across Broad Street on the northwest corner is the latest structure housing Brown's Hardware, a family business which has existed on that same corner for over one hundred years. The Falls Church can be seen in the trees in the foreground. Courtesy of the photographer, Scott W. Boatright

Serving as a symbol for "new towns" built in many different countries in the 1960s and 1970s, this view of the Heron House, Lake Anne, and its village center, and other pictures similar to it, have been published in periodicals and books worldwide since this section of Reston was completed in 1964. Courtesy of Reston Land Corporation

Several windmills were built in Burke Centre in the 1970s with hopes that they could be used for pumping water for the ponds. Although this did not work out, some were left to enhance the nostalgic country atmosphere of the community. Courtesy of Dewberry & Davis

Opened in 1986, the Giant Food Store in Burke Centre is a prototype of the stores being built in the Washington area by this largest local grocery chain. In addition to the regular grocery items, there are special departments of a pharmacy, a florist's shop, an in store bakery, and a gourmet foods kitchen. Of the 155 Giant Food stores, fifty-four are located in Virginia. Courtesy of Dewberry & Davis

In another sense of the concept of community, members of thousands of service, affinity, and religious groups meet regularly and support various projects. These include Lions, Rotary, Kiwanis, Optimists, garden clubs, volunteer firefighters, Business and Professional Women, the Network of Entrepreneurial Women, Black Women United, Zonta, women's clubs, PTAs, the American Legion, the Veterans of Foreign Wars, and many others. Houses of worship reflect the increasing ethnic and religious diversity with Christian churches, Jewish synagogues, Islamic mosques, and Hindu, Sikh, and Buddhist sacred meeting places among them.

With a growing public awareness of the importance of healthy diets, the Farmers' Markets, begun in 1980 in Fairfax, have became popular little centers where one may purchase fresh farm products and at the same time socialize with friends and neighbors. Sponsored by the Fairfax County Extension Service, these occasions give the communities a fleeting look backwards to the agrarian society of the community's past. The markets offer fresh fruits and vegetables, eggs, honey, baked goods, potted plants, and cut flowers for sale. They are held once a week from May through November in Burke Centre, Fairfax, McLean, the Mount Vernon area, and Vienna.

Law and order are also factors in an overall sense of community and pride of place. With a record of more than fifty years of service, the Fairfax County Police Department is now Virginia's largest local law enforcement agency and regularly receives national and international recognition for its professional attainments. Established July 1, 1940, with a complement of six officers and two civilian clerks working in an office which had been converted from a coal bin, the department has grown to a force of nearly 975 officers and more than 430 civilian personnel operating out of eleven facilities, including seven district stations located throughout the county.

Police helicopters are used for patrol duty as well as for emergency rescue service. Here, and officer flies over Route I-95 at Springfield near the Capital Beltway, Route 1495, and Springfield Mall. Courtesy of the photographer, Scott W. Boatright

Fairfax County's 911 emergency service began in 1981. Hundreds of thousands of 911 and non-emergency calls for both police and fire and rescue service are received annually by the Public Safety Communications Center, shown here. Computer terminals in police cruisers also provide officers rapid access to necessary communication and information. Courtesy of the photographer, Scott W. Boatright

Two officers patrol a path around a Reston lake on their trail bikes. Fairfax County has an extensive interconnecting trails system. Courtesy of the photographer, Scott W. Boatright

Fairfax County has an active Neighborhood Watch program which achieves success through continuing cooperative efforts. The police department encourages citizens to take an active role in keeping their communities safe and free from crime. Courtesy of the photographer, Scott W. Boatright

With the increased diversity of population in its ethnic composition, it is important for the Fairfax County Police Department to encourage understanding and cooperation between the various communities and law enforcement programs. Courtesy of the photographer, Scott W. Boatright

Even very small people can get help from a friendly police officer when they get lost in a large shopping mall. (left) Courtesy of the photographer, Scott W. Boatright

Several hundred false and real bomb threats involve businesses each year and the police department responds with several techniques. State-of-the-art equipment includes a disposal unit, a robot, a water cannon, and often, an expertly trained dog like this Labrador, "Black Jack," whose acute sense of smell enables him to locate explosive devices. Courtesy of Fairfax County Police Department

With the automated fingerprint analysis system, NOVARIS, Fairfax County Police Department technicians can compare a suspect's print with thousands of others on file almost instantly, a process which used to take days or even weeks. Courtesy of the photographer, Scott W. Boatright

Officers of the Fairfax County Police Department and children of Reston enjoyed this "Kids 'n' Cops" gathering in a neighborhood park. Photograph by Douglas L. Payne, Sr., Courtesy of Fairfax County Police Department

Fairfax County Police Department's robot named TABS (an acronym for "Think And Be Safe") visits schools to help train students on different aspects of safety. Depending on the age group and setting, five subjects are discussed: strangers, walking, school buses, work with patrols, and latchkey kids. Courtesy of the photographer, Scott W. Boatright

The Fairfax County Police Department's Aries helicopter provides emergency medical rescue service to county residents on occasion. Here, Flight Nurse Nancy Racame, R.N., prepares for a flight at the West Ox Road hanger in 1989. Courtesy of the photographer, Tom Schudel

During the 1980s, the police department met the expanding and increasingly diverse demands for service in a rapidly growing community not only by adding personnel, but also by taking advantage of a variety of technological innovations to enhance the capabilities of its well-trained officers. A state-of-the-art computer-aided dispatch system, which began operation in 1987, expedites dispatching calls to officers on patrol.

The establishment of a helicopter division in 1983 provided the department with greatly expanded capabilities to search for criminal suspects and missing persons, maintain surveillance over the county's ever-increasing volume of traffic, and quickly transport critically injured persons to hospitals. Other applications of technology have included more effective crime scene evidence collections, and explosive device detection and disposal. The latter capability was added in response to the security concerns of the large number of high technology firms which have located within the county.

For the citizens and businesses of Fairfax County, the tangible results of the police department's efforts are reflected in the county's crime rate, which regularly is among the lowest for comparable suburban counties throughout the country.

A key factor in the police department's accomplishments has been the strong support and cooperation it receives from the community it serves. The county's Neighborhood Watch program, one of the largest and most successful in the country, has more than 750 active Watch groups involving some 35,000 citizen volunteers.

The police department encourages two-way dialogue with the community through citizens advisory committees which meet regularly with the commanders at all the district stations and elect representatives to the Citizens Advisory Council which confers with the chief of police. Members of the business community serve on the board of directors of the Crime Solvers program, which pays cash rewards from funds donated by businesses for information while guaranteeing anonymity to informants. Since 1979, the Fairfax County Chamber of Commerce has sponsored the Annual Valor Awards program honoring heroic acts by employees of the police department, the sheriff's office, and the fire and rescue department.

Fire protection and emergency ambulance service are provided by the Fairfax County Fire and Rescue Department. More than one thousand full-time career firefighters serve, and support personnel plus volunteers supplement the career firefighters primarily at night and on weekends. Volunteer fire departments own twelve of the thirty-two fire stations in the county. The county owns the other twenty, and county firefighters staff all thirty-two stations. Fire and Rescue provides service to new businesses and individuals in the county including public education on fire prevention.

A water rescue was made by the police when this fisherman's boat capsized in the Occoquan River. The department's helicopters carry advanced life support equipment and rescue gear. Courtesy of Fairfax County Police Department

The police department and fire and rescue services gather forces to straighten out traffic snarls when accidents occur on busy highways. Rapid response to emergencies effectively minimizes the effects of mishaps like the one shown here. Courtesy of the photographer, Scott W. Boatright

Fairfax Hospital is shown in the center of this aerial view. Mobil Corporation's headquarters building, center background was being enlarged when this photograph was taken in 1989, and Fairview Park, upper right, was being completed. Courtesy of the photographer, Tom Schudel

Beaming parents James and Mary Fulton proudly show the world their triplets, Richard, Michael, and Charles shortly after their birth in Fairfax Hospital on Fathers Day in June 1989. Courtesy of the photographer, Tom Schudel

Personnel in every station have been trained as emergency medical technicians and, when transporting patients, are in radio contact with hospital emergency staffs to relay symptoms and receive instructions. When necessary, cardiac care technicians are dispatched in one of the county's eighteen specially equipped Mobile Intensive Care Units.

In addition to the county's Health Department which supports the physical and mental well-being of residents through numerous services, there are several hospitals, nursing homes, and a hospice program for terminally ill patients and their families. Fairfax Hospital is a 656-bed community hospital and a regional referral center. During 1961, its first year of operation, 1,595 babies were delivered there; in 1990, 8,590 were born at Fairfax. It was the first hospital in the metropolitan area to perform heart transplants. The parent corporation, Inova Health System includes four not-for-profit hospitals: Fairfax, Fair Oaks, Jefferson, and Mount Vernon, and two ACCESS emergency centers, as well as Cameron Glen and Commonwealth care centers. A women's and children's building is scheduled for completion beside Fairfax Hospital in mid-1992 to provide Northern Virginia families with the most up-to-date obstetric and pediatric services. Jefferson Hospital was built as a private doctors hospital in 1965 and was acquired by Inova in 1985. It has 120 beds and no obstetrics department. Mount Vernon Hospital was opened in 1976, has 235 beds, and also has no obstetrics department. Fair Oaks was opened in 1987 with 160 beds. In 1990, 1,558 babies were delivered there.

DeWitt Army Community Hospital at Fort Belvoir serves the military, retired military, and dependent community, as well as employed personnel and civilians. High level government officials and foreign nationals whose countries are parties to treaties with the United States also are eligible for treatment there. The facility opened in 1957, and 1,106 babies were delivered there in 1990.

The Reston Hospital Center's doors opened in November 1966 as a 127-bed full service medical-surgical-community facility. An obstetrical unit was opened February 1989. The operation of the for-profit hospital by the Hospital Corporation of America is overseen by a local board of trustees chosen from among community leaders.

A special awareness of and appreciation for exceptional public service to the larger community is provided by the Northern Virginia Community Foundation (NVCF). It was established in 1978 by a group of public-spirited citizens of Northern Virginia and like most community foundations, it is a philanthropic pool. Thus, even modest charitable contributions are combined to benefit from professional financial management, which produces regular income to help support worthy community causes.

Five areas of concern have been identified by the Foundation to receive benefits from the endowment funds: the arts, education, health, youth, and civic improvement.

The Founders Award is the NVCF's most prestigious. It has been presented annually since 1983 for outstanding community service and dedication to the betterment of Northern Virginia. It seeks to promote awareness of the significance of individual action in improving the quality of life for all persons in the community. The award recipients and their years were: Charles G. Gulledge (1983); Earle C. Williams (1984); John M. Toups (1985); James T. Lewis (1986); Virginia E. Hazel and John T. Hazel, Jr. (1987); Milton L. Drewer, Jr. (1988); Joanne Johnson and George W. Johnson (1989); Joe Gibbs (1990); and Sidney O. Dewberry (1991).

Grants of funds are also given through a prescribed process of application from nonprofit community groups. During 1989, NVCF provided grants totalling $216,990 to help the people of Northern Virginia through the twenty organizations which received the grants that year. The Foundation fosters a sense of community by a collaboration of diverse interests, organized for permanence, which attempts to strengthen a geographically defined community by providing services and nurturing leadership among charitable donors, nonprofit organizations, and the community at large.

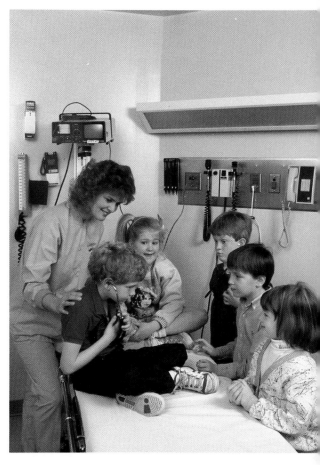

A group of nearby Navy Elementary School students visited Fair Oaks Hospital as a special learning experience, in April 1989. Courtesy of the photographer, Tom Schudel

Virginia's Governor L. Douglas Wilder poses here with Executive Director Judith Mueller and part of the staff of The Women's Center in Vienna, Virginia, the best regional example of "One thousand points of light." A sixteen-year-old non-profit organization, the Center provides psychological, financial, legal, and professional counseling to women and their families. The 60,000 persons who were seen last year were helped by a professional staff of ninety-seven. Over one thousand additional volunteers contribute to the success of this organization, the largest resource for women and their families in the metropolitan area. The role of nonprofits is on the leading edge of privatization in cost-effective human services, increasingly necessary as local and national governments deal with funding crises. Courtesy of The Women's Center

Recipients of the 1987 Founders Award from the Northern Virginia Community Foundation were John T. "Til" Hazel and his wife Virginia E. "Jinx" Hazel. They are shown here, left to right, with the Honorable Clive L. DuVal II; Charles G. Gulledge, Foundation President; the Hazels; and the Honorable Vincent F. Callahan, Jr. Courtesy of Northern Virginia Community Foundation

Recipients of the 1989 Founders Award were George W. Johnson and Joanne F. Johnson, shown here with John M. Toups, right. Courtesy of Northern Virginia Community Foundation

A Place of Honor

The name "Virginia" brings up images of a rich and inspiring past reflecting some of the greatest moments in the nation's history. For years travel surveys have shown that visitors are attracted to Virginia first for its scenery and, closely in second place, to experience it history. Popular perceptions of Fairfax County's place in this history have highlighted the personalities and events that welded the colonies into a nation and later tested its endurance in civil war. But this perception is expanding to recognize the county's importance in other ways and other times, and the commitment to historic preservation has been extended to the county's resources of these types. So, in modern Fairfax County one can experience the Colonial and Revolutionary War periods (Mount Vernon, Gunston Hall, Pohick Church); the early Federal years (Sully Plantation, Woodlawn, Fairfax Court House); the Civil War (Bull Run Stone Bridge, Freedom Hill, St. Mary's Church, Fort Marcy); the Victorian era (Colvin Run Miller's House, Cabell's Mill); railroad towns (Clifton, Herndon and Vienna); rural America (Frying Pan Park, Claude Moore Colonial Farm at Turkey Run); the progress of engineering and technology (Colvin Run Mill, Great Falls Canal, Occoquan Brick Kiln, Hope Park Mill); the history of architecture (Woodlawn and the Pope-Leighey House; Dulles Airport terminal); and the New Town concept (Reston). Few American counties have such reminders of history to reinforce their identity.

In a very real sense the nation's commitment to historic preservation began in Fairfax County with its most famous and

Standing in the footprints of Northern and Southern combatants who fought over the same places in 1861-1865, these reenactors take their recreation seriously in a skirmish staged at Sully Plantation. Fairfax County's wealth of historic sites associated with the Civil War has made it a favored area for visits by Union and Confederate reenactment groups both from Virginia and more distant places. Each year a lengthy list of encampments is scheduled in Fairfax County and thousands of spectators share the sense of living history created by these reenactors. Photograph by Don Sweeney, Courtesy of Fairfax County Park Authority

In 1971, to celebrate the centennial of the Fairfax County public school system, the Legato School, shown here, was restored and moved to the grounds of Fairfax Courthouse and the Massey Building. This one-room schoolhouse served as a school from the 1870s until 1930 on Routes 29 and 211 between Fairfax and Centreville. Its restoration was a cooperative project sponsored by the Fairfax County History Commission and carried out with funds and student labor from several county schools. Courtesy of the photographer, Thomas Schudel.

visited site—George Washington's home at Mount Vernon. In 1856, Mount Vernon and its associated buildings were rescued from destruction by neglect when a determined woman, Ann Pamela Cunningham, organized the national Mount Vernon Ladies' Association of the Union to acquire and maintain the property. America's historic preservation movement started here.

Protection was provided for George Mason's colonial home at Gunston Hall when the Commonwealth of Virginia acquired it as a gift and arranged for it to be administered by the National Society of Colonial Dames. And a third historic landmark was saved when Woodlawn Plantation was acquired by the National Trust for Historic Preservation. Others were not so lucky; some were even turned over to local volunteer fire departments for fire fighting practice.

The need for countywide measures became urgent in the 1950s as population increases encouraged rapid land subdivision. The Potomac Canal site at Great Falls and the home of Richard Bland Lee at Sully Plantation were saved only by heroics that led to their acquisition for park land. The Pope-Leighey House, an architectural landmark designed by Frank Lloyd Wright, survived only by being relocated to the grounds of Woodlawn. Public sentiment for the preservation of history increased.

The call for a countywide preservation program functioning as part of the land use planning and zoning process came in 1965 in a speech by Secretary of the Interior Stewart Udall, himself a county resident, to the Fairfax County Federation of Citizens Associations. His call was heard by these groups and by the Historic Landmarks Preservation Commission, which had evolved from a county Chamber of Commerce committee to promote tourism. Support for county action was dramatized by the recommendations of Virginia's Outdoor Recreation Study Commission in 1965 and by Congressional passage in 1966 of a national historic preservation program. In 1967, an ordinance was adopted authorizing creation of Historic Districts for sites and structures that met criteria of significance. In the 1970s and 1980s, Fairfax County's Board of Supervisors supported its commission of volunteer advisors, the Fairfax County History Commission, and the staff of the Office of Comprehensive Planning in a wide range of activities, the significance of which was later recognized in state and national awards.

Recital of the county's accomplishments in historic preservation not only reflects the recognition they received, but traces the evolution of a public commitment. Promptly after enactment of it zoning ordinance, the planning staff inventoried more than a hundred architecturally and historically significant structures. Where determined to be urgently needed, special planning studies for establishment of historic districts were commenced. In this way the constituencies for preservation and development both gained an opportunity to have their interests fully documented in the planning process.

Many of the planning studies undertaken for historic district zoning ripened into informative and authoritative monographs on the social and economic life of the county in earlier times. Indeed, they refuted the longstanding reputation of local planning reports as being dry or difficult to read and became best-sellers with the public, in several cases reprinted to meet popular demand to learn about the county's history.

As America prepared to celebrate the bicentennial of its independence, communities everywhere undertook special projects to discover or document their own part in the national heritage. Three projects carried out in Fairfax County were particularly successful. In a grass roots effort by citizen groups, a one-room frame schoolhouse of the 1870s was rehabilitated and moved to the grounds of the county office building and the courthouse, serving as a reminder that the county's public school system also was celebrating its centennial at that time.

Some of Fairfax County's historic sites are shown on this poster exhibited at a tourism conference in Philadelphia in 1989. Left to right, from top to bottom are Mount Vernon, Dranesville Tavern, Collingwood, Claude Moore Colonial Farm, Woodlawn, Pope-Leighey House, Gunston Hall, Sully, Fairfax County Court house, River Farm, Colvin Run Mill, and Pohick Church. Courtesy of Fairfax County Economic Development Authority

Dulles International Airport was built in 1962 and straddles the Fairfax-Loudoun County line. The original control tower, terminal, service buildings, and mobile lounges were designed by architect Eero Saarinen. First called Chantilly after an area nearby, the airport was officially named after Secretary of State John Foster Dulles when it was dedicated by John F. Kennedy. Courtesy of Charles Baptie

While Fairview Park was being built in 1985 at Routes 50 and 495, archeologists were given permission by the developers to spend a full year to recover artifacts from the A.D. 200-1500 site while construction went on around it. Shown left to right are Joe Spyrison (front), Tod Creekman (back), Mike Johnson, Fairfax County's senior archeologist (foreground with white hat), and Bob Norton (white shirt). Courtesy of Environmental and Heritage Resources Branch, Fairfax County Office of Comprehensive Planning

The second project involved indexing the records of the Fairfax County Court which served as the governing body of the county from its origin in 1742 until introduction of the Board of Supervisors system in 1870. The books of minutes, orders, and records of this era were gathered from the basements and attics of the old courthouse, and a team of librarians and historians commenced the long task of indexing them. The project, sponsored by the History Commission, working with the cooperation of the Clerk of the Circuit Court, continued through the 1970s and 1980s, earning national praise and the gratitude of the general public, genealogists, and the scholarly community of historians.

The third bicentennial project filled a long-felt need for a comprehensive, authoritatively researched and well-written history of Fairfax County. This task was carried out by the county's planning staff in cooperation with the History Commission, and in 1978 it produced a widely-praised book which would be reprinted five times during the following decade. Added to the existing list of historical and architectural studies of county landmarks and sites, this book increased substantially the source material available to feed the public appetite for local history.

Following closely in the wake of the bicentennial year's celebration, the county's preservation program took on a new dimension by authorizing the study and protection of archeological resources. The action was a bold one since at the time budget-balancing was being made difficult by weak economic conditions in the nation and the region. But a strong case was made for an archeological program by the History Commission, and the Board of Supervisors in 1976 agreed to add professional archeologists to the Office of Comprehensive Planning. This addition was in step with recent Congressional legislation giving greater protection to archeological resources under federal control. It soon proved its worth in helping the county assess the impacts of development proposals on environmental and cultural resources that were protected by state and federal laws.

Through an inventory process, records were made of sites having significance from prehistoric times to the turn of the last century. And through an ongoing educational program the public was introduced to the past inhabitants of Northern Virginia and their lifestyles. This, in turn, became a source of volunteers to help excavate and catalog the discoveries. Lacking a county museum or active archeological programs in any of the local universities, the artifacts obtained from these sites were sent to other centers of Virginia history, such as Colonial Williamsburg, or else stored in the adapted county school building which serves as the program's archeological laboratory.

Measured by the number of archeological sites discovered and registered with the State Archeologist, Fairfax County's program has been a great success, for it is credited with having registered more than a thousand sites. Judged by its service to the county's planners and developers, the archeological program also has earned high praise. As the county's history and prehistoric past became more fully identified, developers ran less risk of unwittingly stumbling into sites having cultural or scientific significance. The county archeology program also has been a useful source of advice on how development plans might be modified to preserve a site without stopping a project, or of how a site that was important only for the information it could reveal might be excavated and made available for development once it has yielded its information. Sometimes developers became personally interested in the special significance of their site and arranged site plans to incorporate an historic or archaeological feature as a focal point.

As land development went forward in the 1980s, conciliation replaced confrontation in many instances where it had not been possible earlier because the preservation of history had not become an element of the planning process at that time. As in many communities, reconciliation of development and preservation interests has not been perfected. Reports of historical and cultural resources being destroyed regularly appear in the news. But the loss of these pieces of the county's distinguished identity has contributed to refining rather than reneging on the commitment to preservation. In the 1980s, this refinement could be seen in several ways.

One was recognition that the socio-economic and cultural values protected by the historic preservation programs were broader than simply perpetuating the memory of heroes in the sites and structures associated with great events or personalities of the past. These values included the symbols and reminders of lifestyles and common heritages that had shaped the identity of a particular place. Criteria for listing clusters of structures, neighborhoods, or even entire communities in the National Register as "Historic Districts" were issued by federal and state historic preservation agencies.

This new concept was promptly applied. In 1980, the county created the Langley Fork Historic District to protect a cluster of historically and architecturally significant structures at the intersection of Chain Bridge Road and Georgetown Pike (Langley Ordinary; Langley Toll House; Gunnell's Chapel; the Friends Meeting House; Hickory Hill; Mackall House) which had been declared eligible to be placed on the National Register. It also moved to preserve the historic and scenic value of Georgetown Pike — the first road in the state to have been designated a "Virginia Byway" — from future improvements that would be incompatible with the atmosphere of the pike.

The tiny town of Clifton is seen from the air in this view taken in 1990. The large L-shaped building is the former Buckley Brothers Store building which now houses the "Heart in Hand" restaurant. Railroad tracks of the Norfolk Southern can be seen to the right. Courtesy of the photographer, Scott W. Boatright

Heron House and Washington Plaza on Lake Anne have served as the symbol of the new town of Reston since they were completed in 1964. The Lake Anne Village Center, shown here, was designated an historic district by the Fairfax County Board of Supervisors in 1984. Courtesy of the Reston Land Corporation

This was followed in 1983 by designation of Reston's Lake Anne Village Center as an historic district, protecting the trend-setting plan which contributed to the "new town" movement of the 1960s. The architectural integrity of the Village Center shops and apartments, designed in a unique semi-circular pattern around Lake Anne, was thus protected against disharmonious renovations. In the following year, the Board of Supervisors approved creation of Centreville Historic District in the old town section of that community. With boundaries drawn to enclose five structures—some dating from the eighteenth century and others from the Civil War—the district represented the last surviving reminder of a place that had helped mold the county's character for over two centuries.

The Centreville Historic District was the twelfth such special zone to be approved since 1967, when the county's preservation ordinance was passed. In and around these districts Fairfax County's commitment to its history was tested repeatedly during the 1980s as its Architectural Review Board (ARB) strove to reconcile the pressures for high - intensity land development with the criteria prescribed to maintain the preservation purposes of the district. As the 1970s ended, the momentum of preservation shifted to defending the values which were essential to the quality of life involved. Within historic districts the spacious settings of protected structures were increasingly considered for more intense developments, and appeals to the Architectural Review Board asked for compromise of protective standards. As each historic district's rules were designed to protect its particular character, results differed from case to case. Case-by-case, the ARB's efforts to achieve compatibility between new development and historic architecture and landscape sought to develop a consensus of quality in design which, if it did not reach the high standards of preservation purists, at least avoided the excesses of development opportunists.

Lessons learned in the architectural review process proved to be valuable in the third major development of the 1980s, namely: incorporation of an historic heritage element in the county's regular comprehensive planning process. When adopted by the Board of Supervisors in Octrober 1988, the plan's Policy Section announced a countywide policy framework for heritage resource preservation where none had existed before, and for integrating the objectives of heritage preservation with other county development objectives and regulatory measures.

In this Policy Plan, the county's commitment to preservation was oriented to "people-benefits" in contrast to more remote "museum-values." The goal of heritage resource preservation was contained in the broader goal of promoting "culture and recreation," and specifically:

> Preservation of the county's heritage resources—its historic structures, landscapes, cemeteries, and its historic and Native American archaeological sites—serves a public purpose by (1) enhancing the quality of life through aesthetic diversity in the landscape, and (2) providing a sense of continuity with the County's historic and prehistoric past. This . . . requires a commitment both from the public and private sectors and from the community.

Concurrently with formulation of the policy for preservation of heritage resources in the new Comprehensive Plan, the county's planning staff developed tools to implement it. These took the form of a Heritage Resource Management Plan, issued in 1988. Based on the National Park Service's "Resource Protection Planning Process," the management plan provides a framework of identifying, evaluating, managing, and interpreting the resources that have shaped community character. With this guide for transforming technical planning data into resource management information, preservation planners were in a better position to work constructively with prospective developers, transportation agencies, utilities, environmental and conservation organizations, and others to reach agreeable and effective development decisions.

The Comprehensive Plan's emphasis on linking the goals of historic preservation with the goals of culture and recreation was, in one sense, recognition of the success of some thirty years of practicing that linkage by the Fairfax County Park Authority and Northern Virginia Regional Park Authority. As agencies authorized to acquire and manage land for park and recreation uses, they have become proprietors of the principal natural and man-made historic sites in the county and the interpreters of the significance of these resources to the county's heritage.

The Fairfax County Park Authority was created in December 1950, after the Virginia General Assembly earlier that same year passed enabling legislation for such action. Two dedicated conservationists and administrators—Charles Robinson and John Brookfield—stand out as the men who gave Fairfax County's park system its start. They started small. Robinson later recalled, " . . . we had no money so we each furnished our own stationery, stamps, and secretarial service." Nevertheless, in 1952 the Park Authority was able to purchase from the Washington & Old Dominion Railroad the property that now is the heart of the park at Great Falls.

By 1959, the Park Authority was able to hire its first Director—Fred Packard—and prepare its first bond referendum to obtain funds for parks. The referendum's success set the course for funding future projects for preservation of history. In 1959, Sully Plantation was transferred by the Federal Aviation Administration to the Fairfax County Park Authority to save it from destruction in construction of Dulles International Airport. And in the 1960s, Park Authority bonds made possible the acquisition and renovation of the Colvin Run Mill and Miller's House, Dranesville Tavern, Green Spring Farm, Wakefield Chapel, Walney, and the picket post at Freedom Hill. In 1980, Cabell's Mill in Centreville was added to the list of historic parks. In 1973, a Division of Historic Preservation was created to develop and administer this growing set of heritage resources, including restoration activities, museum education, and interpretive programs.

The Northern Virginia Regional Park Authority (NVRPA), created in 1959, has actively acquired and protected extensive open space and recreational resources, and currently administers a truly unique historic site in Fairfax County. This is the Washington & Old Dominion Trail, a linear park running from Rosslyn in Arlington County to Leesburg in Loudoun County along the right-of-way of the W&OD Railroad which ceased operations in 1969.

As the decade of the 1980s opened, preservation by private sector efforts was stimulated by the work of the Governor's Commission to Study Historic Preservation. The Commission's report in 1988 led to new legislation by the General Assembly to support statewide programs, but significantly it stressed opportunities for non-governmental organizations to take custody of local heritage resources through the use of easements and other private contractual arrangements controlling use of the land. As early as the 1960s, proposals had been made in Fairfax County by the Chamber of Commerce's tourism committee to create a revolving fund for use in historic landmark protection, but it received no response. Despite the fact that historic preservation in the county had been started by private enterprise at Mount Vernon, Woodlawn Plantation, and Gunston Hall, the thrust which this activity had received since the 1960s came from either public acquisition

Built on the roadbed of the former Washington and Old Dominion Railraod, the W&OD Trail runs through the urban heartland and into the rural open spaces of Northern Virginia. The trail—one hundred feet wide and forty four miles long, and sometimes called "the skinniest park in Virginia"—is a multi-use recreation corridor connecting a series of wayside parks, suburban communities, and local trail systems. Photograph by Rick Buettner, Courtesy of Northern Virginia Regional Park Authority

Dulles Corner's master plan groups twenty-two buildings around a series of landscaped parks and lakes and features sculpture by nationally prominent artists. The Center's award-winning signature sculpture by Lin Emery is "Birds in Flight," a series of eight stainless steel figures representing a flock of geese descending onto the lagoon. Courtesy of Fairfax County Office of Comprehensive Planning

or zoning. Early in 1990, a new start was made by formation of the Fairfax County Heritage Conservancy, a non-profit organization capable of holding and managing property for historic preservation. Initiated almost entirely by individuals, historical societies, and conservation organizations, the Conservancy also works to broaden public awareness of preservation needs and options for participating in the development planning process where historic resources are affected.

A critical commentary on the tendency of some communities to destroy their identity by neglect or indifference to development design is summed up in the quip that, "When you get to the place you're going, there isn't any!" This is not so in Fairfax County. Private sector preservation of heritage resources has gone on in ways that subtly touch the lives of residents daily. Frequently street and place names have been selected so that the personalities, events, and legends associated with Fairfax County's 250 years are brought to mind. To the newcomers who settled the county in the 1950s and 1960s, this was important, for by the names around them they identified themselves with a place in history. The same thing is true of those who came in the 1980s and are coming in the 1990s.

Another indication of progress in preserving Fairfax County's historic identity may be seen in the interest of design professionals in using or adapting heritage resources in the modern man-made environment. In November 1984, the Board of Supervisors established an Exceptional Design Awards program. Administered by the Office of Comprehensive Planning, the program recognizes exceptional architectural and site designs in the county. Since 1985, fifty-eight projects have been honored for their excellence. Significantly, a number of these projects have adapted historic buildings to compatible new uses or designed new construction in styles that carry out historic themes and work to reinforce them. Examples in recent years' awards include: the Chantilly Bible Church (1989 - adaptive use of a rural dairy barn), and Sully Station Community Center (1989 - architectural theme of nineteenth century rural train station).

Modern Fairfax County has a place in history. And it is a place that other communities might well envy, both because of the wealth of resources that represent the county's distinguished heritage and because of the commitment which its residents and their government have made to preservation of those resources. But it is a commitment that has turned out to be one of the most difficult to keep. It deals with elements of the landscape that are fragile and often inconspicuous, and thus easiest to sacrifice in competition with other interests that are more aggressive. It demands vigilance since these heritage resources are vulnerable to continuing pressure from increasing land values and taxes, construction on unsurveyed lands, "by right" development, vandalism, and neglect.

It is a commitment to excellence that seeks to assure a place of honor for the future as well as continuity with the past. It enhances the quality of life by maintaining diversity in the environment and a sense of identity.

This has been recognized in other awards for excellence in architectural and environmental design in Fairfax County sponsored by the American Institute of Architects, American Society of Landscape Architects, and Northern Virginia Community Appearance Alliance.

Preservation of heritage resources always depends for its success on the involvement of the community in its own future. Up through the 1980s, this involvement was mainly in response to short-term goals and specific threats. The 1990s offer a chance to link the preservation commitment to Fairfax County's comprehensive planning process, increase the entire community's awareness of the value of heritage resources, and supplement public planning with broadly-based private sector preservation support. In this way Fairfax County can best assure its place in history.

Located near the entrance to Sully Station and serving as a community center for that 3,272 unit planned development, this building adopted the architectural theme of a 19th century railroad station and provided a visual symbol of the historic context of that area. It was completed in 1987 by the Matrin Organization and Kettler & Scott, with Dewberry & Davis as engineers. It received one of Fairfax County's Exceptional Design Awards in 1989. Courtesy of Fairfax County Office of Comprehensive Planning

Conversion of an 1880s dairy barn into a modern community church was honored for successful adaptive use which preserved the rural quality of western Fairfax County around the turn of the century. The adaptation was made in 1988 by William A. Klene Architects for the Chantilly Bible Church with Charles P. Johnson & Associates as engineers. It was honored by Fairfax County with an Exceptional Design award in 1989. Courtesy of Fairfax County Office of Comprehensive Planning

C H A P T E R

7

The Quality of Life

Fairfax County, once considered a "bedroom community" for Washington, D.C.'s employment centers, has itself evolved into a major business center. The county's highly skilled labor force, proximity to the federal government, and dynamic growth create an attractive location for business. However, it is the quality of life in Fairfax, with its exceptional cultural, recreational, and educational opportunities, that encourages newcomers to call the county home. People from all nations and walks of life make the county a thriving, vibrant community. Other factors that contribute to this exciting environment include a wide selection of housing, an outstanding library system, an extensive park system, a number of significant historical resources and resorts nearby, and a variety of retail outlets, local and regional in nature.

Most of Fairfax County land is zoned for residential development—211,904 acres, or 91.9 percent. Industrially zoned land comprises 4.8 percent, and commercial, 3.3 percent of the county's total acreage. The average number of dwelling units per acre is 1.23, thus preserving the county's spacious, open character.

The county's housing varies in type and price from large homes to condominiums, and from townhouses to garden apartments. Some areas of the county have an urban character, while others are less developed and have a more rural character, sometimes including forests, streams, and nearby hiking, biking, and riding trails. The county has something for almost everyone. From quiet countrysides to bustling urban centers, traditional neighborhoods to planned contemporary communities, upscale boutiques to regional malls, fast food outlets to luxurious restaurants, folk music to opera, and professional sports to soccer and Little League, Fairfax County can satisfy any lifestyle. But the county offers more than just a variety of lifestyles. Its citizens are committed to improving the quality of life, particularly in

Recognized as one of the finest rowing courses in the United States, Sandy Run Regional Park is the site of 1992 Olympic sculling team training as well as national competitions for high school rowing crews. Photograph by William L. Allen of the West Potomac High School rowing crew. Courtesy of Northern Virginia Regional Park Authority

education. The county's high school students consistently rank among the top in the nation in scholastic achievement. Executives and educators work side by side to create new programs and teach concepts that prepare today's graduates for tomorrow's challenges. Educational opportunities are provided for the handicapped as well as work programs.

Fairfax County is nationally recognized for the quality and diversity of its park and recreation system. In "Fairfax Planning Horizons," the policy and concept sections of the county's new Comprehensive Plan, adopted by the Board of Supervisors in August 1990, these parklands and recreational facilities play a key role in shaping both the landscape and the quality of life through conservation of natural and heritage resources, protection of environmental quality, provision of public facilities and human services, and management of urban growth.

Recreation programs began in the county in 1937 when a group of citizens set up programs, with private funding, in three community centers. In 1952, the county's Board of Supervisors began partial funding of programs, and in 1959, a year-round program was inaugurated when Dr. William Dove Thompson was appointed director of the department of recreation.

Today, a wide variety of leisure-time

A 1,400-acre planned residential community, Burke Centre was built in the 1970s and 1980s by the Burke Centre Partnership, preserving open space and farm ponds to provide an attractive environment. An extensive pathway system ties together neighborhoods of single-family homes, townhouses, condominiums, apartments, schools, commercial, and employment centers and recreational areas. Burke Centre Parkway is the main thoroughfare through the community. Courtesy of Dewberry & Davis

and human service programs are provided for children, youth, adults, and senior adults. These include summer and after-school playgrounds; youth drop-in centers; organized community baseball, basketball, football, soccer, lacrosse, and softball for youth; softball, volleyball, basketball, soccer, lacrosse and touch football for adults; hobby-related classes; seasonal sports, clinics, leagues, and tournaments; indoor athletic activities; activities for senior adults; special programs for mentally and/or physically disabled citizens; special summer programs for the learning disabled; nutrition and leisure programs for seniors; cultural opportunities; assistance to arts groups; and making recreation services available to individuals with disabilities.

Through its youth services division, the recreation department provides short-term interim counseling for troubled youth. The counseling program focuses its efforts on four main areas of service to the youth of Fairfax County: problem solving, information channeling, referral, and crisis intervention.

In the decade that the recreation program was growing in size and stature, both the county and regional park systems were established. In the same year, 1950, that the Virginia General Assembly passed the Park Authorities Act, the Fairfax County Board of Supervisors established a county authority to make decisions concerning land acquisition, park development, and operations. The goal and purpose were to contribute to the quality of life and environment for the citizens, visitors, and tourists of Fairfax County. With the support of the county Board, and the approval by voters of six park bond referenda between 1959 and 1988, the Fairfax County Park Authority (FCPA) now has over three hundred parks on over 14,000 acres of land. In forty-one years, the Authority has grown from a seasonal outdoor park system into a year-round leisure services agency.

The Lake Braddock residential community was an award-winning land development project begun in 1967. Courtesy of Dewberry & Davis

Franklin Farm is an 828-acre planned residential community initially built in 1987 on the site of a former dairy farm. Despite the rural setting and 165 acres of open space and farm ponds, there are 1,300 single family dwellings, 330 townhouses, community centers, and a neighborhood commercial center. Photograph by Larry Olsen, Courtesy of Dewberry & Davis

The interior of a fifty-year-old grain silo on the edge of the Franklin Farm community near
Herndon was redesigned as a contemporary home in the 1980s. A one-story tin-roofed
addition was constructed as a garage and foyer. A large Dutch barn on the site was
renovated and an adjacent milk parlor was converted into a community day care center.
The entire conversion won awards from the American Institute of Architects and the
National Trust for Historic Preservation. Exterior of silo photographed by Joe Grimes,
Interior of silo photographed by Maxwell MacKenzie, Courtesy of Dewberry & Davis

Kids enjoy playing on the Oak Marr Recreation Center's pool float, one of several at park authority centers. Courtesy of Fairfax County Park Authority

Recreational ice skating, ice hockey, and private lessons are available for all ages at the Mount Vernon Recreation Center's rink. Courtesy of Fairfax County Park Authority

Providence Recreation Center gets the spring racing season off to a running start with annual 10K and 2K Fun Runs. T-shirts are awarded to early registrants and medals to winners. Courtesy of Fairfax County Park Authority

Recreation centers have been built by FCPA throughout the county since 1977, when Wakefield was first opened. Since then, Mount Vernon, Providence, George Washington, Robert E. Lee, Oak Marr, Spring Hill, and South Run have been opened. A variety of classes is available at the centers, where indoor pools cater to the "Bitsy Bubble Babies" (six to 17 months old), the "Pee Wee Paddlers" (three to five years old), swim and dive team training, aquatic aerobics, and scuba diving among other water-related skills. Other classes teach tumbling, gymnastics, racquetball, wallyball, volleyball, golf, fencing, tennis, weight lifting, back packing and orienteering, triathlon training, jogging, hiking, biking, ice skating, cross-country skiing, martial arts, rock climbing, and caving. Although no riding lessons or horses are provided, there are riding trails and horse show arenas in the system. Classes are offered in arts, crafts, and the performing arts.

Movement for Children classes are available at recreation centers throughout the county. The program is designed to develop muscle strength, sensory perception, and motor skills. Courtesy of Fairfax County Park Authority

Karate classes at the Fairfax County Park Authority's recreation centers teach young boys and girls basic hand and foot techniques and self defense. Personal pride and a positive mental attitude are also encouraged. Classes in martial arts are offered to both children and adults. Courtesy of Fairfax County Park Authority

Huntley Meadows, with its 1,261 acres in Hybla Valley, is the Fairfax County Park Authority's largest park. It has a two-mile interpretive trail system and a boardwalk wetland trail and wildlife observation tower. Resident animal species include deer, fox, beaver, heron, hawks, and many other animals. Nature programs are provided by on-site naturalists. Courtesy of Fairfax County Park Authority

Symbolic of the historic interest in equestrian sports in the county, quarterhorse Walter Mitty is shown with his owner, Anita Ramos, at Bay Ridge Riding Stables. This is one of the facilities used by the Fairfax County Park Authority for riding classes. Riding and hunting on horseback have been popular in Fairfax County since the eighteenth century, when Fairfaxes, Washingtons and Masons and other families rode together in a relative wilderness. Currently, local horse and pony club members train and ride regularly; the Fairfax Hunt now rides in Loudoun County. Photograph by Donald L. Light, Courtesy of Anita Ramos

Summer activities in the county's park system provide a contrast to high technology and urban living which has in relatively recent times altered their lives. In outdoor settings, in amphitheaters ringed by trees, where birds add background music, restful shade and gentle breezes demonstrate nature's air conditioning. Players, singers, storytellers, and puppets sing songs and weave tales about places near and far, real and mythical, and exotic animals with human traits and conversation.

Specialized types of park facilities, in addition to the recreation centers, include a horticultural center at Green Spring Farm, the Kidwell Farm and an activities/ equestrian center, both at Frying Pan Park, an indoor ice skating rink, five nature and visitors' centers, lakes, two camp grounds, five golf courses, and a working mill at Colvin Run.

Forests, meadows, and wetlands surrounding the nature centers offer settings where one can appreciate experiences away from climate-controlled homes and giant shopping malls. On weekdays and weekends, short programs are given to audiences of all ages about bugs, snakes, birds, bats, beavers, frogs, wolves, turtles, and rocks from the natural world. Some of the classes and programs have intriguing names like "Nature Detectives," "Snakes of Fairfax," "Nature Snoopers," and "Damsels and Dragons" (insects).

The four waterfront county parks offer different out-of-doors experiences. Burke Lake, Lake Accotink, and Lake Fairfax, and Riverbend Park on the Potomac offer

Burke Lake and its Vesper Island, a state wildfowl refuge, are seen from the air in this Fall 1988 view. An airport was once planned for the area but the idea was abandoned in favor of the present Dulles International Airport site. Small streams were then dammed here and valleys were flooded to create the lake in the late 1960s. Courtesy of the photographer, Scott W. Boatright

fishing, boating, canoeing, pedal boating, pontoon excursion boat rides, miniature train rides, miniature golf, carousels, playgrounds, trails, and picnicking at some or all of these special parks.

Arts in the Parks programs give parents a welcome alternative to commercial television. Instead of watching a small, two-dimensional screen, the kids in the audience become part of the show as performers invite them to help write a story or act a part. In the summer of 1991, productions given at Lake Fairfax, Burke Lake, Mason District, and E.C. Lawrence parks were free to the public, the cost having been underwritten by a grant from the McDonalds Corporation. Summer concerts in the parks, some given by members of the Fairfax Symphony, fill the air with sounds of many kinds of music—country-western, ragtime, boogie-woogie, Dixieland, bluegrass, folk, jazz, classical, and oompa—to audiences of all ages.

The Fairfax County Park Authority is governed by a twelve-member board who set policy and establish priorities. Nine members represent the nine supervisory districts and three are members at large, all appointed by the Board of Supervisors.

Volunteers are an important group of people who have become involved in various aspects of the overall parks program through the years. In 1985, the total number of hours contributed to the Authority by volunteers was 32,859, equivalent to sixteen full-time employee positions. The figure in 1990 had more than doubled, to 67,128 hours.

The Junior Symphony gives a summer concert under the trees at Mason District Park near Annandale. Photograph by Don Sweeney, Courtesy of Fairfax County Park Authority

Since the Fairfax County Park Authority was established in 1950 by the Board of Supervisors, its board of directors, staff, and programs have received numerous awards. National recognition came in 1983, when Joseph P. Downs was director. The Authority received the National Gold Medal award from the National Recreation and Park Association "for Excellence in the Field of Parks and Recreation Management."

Concern for environmental conservation is growing with individuals, private industry, and public agencies. An interesting example of this awareness was provided by the Summer 1991 edition of seventy-two-page *Parktakes* planning guide magazine of the Authority. In a letter to the readers from Director William C. Beckner, he pointed out that the publication was now being printed on recycled paper with soy-based inks for the following reasons: "Using recycled paper saves trees, electricity, water, and landfill space and prevents unnecessary release of contaminants. Using soy-based ink removes petro-chemicals from the waste stream and helps lessen in a small way the demand for imported oil." Other organizations and individuals will surely follow with their conservation ideas in the decade of the 1990s.

Music of the eighteenth century is performed here on period instruments at Sully Plantation by musicians in costumes appropriate to those times. Courtesy of Fairfax County Park Authority

In addition to the Fairfax County Park Authority's eight recreation centers, there are several community centers operated with town taxes or homeowners association fees. Both county and regional park authorities have built and maintain golf courses. Centers have been built in Vienna, Herndon, Reston, McLean, Falls Church, and five neighborhood buildings with outdoor pools are in use at Burke Centre.

Although participation in sports of all kinds is a major activity throughout Fairfax County, including numerous privately sponsored sports organizations, spectator sports are enjoyed as well. In July 1985, George Mason University added a regional sports and entertainment facility with the opening of its ten thousand-seat Patriot Center on the campus. Managed by the Capital Centre organization, the center offers the public such events as commencements, basketball and soccer games, ice shows, concerts, trade shows, and the Fairfax Fair.

Another favorite sport in the entire metropolitan area is watching professional football games. The Washington Redskins team has a practice field near Dulles Airport, and a number of players and former players live and have businesses in Fairfax County.

Competitive swimming, which got its start in privately funded community membership pools in the county in the 1950s, produced an Olympic star at the 1972 games in Munich, Germany. Melissa Belote had learned to swim at the age of three at a private Springfield pool and from this start went on to win three gold medals swimming the backstroke at the Olympics.

The Patriot Center at George Mason University was opened in July 1985 and added a major regional sports and entertainment facility which seats ten thousand people. It is the site of events such as commencements, basketball and soccer games, trade shows, concerts, and ice shows. Photograph taken in 1989, Courtesy of the photographer, Tom Schudel

The dual demands for active recreation facilities and room for future growth led to creation of the Northern Virginia Regional Park Authority under state legislation passed in 1959. During the first decade of its existence, emphasis was on land acquisition for conservation purposes, particularly for protection of the Bull Run/Occoquan River watershed and Occoquan Reservoir, operated by the Fairfax County Water Authority. Later, the regional park authority responded to public demand to provide a variety of family-oriented, outdoor recreational facilities. User fees for some of these facilities supply well over half of the funding needed to operate the parks.

The Redskin Park training facility was established for the Washington Redskins football team, off Route 28 near Dulles International Airport, in 1971. There are two practice fields; one of Astroturf on the left, the other of natural turf. Courtesy of Fairfax County Economic Development Authority

Soccer fields see heavy use at Bull Run and other regional and county parks in Fairfax County. Both park systems also maintain public golf courses and boat launching ramps. Courtesy of Northern Virginia Regional Park Authority

A family enjoys their picnic at "a table by the window" in the regional park overlooking Pohick Bay. Boating, camping, golf, and other activities are also available on the bay which is part of the Potomac River. Courtesy of Northern Virginia Regional Park Authority

Policy for managing the sixteen regional parks, now including more than ten thousand acres, is made by a twelve-member board, two appointed from each of the six participating jurisdictions: Alexandria, Falls Church, and Fairfax cities, and the counties of Arlington, Fairfax, and Loudoun. The members serve four-year terms and together provide a mechanism for regional communication. The Authority's purpose was well stated by Chairman Walter L. Mess: "Nature has endowed Northern Virginia with a vast and beautiful legacy of scenic land and water within easy reach of our urban population. Preserving this priceless heritage for the enjoyment of present and future generations has been a primary policy goal of the Regional Park Authority."

Special events in different years have been Civil War reenactments, one of the largest dog shows in the United States, and an air show with vintage planes, skydivers, hot-air balloons, and kite flying. But the most popular event is the Annual Bull Run Country Jamboree, held rain or shine. In addition to five hours of country music played and sung by nationally-known entertainers, there are competitive country-style events for all ages. The attendance averages between 10,000 and 12,000. In 1990, 70.8 percent of the Regional Park Authority's funds were generated through park revenues, partly from the Jamboree.

Of the total of over ten thousand acres in the regional park system, 7,860 acres are within Fairfax County's borders. Four of the most unusual parks are Hemlock Overlook, Meadowlark Gardens, Sandy Run, and the W&OD Trail.

The Bull Run/Occoquan Regional Parks offer twenty-five miles of trails along the continuous Fairfax County shoreline of the two watercourses. The stream valley was once inhabited by Taux and Doag Indians of the Powhatan chiefdom. Streams and scenic woodlands offer solitude and silence and encourage walking and unwinding. The park is a valuable conservation area where forests, marshes, wild flowers, and wild animals are protected, as well as the Occoquan Reservoir, which is part of the water supply for Northern Virginia. Courtesy of Northern Virginia Regional Park Authority

Bull Run Regional Park's spacious fields accommodate groups by the hundreds for picnics, camping, and special events like dog shows, soccer, and the annual Country Jamboree with concerts, contests, and special events. Courtesy of Northern Virginia Regional Park Authority

Hemlock Overlook Regional Park is an outdoor learning center jointly operated by the Northern Virginia Regional Park Authority and George Mason University. Summer camps and year-round programs stress "outward bound" types of challenges for all ages. Courtesy of Northern Virginia Regional Park Authority

Top photo: Meadowlark Gardens Regional Park opened in 1987 and is becoming a botanical garden of regional significance. Curving, meandering trails lead to three sparkling lakes, gazebos, and picturesque hillsides covered with blooming plants and specimen trees. Courtesy of Northern Virginia Regional Park Authority

Bottom photo: The Washington & Old Dominion Railroad Regional Park is 100 feet wide and 44 miles long. Built on an old railroad right-of-way, the multi-use W&OD trail serves as a recreation corridor connecting a series of wayside parks and linking other trail systems. A separate bridle trail runs parallel west from Vienna. Courtesy of Northern Virginia Regional Park Authority

Hemlock Overlook, an outdoor learning center with an impressive stand of two hundred-year-old evergreens, is operated jointly by the Regional Park Authority and George Mason University. Classes are offered to youngsters, senior citizens, international sports or cultural groups, and business executives who conduct "outward-bound"-style programs.

Meadowlark Gardens opened in 1987 on Beulah Road near Wolf Trap and I-66. It is becoming a botanical garden of regional significance. On ninety-five acres of rolling hillsides, sparkling miniature lakes, and meandering trails, this budding arboretum already has the beginning of a separate endowment fund to help with the garden's new plants and continued maintenance. Within twenty years, the master plan should be fully developed and the trees, shrubs, and herbaceous plants mature.

Sandy Run Regional Park is located on the shores of Lake Occoquan reservoir. The site was used for the 1984 U.S. Olympic Trials in canoeing and kayaking, and the 1992 trials for rowing. It is also used for national competitions of high school rowing teams, and local college and university teams. The calm water, absence of wind, and strong current, and the long racing course at Sandy Run have won praise from racing experts who believe it to be "one of the finest rowing courses in the country." A natural amphitheater and a grandstand which seats five hundred have been constructed on the hillside to provide space for spectators to observe the finish line.

The Washington & Old Dominion Railroad Regional Park is one hundred feet wide and forty-four miles long, using an old railroad right-of-way which has been black-topped. Described as the "skinniest park in Virginia," the hiking/biking/riding trail runs through urban Northern Virginia, a recreation corridor which connects with other trails and parks along the way. An annual fifty-two-mile Wheelchair Race of Champions is a special event run from Purcellville to Washington, D.C., primarily on the Washington & Old Dominion Trail.

An annual fifty-two-mile Wheelchair Race of Champions runs from Purcellville to Washington, primarily on the Washington & Old Dominion Trail. Photograph by Julie Maloney, Courtesy of Northern Virginia Regional Park Authority

Since its organization in 1959, the Regional Park Authority, like the County Park Authority, has received many awards and citations for its accomplishments from national, state, regional, and county organizations including the U.S. Department of the Interior, the American Institute of Architects, and several conservation, sports, and recreation groups. This recognition underlines the wide variety of programs and facilities which the Regional Park Authority offers. Darrell Winslow is the executive director.

Individuals are not forgotten for their contributions. The National Recreation and Park Association gives annual awards nationwide. In 1990, two Fairfax Countians received national citations. Dr. Thomas L. Goodale, Professor and Coordinator of Parks, Recreation and Leisure Studies at George Mason University, received the literature award for his two recent publications, *The Evolution of Leisure: Historical and Philosophical Perspectives*, and *Recreation and Leisure: Issues in an Era of Change*. One of the National Voluntary Service Awards for 1990 was given to Joseph T. Flakne of Mason Neck, whose voluntary contributions of time and effort over a period of years have improved the quality of leisure opportunities through recreation, parks, and conservation programs and projects.

The era when large parcels of county and regional park lands could be acquired has probably passed. In recent years, the pressure of population growth, changing land use patterns, and changing lifestyles has greatly strained the county's capability to maintain service levels which citizens have come to expect. At the same time, the pace of urban development is rapidly limiting the availability of land suitable for future parks, while escalating land costs further constrain opportunities for purchase of public lands.

The existing and proposed system of parks, recreation, and open space is intended to offer residents, workers, and visitors the opportunity to make constructive use of their leisure time in safe, accessible, and enjoyable parks and community recreational facilities and programs. The park systems also serve as primary public mechanisms for the preservation of environmentally sensitive land and water resources, and areas of historical significance.

In addition to the county and regional parks, Fairfax County is the site of other unusual parks and wildlife refuges. The Mason Neck State Park is administered by the Commonwealth of Virginia and Gunston Hall Plantation is owned by the Commonwealth and administered by the National Society of Colonial Dames. The Mason Neck Wildlife Refuge is managed by the United States Fish and Wildlife Service. One of the sensitive areas on Mason Neck is a bald eagle nesting area which is protected by these preserves. Great Falls National Park, the George Washington Memorial Parkway, Wolf Trap Farm Park for the Performing Arts, Fort Hunt, and Fort Marcy are all part of the National Parks system within the borders of Fairfax County.

Cameron Run Regional Park is a water-oriented recreational facility located on Eisenhower Avenue inside the Capital Beltway. In addition to having been Virginia's first wave pool, it has a three-flume water slide and a new water playground. Courtesy of Northern Virginia Regional Park Authority

A tranquil woodland spot within an urban area is located on the boundary line between Fairfax and Arlington counties. The Upton Hill Regional Park offers several opportunities for leisure time activities. In addition to a waterfall, reflecting pool, gazebo, and picnic facilities, the park has a large swimming pool complex, a miniature golf course, a practice batting cage, and other game facilities. Courtesy of Northern Virginia Regional Park Authority

Mason Neck was an endangered nesting site for the American Bald eagle, our national symbol, shown here. As a result of years of dedication by former NVRPA board member Elizabeth Hartwell and others to preserving and protecting the fragile ecosystem on the peninsula including the nesting area, the Regional Park Authority established Pohick Bay Regional Park and acquired additional acreage, now managed by the U.S. Fish and Wildlife Service. Courtesy of Fairfax County Economic Development Authority

The Fairfax Symphony is shown at the concert hall of the Kennedy Center in 1990 with Conductor William Hudson. Photograph by Donna Cantor-Mclean, Courtesy of Fairfax Symphony

During the decade of the 1950s, cultural amenities as well as parks and recreation were becoming important to the county citizens. The Fairfax Symphony was founded by violinist Dorothy Farnham Feuer in 1957 and grew from an initial group of fifty-four mostly volunteer avocational musicians to a group of auditioned players who began to receive stipends in 1980. After Mrs. Feuer's death in 1964, an annual memorial scholarship fund was set up in her name for young string players. The same year, the symphony started the Northern Virginia Youth Orchestra and sponsored it until it became independent in 1978.

Since 1971, the Fairfax Symphony has been conducted by William Hudson. It has been hailed as a "first-class orchestra in a first-class community." It stages more than fifteen concerts each year, runs a chamber music institute, and conducts musical education programs in the public schools and parks. As the symphony players have grown in technical excellence and repertoire, they have received wide critical acclaim and substantial economic support from the business and educational communities. For many years, the symphony played concerts in the Fairfax High School, at Wolf Trap Farm and Orkney Springs, and in the Kennedy Center. After the Center for the Arts opened at George Mason University in 1990, the Fairfax Symphony was able to schedule the 1990-1991 season — their thirty-fourth — in the brand new acoustically designed symphony hall. For that first season in the new location, substantial support for this significant musical asset came from the business community. Principal underwriters and benefactors were Mobil Foundation, Inc., West*Group, AT&T, KPMG Peat Marwick, William A. Hazel, Inc., Coopers & Lybrand, Boeing Computer Services, Crestar Bank, Emhart PRC and ATI, First Virginia Bank, Unisys, C&P Telephone of Virginia, Sovran Bank, BDM International, Inc., First American Bank, TRW, Federal Systems Group, and Dyncorp.

Since 1985, the Fairfax Symphony's board of directors has presented Pyramid awards. These are given at an annual gala to individuals, corporations, and organizations, recognizing significant support for the orchestra.

The arts movement in the county became community-wide and broadly based in the decade of the 1960s. The Fairfax Choral Society was formed in 1962. Under the direction of Robert E. McCord, it has performed with the Arlington, Fairfax, and National symphonies and on the stages of Constitution Hall, the Kennedy Center, the Filene Center at Wolf Trap, and at National Presbyterian Church. The same year, the American Symphony Orchestra League, at the invitation of Mrs. Jouette Shouse, moved down to what was later to become Wolf Trap from Charleston, West Virginia. County women's clubs and other groups, aware of the burgeoning of independent groups, approached the Board of Supervisors urging the creation of an arts council to coordinate performing and graphic arts groups activities in the county for greater recognition of and education in the arts. First chartered as the Fairfax County Cultural Association in 1964, the organization was renamed the Fairfax County Council of the Arts in 1971. One of the first private nonprofit art agencies in the Commonwealth of Virginia, its mission is to create an environment in which the arts and artists may flourish and enrich the quality of life for all Fairfax County citizens.

As if to emphasize the importance of the decade for the arts in the county, in 1966 Mrs. Shouse gave her country residential property near Vienna to the Department of the Interior to establish the Wolf Trap Farm Park for the Performing Arts, to be administered by the National Park Service. It was the first national park established for this specific purpose. Here, public performances by local and international artists are given each summer to capacity audiences who sit in the pavilion or on the surrounding lawn. After the Filene Center had been built a second time following a fire, Mrs. Shouse had two old weathered barns moved down from upstate New York to Wolf Trap and had them joined together. As "The Barns of

Wolf Trap," they have served for the winter seasons since 1981. They provide an intimate showcase which seats 350 people for programs by some of the finest entertainers in folk, country, bluegrass, jazz, and classical music.

As originally planned, Reston was to be an idyllic place where people could live, work and play, enjoy nature and the out-of-doors, live in harmony without regard to race, creed, or color, and feel free to enjoy the arts and be creative if they so desired. The first residents had moved into their businesses and residences by the end of 1964. Shortly after the new town's dedication in May 1966, a community theater called the Reston Players was incorporated by entrepreneur Frank Matthews. The troupe almost immediately put on an original musical in July in the Hunters Woods stable. There have been other community theaters in the county but none with their home community backing them from their inception with the enthusiasm shown by Reston residents. After twenty-five years, Reston continues to support the troupe and its productions financially and with their attendance at the regular productions. The Northern Virginia Theater Alliance holds their one-act play competitions every year at the Reston Community Center's theater as an added theatrical experience.

A second Reston arts group, the Reston Chorale, was formed in December 1966 under the direction of Dr. James Christian Pfohl. The chorale sang with the Fairfax Symphony during the 1990-1991 season at George Mason University's Center for the Arts. The present conductor is Fred Wygal.

The Reston Community Players, the Reston Chorale, and the Fairfax Symphony are all members of and benefit from the activities and annual budget of the Fairfax County Council of the Arts. The Council assists numerous other arts programs as well.

In honor of Mrs. Jouette Shouse, a founding member of the Council of the Arts and chairman emeritus of the International Children's Festival, the Council established the Catherine Filene Shouse Endowment Fund in 1986, with annual awards going to local high school seniors in good standing who are planning to pursue further preparation in the field of the performing arts.

The Reston Community Players are shown here in a performance of Hello, Dolly!, *produced at the Reston Community Center Theatre in 1989. Courtesy of the Reston Community Players, Inc.*

Catherine Filene Shouse has for years been a significant patron of the arts. It was she who gave her estate outside of Vienna, Virginia, as well as partial funding, to establish the first national park for the performing arts. She continues to have an active interest in Wolf Trap and its programs, and is involved with the Fairfax County Council of the Arts as well. Courtesy of Catherine Filene Shouse

The annual International Children's Festival at Wolf Trap is a treat for both eyes and ears with colorful native costumes, music, and dancing from around the world. In this photograph, taken at the Festival in 1984, young dancers perform from the Grupo Folklorica di Argentina of the Hispanic Institute for the Performing Arts. Courtesy of the Fairfax County Council of the Arts

One of Mrs. Shouse's favorite projects, the International Children's Festival, is held for three days each Labor Day weekend at Wolf Trap. The proceeds help in large measure to fund programs for the Council. The festival celebrated its twentieth year in 1990 with an appearance of Bob McGrath of "Sesame Street" as master of ceremonies, with approximately 35,000 county residents and visitors in attendance. In addition to the international performances by children and adults, the children participate in workshops oriented to international arts and crafts such as Chinese kitemaking, Mexican paper flower construction, English brass rubbing, and American weaving. The festival illustrates an important concept: that people of all nations, states, and areas can share their cultural traditions through the international language of the arts, creating an atmosphere of friendship, trust, and harmony.

Although the festival has been an important event in its overall program and outreach, assistance with the Council's mission has come from the community as well. At its twenty-fifth anniversary celebration in 1989, the Council focused on the people of the county who had given freely of their time and treasure to establish the arts as a vital force in the community. Help has come from many areas—government, educators, industry and commerce—with each of these components represented in the membership of the Council.

Toni McMahon has been President and Chief Executive Officer of the Fairfax County Council of the Arts since 1983. In that period of time, with the dedication of the Council's Board of Directors, and their development committee, the Council's budget has risen from $100,000 annually in 1983 to $1.2 million in 1991. During this period, the business community's share of the funding for Council activities grew to over one-third of the total. In recognition of the importance of the arts in the community, the Fairfax County Chamber of Commerce initiated a Business Salutes the Arts annual luncheon in 1989 to show its support. Photograph by Toni Webb. Courtesy of Fairfax County Council of the Arts

Dingwall Fleary, music director for the International Children's Festival at Wolf Trap, and Bob McGrath, artistic advisor and host of the Festival are shown here in a rare moment of quiet. Fleary is founder and conductor of the McLean Symphony and McGrath is a member of television's "Sesame Street" company. Continuous interest and support from the Wolf Trap Foundation, the National Park Service, and the production staff of the Filene Center help to make this annual event the great success it is year after year. Courtesy of the Fairfax County Council of the Arts

The Thomas Jefferson High School for Science and Technology was converted to a technical high school in 1985. It boasts its own outdoor sculpture designed by student Bobby Koo, who was the winner in a design competition sponsored by the Northern Virginia Building Industries Association. It is titled "Today is Tomorrow." Photograph by James Corrie, Courtesy of Fairfax County Public Schools

Dozens of patrons of the arts have generously given funds to the Council for its program. In 1990, the principal benefactors were: Boeing Computer Services, Fairfax County government, Mobil Corporation, National Endowment for the Arts, TRW Federal Systems, Virginia Commission for the Arts, The Washington Post, and First Virginia Bank, all strong indications of support from local, state, and national government, and the corporate community.

Opportunities for visual cultural enrichment have increased markedly in Fairfax County in the past few decades. Art can be seen in sculpture in front of public buildings or in paintings hanging in corridors and reception rooms in offices, and more and more in private homes. Swedish sculptor Carl Milles was commissioned to design thirty-eight bronze figures in 1952 for the Fountain of Faith at National Memorial Park. He has left an important artistic legacy. Architectural historian William O'Neal of the University of Virginia has written of Milles' work: "The Fountain of Faith is, without doubt, one of the nation's greatest fountains." Artist Azriel Awret of Falls Church, born in Poland, has done several commissioned bronzes for George Mason University for the campus as well as inside the new Center for the Arts.

The Northern Virginia Community College has for some time had an important program related to the arts and artists. For over twenty years, the Annandale Campus has been systematically acquiring art for a permanent collection. In the early years, donations from organizations that included the Annandale Women's Club, the Fairfax County Council of the Arts, and the Philip Arnow Foundation were used to purchase art from the annual student art exhibitions. In addition, donations of works were made by visiting artists featured in exhibitions on campus, and by students and alumni.

In the 1980s, money for purchase prizes has come almost exclusively from the Philip Arnow Foundation, from artist donations, and from individual gifts. Since 1980, over fifty works have been added to the collection, bringing the total holdings to over one hundred paintings, prints, drawings, and sculptures.

For those individuals who wish to have a revolving display of art in their home or office, the Fairfax County Public Library has two lending collections of reproductions. Sculpture reproductions may be borrowed for a limited period from the Martha Washington Branch Library, and reproductions of famous paintings may be borrowed from George Mason Regional Library.

The Greater Reston Arts Center (GRACE) was incorporated as a nonprofit organization in 1973 and began an Art in the Schools program in 1977, which has received commendations and continues as a major activity in the community. Their Gallery Shop expands the opportunities for local artists and craftsmen to show and sell their work.

Cultural organizations and interest groups continue to proliferate. There are now more than 150 arts organizations in Fairfax County. The Fairfax County Council of the Arts, with Toni Winters McMahon as President and Chief Executive Officer, has since 1988 occupied the Fairfax County Park Authority's Fred M. Packard Center on Hummer Road in Annandale. Offices of nine other Fairfax County arts and civic organizations share the Center. They are: Artists United, the Springfield Art Guild, the Fairfax Symphony Orchestra, the Northern Virginia Youth Symphony Association, the Virginia Chamber Orchestra, the Fairfax Choral Society, the Fairfax County Federation of Citizens Associations, the League of Women Voters of the Fairfax Area, and the National Association for the Advancement of Colored People, Fairfax Branch. The close association of these groups has been mutually beneficial in the continued improvement of the quality of life in Fairfax County.

Sculptor Carl Milles was commissioned by the proprietors of National Memorial Park near Falls Church to design a fountain and bronze figures to express the "warmth and tenderness, the joy and strength of supreme love in all human relationships." The "Fountain of Faith" has been called one of the nation's greatest fountains. Courtesy of the photographer, Tom Schudel

Taking a rare moment of relaxation on the George Mason University campus is this "Woman on a Hammock," a life-size bronze figure sculpted by Azriel Awret of Falls Church. The artist, who was born in Poland and studied in Belgium, has created other sculpture, some of which is on display in George Mason University's new Center for the Arts. Photograph by Carl Zitzman, Courtesy of George Mason University

CHAPTER

8

Business and Professions

Fairfax County's business and professional community is unparalleled in its excellence and expertise.

Fairfax County Chamber of Commerce   120

Fairfax County Economic Development Authority   122

Freddie Mac   124

Dickstein, Shapiro & Morin   126

Dr. Michael Bermel, O.D., Optometrist   127

Pace Consulting Group, Inc.   128

Temps & Co.   129

Vance International, Inc.   130

Tysons Corner showing the Marriott Hotel and Tycon building in the foreground. Courtesy of the photographer, Scott W. Boatright

FAIRFAX COUNTY CHAMBER OF COMMERCE

The Fairfax County Chamber of Commerce has, throughout its long history, been an active partner of Northern Virginia businesses. As a vital part of the business world, the Chamber has maintained an unparalleled record of service to its membership and to the community at large.

Since its re-incorporation in April 1954, the modern Fairfax County Chamber has served as the preeminent voice of the business community in Northern Virginia. Today, the Chamber continues to play a vital role in the life of Fairfax County. Offering programs, benefits, and activities for every level of interest, the Chamber meets the needs of its large and diverse membership in ways unmatched by other organizations.

Today, the two-thousand member firm Chamber is very much a member-driven organization, with an eighty-member elected Board of Directors setting policy and determining overall goals and activities. Fifteen committees and over 1,200 volunteers interact with a staff of twenty to guide the Chamber's actions in areas as diverse as federal, state, and county legislation; leadership development; education; planning and land use; small business support and development; and Chamber programs and publications.

The Fairfax County Chamber is highly regarded for its long-standing reputation as an "issues" Chamber, testifying regularly before government bodies, lobbying for the interests of its members, and educating the business community on potential matters of concern. Among the Chamber's many accomplishments over the years have been initiatives resulting in key achievements on transportation needs, the founding of a Community Development Corporation to provide funding for affordable housing initiatives, the formation of a technology council to support the specific needs of that important and growing business sector, and the establishment of a local development corporation to provide startup funds for small businesses.

Recent Chamber efforts include an in-depth report to the Board of Supervisors on ways to re-invigorate the region's economy. Actions recommended in that study, a product of the Chamber's blue-ribbon Economic Potential Task Force, are forming the foundation for the county's fiscal planning strategies and for the way county government interacts with area businesses in the future.

Known for its legislative efforts, the Chamber, through its staff and volunteers, monitors sessions of the Virginia General Assembly and meets regularly with members of the Northern Virginia delegation to that body. The value of this effort is clear, as each year the Chamber enjoys a legislative success rate of over 90 percent on bills that would affect Northern Virginia. The Chamber also works closely with the Fairfax County Board of Supervisors, playing a key advisory role on issues affecting county businesses. From tax policy to zoning issues to land use and environmental legislation, the Chamber has been at work representing the views of the business community. Through its testimony at virtually every public hearing and representation on nearly fifty task forces and commissions, the Chamber ensures business community input on every issue affecting business or the quality of life in Fairfax County.

While the Chamber's legislative work may be the primary interest of large corporate members, smaller firms come for the incredible variety of networking opportunities. Including breakfast programs, Small Business Executive Forums (training programs for new business men and women from seasoned business leaders), the Professional Services Network, and evening Power Mixers with more than 300 in attendance, the

Committee members help guide the activities of the Chamber through regular meetings with staff.

Chamber offers a myriad of small business services and opportunities.

Chamber seminars cover timely topics, such as employment law, marketing and promotion, bidding on government contracts, and strategies for coping with changing economic times. The format includes panel presentations by leaders in the field, round table discussions with the panelists and other experts providing one-on-one counseling, and question and answer sessions with the whole audience.

General Membership Luncheons feature prominent speakers from business, government, and the arts. Proximity to the nation's capital has helped to attract speakers from the White House, the Cabinet, the United States Senate, and the House of Representatives. Special luncheons include those honoring the Chamber's "Captain of Industry" (a leader in business and the community at large), the Candidates Debate (with opponents for key political offices presenting their views before a panel of top journalists and the business community), a salute to partnerships between business and the arts community, the Chamber's Small Business Awards winners, and Valor Awards, medals of honor for public safety heroes.

In addition to publicly honoring Valor Award recipients, the Chamber has organized and maintains a scholarship fund providing grants for post secondary education for their children.

Topping the Chamber's social calendar is the annual "Turkey Roast," a black tie dinner celebrating, in a light-hearted manner, the accomplishments of key community leaders. Recipients of the Chamber "Turkey" have included present and former senators, Congressional representatives, governors, state legislators, members of the Fairfax County Board of Supervisors, and luminaries from the business world and the community. While the evening is festive, and the speeches tend to relate the more humorous and occasionally embarrassing "highlights" of the recipient's life, the honor is taken most seriously by the recipient and by the community at large.

A key part of any community's future is the development of the talent needed to lead it there. The Fairfax County Chamber is a vital link between the present and future through its sponsorship of Leadership Fairfax, a year-long educational program for up-and-coming community leaders. In monthly sessions, participants acquire a thorough knowledge of the history of their community, questions facing it now and in the future, and how they can become involved in finding solutions. Chosen from local businesses, community organizations, non-profit agencies, and government offices, the Leadership Fairfax class members comprise a cross-section of the community's character and of its potential.

The Fairfax County Chamber, like the county itself, grew tremendously in the 1980s. The Chamber of 1992 is a far cry from that of 1954, but the mission remains the same:

To foster a better understanding of the business community, its aims, responsibilities, efforts, contributions, and needs by encouraging healthy economic growth which provides jobs and opportunity for Fairfax County citizens.

1954 Statement of Mission

When you consider all the services, programs, and benefits available to members of the Fairfax County Chamber of Commerce, it is no surprise to find that nearly 5,000 of the region's most influential business men and women regard the Chamber as their most valuable business partner.

INNOVATIONS, *the Chamber's annual business-to-business trade show, attracts crowds of over 6,000 to visit the booths of its participants.*

Chamber networking functions offer members the opportunity to highlight their company before potential clients.

FAIRFAX COUNTY ECONOMIC DEVELOPMENT AUTHORITY

The advantages of living and working in Fairfax County have long been appreciated by its residents, but not until 1964 was an organization created to communicate these advantages to businesses and employers in other parts of the country.

That year, the Virginia General Assembly enacted legislation to create the Fairfax County Economic Development Authority to promote business development in the county.

Seven prominent business leaders were named by the County Board of Supervisors to serve as Commissioners of the Authority, but the activities—and those conducted by a small professional staff— were fairly limited in nature until more data about the county's economic condition was revealed in 1976.

Under the direction of the Board of Supervisors, a Blue Ribbon Panel was appointed to study the economic future of the county.

Among their findings was the fact that every tax dollar collected through real estate assessments generated a greater than proportionate demand for services by residents of the county, but a far less than proportionate demand for services by businesses.

Until this time, the sleepy, bedroom community in the suburbs of Washington, D.C., had been growing by the number of residents it housed, but not by the number of businesses it attracted or jobs it created. Thus, the demand for public services—particularly schools—had surpassed the amount of taxes residents could afford to pay.

The release of this information prompted the Board of Supervisors to authorize an ambitious program to increase the amount of real estate taxes contributed by businesses to the overall county budget from the existing level of 11.7 percent to 25 percent.

Over the ensuing ten years, the Economic Development Authority combined an aggressive program of marketing, advertising, and research to lure quality business development to Fairfax County. As their successes mounted and predominantly high technology firms relocated to Fairfax and existing companies continued to grow, residents and businesses alike enjoyed numerous successive real estate tax cuts.

By 1987, the Authority had reached the goal. An all-time high of 27-1/4 percent of the county real estate tax base was raised by business while the actual tax rate for both business and residential properties was reduced over the same period from $1.74 to the current $1.11 per one hundred dollars assessed value.

Over 68 million square feet of office space was needed to house all the businesses, ranking Fairfax County amongst

Business growth has been an important element in the vitality of Fairfax County's economy.

Economic vitality translates into an exceptional quality of life.

the largest in office space development in the nation, behind the central business districts of New York, Los Angeles, Chicago, Atlanta, and Washington, D.C. The Tysons Corner area, alone, offered over 19 million square feet of office space by 1991, ranking it among the leaders on the same list. This size surpassed the office space available in cities such as Miami, San Diego, St. Louis, or the combined Virginia areas of Richmond, Roanoke, and Norfolk.

While business was growing in Fairfax County, the Authority was also expanding its breadth of services. In addition to providing support for small businesses and assisting companies with expansion plans, the Economic Development Authority entered the new industry of convention and travel promotion.

The Board of Supervisors commissioned a study group on the travel industry in 1985 and created the Convention and Visitors Bureau in 1987. Advertising, marketing, and convention support are primary services provided by the Bureau for business travelers, travel writers, and meeting planners. For the leisure traveler, a Visitors Center was established in 1990 to promote area attractions and the county's thriving hospitality business. In 1991, nearly 10,000 hotel rooms exist for visitors to Fairfax County.

Since 1964, the Fairfax County Economic Development Authority has been an integral part of the prosperity both business and residents have enjoyed in Fairfax. As communities throughout the country compete for foreign and domestic business investment, the successful partnership of private and public sectors in Fairfax County will continue to be the standard by which others are judged.

County businesses are at the forefront of emerging technologies.

School children prepare for new and exciting futures.

Freddie Mac employees celebrate the dedication of the new McLean headquarters in June 1991.

Freddie Mac (Federal Home Loan Mortgage Corporation) is a congressionally-chartered corporation created to ensure a steady flow of mortgage funds for home buyers. Armed with a mission to make the American dream of home ownership a reality, Freddie Mac has helped finance one in eight American homes, including more than 700,000 apartment units, since the company's creation in 1970. In 1989, Freddie Mac became a publicly-held stockholder-owned corporation with a board of directors comprised of some of America's foremost business leaders.

How does Freddie Mac assist home buyers? The corporation replenishes primary market funds by purchasing mortgages from savings and loans, commercial banks, and other financial institutions, thus providing lenders with funds to make more mortgages. Freddie Mac packages these mortgages into securities, adds a payment guarantee, and sells the securities to investors.

By linking the capital markets with the mortgage markets, Freddie Mac brings the efficiencies and lower costs of the secondary mortgage market to the lender, the investor, and the home buyer. The result? Mortgage interest rates which are one-half percent lower on average, than if there were no secondary mortgage market.

Freddie Mac's corporate headquarters is located on more than thirteen acres in Tysons Corner, Virginia. Other buildings are located throughout Fairfax County with regional offices scattered around the nation. Sixty-three percent of the corporation's 2,500 employees live in the Northern Virginia area.

With an average age of 33, Freddie Mac employees are diverse, dynamic, and energetic. The corporation employs a wide variety of professionals—financial analysts, accountants, attorneys, computer specialists, and others. Employee enthusiasm is evidenced by the aggressive support of Freddie Mac's corporate philanthropic efforts to address the needs of children at risk. With these efforts the company has strived to call public attention to the devastating problems so many of our children are facing. The company is working to raise the awareness of the need for foster care and adoption as well as related volunteer services in the

Leland Brendsel, Chairman and Chief Executive Officer, delivers opening remarks at the School for Contemporary Education building dedication in Annandale, Virginia, as First Lady Barbara Bush looks on.

Washington area. Helping to find homes for over four thousand neglected, abused, and abandoned children fits perfectly with Freddie Mac's corporate mission of making the American dream of home ownership a reality.

Freddie Mac's community relations program enjoys widespread participation from employees throughout the corporation. The program's goal of establishing continuing relationships with community groups is exemplified by the success of the corporation's partnership with Hunters Woods Elementary School in Reston, Virginia. Through this partnership Freddie Mac employee volunteers are matched with students to form mentor/mentee relationships. Freddie Mac employees also volunteer their time for county-wide events such as Special Olympics, Christmas in April, and the Fairfax Fair.

In keeping with the goal of making home ownership a reality for everyone, Freddie Mac has made a focused commitment to support shelter initiatives for low-and moderate-income borrowers and renters. In 1991, Freddie Mac designed initiatives in the state of Michigan, in Greensboro, North Carolina, and for AFL-CIO union members. Each of these programs helps low-and moderate-income families qualify for home ownership by providing counseling and modifying underwriting guidelines. For example, instead of the usual 10 percent down payment that is required to buy a home, the borrower is required to make a 5 percent down payment combining up-front cash with loans, gifts or grants. To assist renters, Freddie Mac has invested approximately $87 million in tax credit equity funds which will help create affordable rental homes for more than 10,000 Americans.

From affordable housing initiatives to volunteer activities and programs for children at risk, Freddie Mac is committed to improving the lives of those around us.

Freddie Mac employees man the awards stand at the Fairfax County Special Olympics in April 1991.

DICKSTEIN, SHAPIRO & MORIN

For more than thirty-five years, Dickstein, Shapiro & Morin's (DS&M) goal has been to achieve results for its clients.

The firm has long served as litigation counsel in numerous cases of national importance. During the past two decades, however, DS&M's capabilities have grown far beyond the litigation arena where it first earned acclaim. DS&M's attorneys counsel individuals, corporations and associations, as well as local and state governments. The firm's practice areas include: banking and bankruptcy, corporate, securities and finance, energy, enforcement, environment and natural resources, government contracts, immigration, intellectual property, international trade, litigation, public policy and tax. Broad experience across these legal disciplines enables DS&M to respond immediately and efficiently, with a team approach, to a client's most complex and pressing legal problems.

Based in Washington, D.C., with offices in New York, Paris and a correspondent office in St. Petersburg, Russia, Dickstein, Shapiro & Morin opened offices in Vienna, Virginia, in 1986 to serve the growing presence of high technology firms located in Northern Virginia.

Located in Virginia, the Government Contracts Section takes pride in its ability to keep pace with today's volatile and constantly changing high technology marketplace. The section has been active in representing domestic and foreign high technology and computer companies and has been extremely successful in winning and resolving significant technology-related protests, claims and other disputes. DS&M's ability to serve the needs of this high technology community is solidly grounded in the engineering and scientific training of many of its attorneys.

Other strengths of DS&M's Virginia attorneys include their hands-on experience in negotiating and implementing the sale, financing and acquisition of high technology companies and other corporate entities. In connection with such matters, DS&M has the ability to represent its clients at all government levels—federal, state and local.

In addition, DS&M's Virginia attorneys have capabilities in real estate transactions, including zoning, leasing, financing and related environmental matters. All of these activities are supported by DS&M's Washington, D.C. office.

Through the years, DS&M has remained intensely and personally devoted to its clients. The firm's growth has been nourished by its attorneys' ability to understand clients needs and by its zeal and tenacity in providing cost-efficient solutions to clients' legal problems. DS&M is now a large national firm with growing international reach, but with a strong belief that its future will be measured by the successes achieved for its clients.

Dickstein, Shapiro & Morin focuses on high technology at its Virginia offices.

DR. MICHAEL J. BERMEL, O.D., OPTOMETRIST

As recently as 20 years ago, most eye doctors corrected poor vision simply by prescribing glasses. Today, new procedures make it possible to halt the degeneration of eyesight, and in some cases, to permanently improve vision.

Dr. Michael Bermel is a firm believer in keeping abreast of innovative eye care technology. "Take eye spasms for instance," explains Bermel. "More than 10 percent of my patients who come to me complaining of nearsightedness actually have an eye spasm. In other words, the patient may actually have 20/20 vision, but because they work at a job that requires constant close-up vision—word processing, writing, accounting—their vision gets locked into a "near focus" and objects in the distance appear blurry."

To correct eye spasms, Dr. Bermel often prescribes eye exercises and special reading glasses. "The scary thing," says Bermel, "is if this temporary affliction is not tested for, patients may be prescribed lenses that are too strong for them, resulting in further eyesight deterioration."

In some cases, actual nearsightedness can be permanently repaired. When Kyle Smith was referred to Doctor Bermel, his vision was 20/200 in his left eye and 20/100 in his right eye. Bermel prescribed a treatment called Orthokeratology. Proven successful in treating nearsightedness caused by an irregularly shaped cornea, this process uses a series of hard contact lenses designed to gradually change the shape of the cornea, allowing for more normal vision. Today, Kyle Smith has uncorrected 20/20 vision in both eyes.

"With technology available to correct dozens of problems that could not be detected or treated before, you can't settle for 'good enough,'" affirms Bermel. "Sure, my exams are long—usually 45 to 50 minutes—but if it means saving someone's eyesight, isn't it worth it?"

When prescriptions are required, Dr. Bermel stresses precision and service. He custom grinds lenses in his own lab so they match his prescription perfectly. He also stocks a large inventory of contact lenses, everything from common prescriptions to highly specialized bifocals, so patients can test them before they buy or are able to borrow an emergency pair if they have lost or damaged their own lenses.

"Eye care is more important than many of us think," advises Bermel. "After all, 80 percent of what we learn is through our eyes."

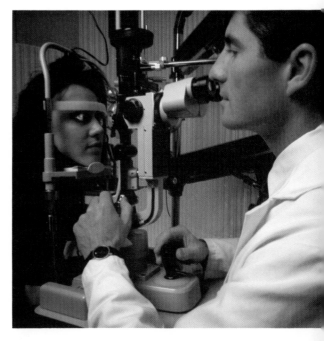

Dr. Bermel looks for eye disease that could cause loss of eyesight.

Certified on-staff fashion consultants present the best choices for each patient from more than 1,000 designer frames in stock.

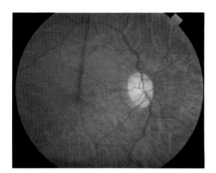

A retinal hole behind the eye was diagnosed in time to save this patient's vision.

Dr. Michael J. Bermel.

PACE CONSULTING GROUP, INC.

Dr. Barbara Pate Glacel is the president and managing partner of Pace Consulting Group, a Fairfax County firm serving national and international clients in executive and organizational development.

Pace Consulting Group, Inc., specializes in assisting organizations with leadership, quality and change. Founded in Fairfax County in 1988, Pace's programs and services in executive development, organization development, strategic planning, and human resource planning focus on preparing organizations and individuals for the demands of the 1990s and the twenty-first century.

Pace tailors its services to the individual needs of its clients in the areas of planning, assessment, and development of the organization, executives and managers. Consulting services assess the climate and performance of an organization and its work force in order to develop a plan to meet future needs for productivity and quality. Proprietary Pace programs assist organizations in developing the alignment of goals and leadership skills to motivate the highly skilled work force of our times.

Pace Consulting Group is a network associate of the Center for Creative Leadership, presenting two flagship technologies for executive and organizational development. "The Looking Glass Simulation" is state-of-the-art assessment for executive development and assessment of organizational culture. Over time, the application of the Looking Glass simulation measures the change in organizational culture as a result of the organization's efforts to meet changing business requirements.

In addition, Pace is the exclusive agent for the Center for Creative Leadership's "Systems Leadership" program. The systems leadership concepts aim at developing highly productive organizations through the creative integration of all behavioral operating systems. Focusing on the alignment of goals, climate of leadership and trust, and measurement of results, it is based on the leadership and organizational practices which are required for quality performance.

Pace Consulting Group uses research-based survey techniques such as the Myers-Briggs Type Indicator, the Campbell Work Orientations (NCS) and the Profilor (PDI) to assess leadership and organizational performance.

Pace is a group of interdisciplinary consultants with backgrounds in organization behavior, industrial and clinical psychology, human resource development, business administration, and public administration who bring both academic credentials and line management experience to the client organizations it serves. Producing quality, performance and leadership results, Pace Consulting Group assists such national and international clients as Atlantic Richfield Company, GE, Johnson and Johnson, Life Technologies, Inc., Martin Marietta Corporation, MCI Communications Corporation, The MITRE Corporation, NASA, and TRANSNET.

The senior consultant staff at Pace Consulting Group, with Headquarters in Fairfax County, Virginia, provides clients with years of experience in leadership within organizations, as well as the interdisciplinary academic credentials to relate theory and reality in the changing world of the 1990s. Pictured are, left to right: Mr. William Dunn (Johannesburg), Dr. Larry Kahn (Philadelphia), Dr. Barbara Pate Glacel (President and Managing Partner, Pace West), Ms. Gretchen Hannon (Fairfax), Ms. Patricia Ryan (Partner, Fairfax), Dr. Emile A. Robert, Jr. (Vice President, Fairfax), and Dr. Todd Greenberg (Boston).

T E M P S & C O .

In October 1981, Steven Ettridge sold his car and took a third mortgage on his home to raise $20,000. He recruited his sister, Crystal, from academia and the co-founders bet the whole stake to create their own temporary personnel service.

In recession-ridden 1981, only one other temporary service tried to start up in Washington, and it quickly went out of business. Yet despite the long odds and the entrenched position of national services, Steven and Crystal Ettridge succeeded in making Temps & Co. an immediate leader through innovation.

Today, Temps & Co. is Washington's largest temporary service, with fourteen offices and 5,100 active temporaries. By their fourth year in business, they had surpassed all the national temporary services (including Kelly, Norrell, and Manpower) in regional sales, and have gone on to dominate the Baltimore-Washington market.

Washington Business Journal recently rated Temps & Co. Washington's most frequently chosen secretarial service in their annual Book of Lists. The reasons are many and varied. With its computerized offices, Temps & Co. can access its entire temporary and client roster within seconds of a call, a service that assures an immediate response and a more accurate matching of a client's needs.

The philosophy of Temps & Co. is simple: meet the needs of your temps and they will meet the needs of your clients. Thus, Temps & Co. attracts and retains its temporaries 50 percent longer than the industry average.

Temps & Co.'s Guaranteed Work Program pays between fifty and one hundred proven temporaries to report to its offices every morning. This preparedness generates industry-leading numbers: Temps & Co. is placing temporaries on-site within thirty minutes, 97 percent of the time.

The MATCH Program—Management Alternative Toward Career Hiring—has proven particularly successful for clients of Temps & Co. The MATCH Program gives the firm and the potential employee the chance, on the job, to evaluate the working relationship before a hiring commitment is made.

Temps & Co. has developed proven methods that make managing a client's temporary needs easier and more profitable. They even offer to be put to the test by offering a no-fee, four-hour trial assignment program.

President Steven D. Ettridge and his sister, Vice President Crystal Ettridge, pose in front of one of their fourteen Washington area locations.

Steven D. Ettridge receives the Inc. *magazine Entrepreneur of the Year award in 1989 from Richard W. Dugan, managing partner of Arthur Young, and John Rosato, president of ComSite, the 1988 recipient of the award.*

VANCE INTERNATIONAL, INC.

L ADIES AND GENTLEMEN, the President of the United States of America...

This honored greeting was heard frequently by Charles F. Vance, founder of Vance International, during his fourteen years as a Special Agent of the U.S. Secret Service. With a spirited zest for the professionalism, reliability, and responsiveness which made him one of the Service's most respected and knowledgeable agents, Chuck Vance has honed Vance International into the quality leader of the private security industry. ·

At Vance International, leadership is defined as striving to be the best. While their office walls are adorned with letters and commendations from many nationally and internationally prestigious clients, Chuck Vance states, "Such accolades of the past are not enough." Indeed, the success of this organization comes from their dedicated effort to continually satisfy the needs of their clients for professional security services. Since the company's inception in 1984, Vance International revenues have shown dramatic annual growth.

Oliver North, Imelda Marcos, strike torn companies, Saudi Arabian potentates, international espionage, anti-terrorist strategies, security management of billions of dollars of real estate assets, complex investigations—Vance International has experienced it all through its five dynamic subsidiary companies:

Founder and President, Charles F. Vance.

Vance Executive Protection, Inc. offers discreet executive protection services once available only to high ranking U.S. and foreign government officials. Vance is second to none in serving the executive security needs of the private sector. Agents are specially recruited from various government and municipal security forces, and bring to the client years of experience, worldwide intelligence, and invaluable contacts on the law enforcement and political fronts. From the United States to the Far East, Vance's client list is a Who's Who of the powerful and the respected in business and government.

Asset Protection Team, Inc. (APT) provides highly-trained security strike specialists who are dispatched anywhere in the United States to protect people, property, and facilities. They have provided security during highly charged work action at paper mills, coal mines, metal manufacturing plants, and other private and publicly held companies. The key to APT's success is its policy of maintaining a nonviolent profile even in the face of serious and threatening provocation. Their use of photo documentation teams are an integral part of each operation. An APT division, Vance Emergency Response Services Team (VEST), is specially trained and able to respond swiftly to the most serious of security challenges during natural or man-made disasters.

Vance Uniformed Protection Services, Inc., specializes in providing the private and governmental sectors with uniformed security officers, acclaimed by clients and competitors alike to be a cut above. Their specialty is to provide protective services exclusively to premier, prestigious, and sensitive clients who expect and demand exceptional services. Each Vance officer is investigated, screened for job suitability, professionally trained at Vance's own academy, and completely familiarized with the client's specific requirements. The Officer Training Program exceeds all state and federal expectations and requires Emergency First Aid and CPR Red Cross certification of all security officers. The result is courteous, efficient, highly skilled, professional security personnel.

Vance Education and Training Services, Inc., offers a selection of state-of-the-art professional security training programs. Courses can vary in length from one day seminars to six month skill mastery programs. Popular offerings include Executive Protection Training, Proprietary Guard Force Training, Firearms, Evasive Driving, Bomb Threat Management, Counter-espionage, and Electronic Surveillance Countermeasures.

Vance Executive Protection Agents.

Vance International Investigative Services, Inc., staffed with former senior level U.S. Secret Service personnel, provides expertise in due diligence investigations, financial risk analysis, personal threat analysis, computer fraud, counterfeit product/gray market, embezzlement and theft of trade secrets, along with others. Through their worldwide network of investigative professionals, Vance has helped to solve some of the most intriguing investigative cases ever experienced by the corporate and legal world.

The challenge and opportunity welcomed by Vance International personnel is to position the company for even greater success in the 1990s and beyond. Their Senior Management Team, lead by Executive Vice President David P. Johnson, feels this challenge will be met by being a company which "continues to redefine client expectations." Their goal is to constantly expand and improve upon the standards by which true quality performance is measured. Virtually every aspect of their operation focuses on exceeding traditional industry standards.

Being an industry leader is not an easy position to reach and even more difficult to maintain. Regardless of their positions, jobs, or assignments within the organization, Vance International security professionals have developed this organization exponentially through their professionalism, reliability, and responsiveness in providing the best security services possible.

Vance International is proud to be a prominent member of the Fairfax County business community. There is a strong mandate in Fairfax County to support and encourage the success of the business community and at Vance International, great benefit has been realized from this dynamic, can-do spirit.

Vance officers protecting the National Archives and its most important documents — Our Constitution and the Bill of Rights.

CHAPTER

Networks

A diverse range of organizations and businesses ensure the quality of life in Fairfax County.

Inova Health System   134

Washington Gas   135

Northern Virginia Community College   136

Northern Virginia Public Television   138

Little children have always seemed to enjoy a ride on a hay wagon whether it happened in earlier times or presently at the Claude Moore Colonial Farm at Turkey Run in Langley. The living history exhibit offers a view of the subsistence farmer in Northern Virginia during the latter part of the 1700s. Courtesy of Fairfax County Economic Development Authority

INOVA HEALTH SYSTEM

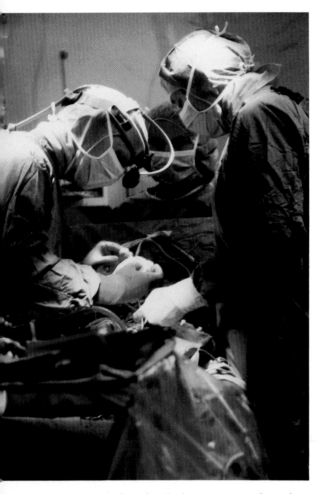

From routine to "first-of-its-kind" surgeries, Inova hospitals are leaders in high quality patient care.

Inova Health System is a comprehensive, not-for-profit health care organization with one goal: to serve the community. It does so through a strong mission of making quality health care accessible to all Northern Virginia residents.

With a network of four hospitals, nursing homes, urgent care centers, free-standing emergency rooms, and home health services, Inova Health System is the largest community-based health care provider in Northern Virginia—and the Washington, D.C. area.

From bumps and bruises to major illnesses and trauma, Inova provides health care to all Northern Virginia residents regardless of ability to pay. It also offers comprehensive birth and family education as well as programs to help community members maintain and improve their health.

Above all, Inova is people helping people—over 12,000 physicians, employees, and volunteers dedicated to bringing quality health care to the people of Northern Virginia. Among Inova's many contributions, it performed the first heart transplant and the first lung transplant in the Washington, D.C. area.

Included in the Inova family of hospitals are Fairfax Hospital, Fair Oaks Hospital, Jefferson Hospital, and Mount Vernon Hospital. In addition, Inova offers: the Office of HIV Services, an AIDS information and awareness program; the Cameron Glen Care Center and Commonwealth Care Center, long-term care facilities; and The Kellar Center, a behavioral health program for adolescents.

Other services include: CATS, (Comprehensive Addiction Treatment Services); Inova Home Care, a Medicare-certified home care system; and Inova Health Professionals, which offers private duty nursing care. ACCESS of Fairfax and ACCESS of Reston/Herndon are freestanding emergency rooms, the first such 24-hour emergency facilities in the United States.

Inova Health System serves its communities through an ongoing commitment to quality improvement. Inova educates future physicians through its residency programs, and trains nurses, physical therapists, and other technicians. Inova provides continuing medical education to its over 1,700 active physicians, a vital part of its mission of assuring the quality of health care to the people it serves.

Dramatic changes took place in health care during the 1980s, with diagnostic technologies that gave physicians extraordinary new insights into the body and new drugs that saved the lives of many. The 1990s will bring even greater challenges to Inova's commitment, resourcefulness, and ingenuity as a premier health care provider in the community.

Through these challenges, Inova Health System will continue to meet the three fundamental values it strives to achieve: Innovation, Caring for and about People, and Responsiveness to the Community.

Inova provides care to the growing elderly population through specialized services such as respite care.

Fairfax Hospital's new Women and Children's Center is everything you asked for.

W A S H I N G T O N   G A S

Commercial customers account for nearly one-third of the company's sales in the county.

A vibrant commercial sector. Strong public and private education systems. Perhaps the best-educated workforce in the country. These are just a few of the reasons why Fairfax County stands out as a premier business location. Washington Gas, one of the county's foremost business partners, is proud to play a part in Fairfax's progress.

Founded in 1848, Washington Gas claims the honor of being the first gas company in the United States to be chartered by Congress. That year, the company provided gas to light the Capitol Building and grounds. With the advent of the electric light later in the century, gas use for lighting declined, but new markets developed in home heating and cooking.

The company extended service into Virginia in 1917. Soon afterward, Washington Gas began supplying customers in Fairfax County. By 1930, it was replacing manufactured gas with clean natural gas brought in by pipelines from the southwest United States.

Today, the company provides natural gas service to more than 135,000 homes and offices in Fairfax County. More than 90 percent of these customers are residential users, but 30 percent of the sales are to commercial customers such as restaurants, department stores, health spas, and office buildings.

Natural gas is versatile. It can be used to fuel clean-burning fireplaces and to heat spas, swimming pools and patios, as well as for basic uses such as home-heating and cooling, cooking, water heating, and clothes drying.

Clean-burning natural gas is expected to play a significant role in helping our country meet environmental challenges. One of the major causes of air pollution is automobile emissions. Emissions of carbon monoxide, for example, can be reduced by more than 90 percent when using natural gas as a vehicle fuel. Washington Gas has operated a fleet of natural gas vehicles since 1979.

The emphasis at Washington Gas is on delivering the Best Energy Value to its customers and contributing to the high quality of life in its service area.

Each year, company employees donate thousands of hours to community organizations and projects in Fairfax. They perform tasks as diverse as making home repairs for elderly citizens, judging high school science and social studies competitions, and helping area fire departments distribute safety information. Washington Gas employees have teamed up to deliver some volunteer services. A clown group entertains at local hospitals, nursing homes and community celebrations and fairs, while the employee running club participates in fund-raising marathons for worthy causes.

Washington Gas employees are energetic in promoting the economic vitality of Fairfax as well. They serve in numerous business, professional, and neighborhood associations, and help champion the county's interests in the state capital. The company is committed to continuing to support the special blend of tradition and progress that is Fairfax County.

The Community Clowns appear at more than one dozen events annually in Fairfax, bringing joy to thousands.

Washington Gas strives to provide superior service and the Best Energy Value.

NORTHERN VIRGINIA COMMUNITY COLLEGE

Northern Virginia Community College is an unparalleled success story—successful because of the student accomplishments and what the college has meant to a thriving Northern Virginia community. Known as NOVA, the college recently celebrated twenty-five years of providing the highest quality programs and services by opening numerous doors of opportunity and touching the lives of so many people.

The multi-campus system of the college provides traditional and nontraditional higher education through the five campuses and the Extended Learning Institute. Increasing numbers of international and minority students are being serviced within a student population that totals almost 60,000 different credit students each year. About 42 percent of the students are residents of Fairfax County.

Even though the college first opened in temporary facilities at Baileys Crossroads, the first permanent building was built on the Annandale Campus in 1967. The campus has remained the largest of the five campuses with a Community Cultural Center being the latest building added to the seven building complex. Located on Little River Turnpike just one-half mile outside the Beltway at Exit 6, the 76.4-acre Annandale Campus specializes in health technologies and light engineering programs.

Each of the five campuses has occupational/technical programs which are unique to the campus. All campuses have a basic core of general education courses and college transfer curricula such as Business Administration, Computer Science, Education, Fine Arts, Science, and Liberal Arts. And, General Studies is a specialized program where students develop their own curriculum based on the needs for transfer to a specific baccalaureate degree major at a four-year college or university.

Curricula unique to the Annandale Campus include Emergency Medical Services Technology; Cardiac Care Technician; Electrical Engineering specialization under Engineering; Fire Science Administration; Fire Protection Technology; Fire Science Investigation; Hotel, Restaurant and Institutional Management; Food Service Management; Mechanical Engineering; Machine Tool Operation; Medical Laboratory Technology; Histotechnology; Phlebotomy; Medical Records Technology; Medical Office Assisting; Nursing; Physical Therapist Assistant; Radiography;

An outstanding atmosphere for learning.

Recreation and Parks; Respiratory Therapy; and Travel and Tourism. The campus enrolls almost 14,000 students each fall. There are eighty-five different curriculum areas with over 1,700 different classes available.

Activities during the year are highlighted by drama and chorale productions, an international festival, black history week, noted guest speakers, band concerts, and intramural sports. In addition, many community groups, government agencies, and businesses use facilities at NOVA for special events, meetings, and seminars. The Annandale Campus Community Cultural Center has a 520-seat theater, dance studio, forum area, seminar rooms, gymnasium, art gallery, and dining room to accommodate college and community functions. The Festival of the Arts, for example, is held both indoors and outdoors with participation by many citizens of Fairfax County.

It's a beautiful campus, with a lake, trees, and a very open atmosphere. Everyone, even visitors, feels welcome because of the caring attitude of faculty and staff. In addition to the academic excellence, it is one of the reasons that the college continues to be successful. NOVA is "the community's college."

The Annandale Campus Community Cultural Center.

The Annandale Campus.

NORTHERN VIRGINIA PUBLIC TELEVISION

Thomas C. Boushall, First President and Chairman of the Board of CVETC.

In the early 1950s, the Federal Communications Commission began to address the special needs of viewers by enabling alternative programming to air in addition to the regular commercial schedule.

By the 1960s, Virginia had its first educational station, WHRO, in Norfolk and in Richmond, several community leaders formed the Central Virginia Education Television Corporation (CVETC). Their goal was to provide educational television broadcasts directly to schools in the entire Central Virginia area.

By April 1965, evening hours of cultural and informative programming were added to the broadcast schedule to provide general interest programs for the public. When results showed that a single station could not meet the demand for instructional programming, WCVW-TV Channel 57 was placed in service in 1966 to help channel 23 in its overwhelming effort to provide more comprehensive educational opportunities for students in schools across fifty-two counties.

In the following year, the Carnegie Commission under President Johnson recognized the potential for educational television to serve a greater audience and recommended the Public Telecommunications Act. This act eventually passed Congress and enabled the creation of public television as we know it today.

A study commissioned by Governor Holton in 1970 showed there was an unfulfilled need for a station to provide instructional TV from Fredericksburg north. As a result, the Virginia Public Telecommunications Council (VPTC) was formed.

The Northern Virginia Education TV Association was formed in 1972 to fill the gap in service and the same year WNVT Channel 53 was licensed to that body. On March 1, 1972, WNVT began its transmission with live coverage of the Virginia General Assembly. Educational and public television service to the Northern Virginia area began when, at the request of the State of Virginia, the Central Virginia Educational Television Corporation assumed operation of WNVT Channel 53 in 1974.

Today, WNVC-TV, situated on the corners of Lee Highway and Gallows Road in Merrifield, Virginia, is a fully-accredited, independent, viewer-supported public television station serving Northern Virginia and the greater Washington, D.C., area with a 4.6 million audience potential.

Channel 56 carries locally-relevant programs such as Congressional coverage daily, Fairfax County meetings, and other programs that satisfy a diverse range of interests. WNVC offers collegiate wrestling, football, and basketball; how-to series; music programs; international programs; movies; as well as news and international programming for a minority ethnic audience in their native language.

WNVC presents daily the "U.S. State Department Report," a summary of the State Department briefings. The Channel 56 news bureau in Richmond produces

B. W. Spiller, second from left in front of the WCVW/WCVE building in 1967–1968, with Holladay Aero representatives.

"Making of Virginia Laws" and "Virginia Legislature," daily reports on legislative activities in the state capitol, and "The Virginia Capitol News Report," in-depth reviews of the major issues facing Virginians. Since 1974, WNVC has aired Virginia candidate and election coverage.

In May 1989, WNVC-TV in cooperation with China Central Television and Shandong Television, produced five hours of live programming, fed by satellite from the People's Republic of China to public television stations across the United States. The series, "Shandong: China's New Open Door" included the first live satellite education exchange between high school students in China and the United States. The series was also broadcast on China Central Television.

Also internationally, in cooperation with Radio Telefis Eirann (RTE), WNVC has produced the Dublin St. Patrick's Day Parade every year since 1987 for live satellite broadcast to the United States. WNVC production teams have travelled to Israel to produce a program on political unrest in that country, and to Togo and to London for the ill-fated *Godspell* voyage.

Top left: Taping an international program at WNVC studio.
Top right: Master control air switchers at WNVC.
Bottom left: Record technician recording a feed at WNVC.
Bottom right: Master control room at WNVC.

In May 1991, WNVC along with the Fairfax County Chamber of Commerce hosted "The Rebuilding of Kuwait" following the events in the Persian Gulf crisis. Joining the discussion were former Virginia Governor Gerald Baliles and the state's Secretary for Economic Development, Lawrence Framme.

The following month, Gov. L. Douglas Wilder launched a statewide anti-drug campaign with the broadcast of a half hour statewide television simulcast special, "Keep Your Kids Drug Free." Following in October with a statewide public TV simulcast "Parents, Kids, and Drugs," both programs were designed to teach parents and children how to recognize and deal with the drug problem. Both programs were produced at WNVC.

The bi-weekly public affairs program, "The Fairfax County Report" features interviews with members of the Fairfax County Board of Supervisors. The monthly WNVC international affairs production "Program International," presents interviews with diplomatic officials from such nations as India, Czechoslovakia, Malaysia, and the Soviet Union.

Today, the CVETC through its five public TV stations reach 540,462 students in sixty-four school divisions with 2,400 hours of yearly in-school programming, provide 13,972 hours of annual public television programs and 8,760 hours of quality programming tailored to the needs and interests of Virginia listeners and viewers including thirty-four hours a week of international programming. This service provides in the truest sense what public television is really about, alternative programs for viewers with special interests.

WNVC/WNVT *studio in Fairfax, Virginia taping a program.*

C H A P T E R

10

High Technology

Fairfax County's High Technology community is in the forefront of technological progress.

BDM International, Inc.	142
Comprehensive Technologies International, Inc.	144
DynCorp	146
EDS Corporation	148
Ogden Environmental and Energy Services	150
James Martin & Company	151
Mandex, Inc.	152
PRC	153
SEMA, Inc.	154
User Technology Associates, Inc.	156

The Dewberry & Davis environmental laboratory is the site of a variety of testing procedures, including metals analysis, microbiological investigations, inorganic chemistry processes, and atomic absorption spectroscopy tests to identify lead-based paint. Courtesy of Dewberry & Davis

BDM INTERNATIONAL, INC.

Senior BDM executives include, left to right, Dr. William E. Sweeney, Jr., Executive Vice President and Chief Operating Officer; Earle C. Williams, President and Chief Executive Officer; and Michael J. Mruz, Executive Vice President and Chief Financial and Administrative Officer.

What defines a professional and technical services company like BDM International, Inc.? Here are some of its business areas where, in turn, BDM is helping to define the future: National planning and policy research. Information and communications systems and networks. Advanced manufacturing. Logistics. Analysis, test, and evaluation. Education and training. Security and access control. Space. Transportation.

The BDM story is distinguished by a track record of growth, diversification, and achievement spanning more than 30 years. Today, from McLean, Virginia, site of BDM's corporate headquarters and its largest operational complex (out of 50 worldwide locations), the company addresses problems and issues of concern to hundreds of clients in both government and the private sector. BDM's men and women apply appropriate modern technology to a wide variety of problems and issues, seeking to develop and implement the best solutions and results, with due consideration to the constraints of time and resources.

A Capital Location Is Catalyst to BDM's Growth

Founded by university scientists in 1960, BDM was first headquartered in the Southwest, where it still maintains a major presence, especially in New Mexico. At the time the company relocated its headquarters to Fairfax County, BDM comprised only a few hundred people, and its annual revenues had yet to reach the $10 million mark. Two decades later, BDM had grown 30-fold, with revenues of $300 million and employees in the thousands, more than one-third of whom are in Fairfax County, with other Capital area operations in Columbia and Germantown, Maryland; Arlington and Alexandria, Virginia; and Washington, D.C.

BDM is an independent company, partially employee-owned, with a long tradition of objectivity and autonomy essential to the analysis and design of systems and programs which are responsive to the paramount interests of BDM clients. This means both a freedom from hardware manufacturing involvement (which might otherwise color or compromise recommendations and analyses) and a relentless insistence on quality performance. In this era of emphasis on quality, BDM helped write the book. Over 20 years ago it established a guiding principle called Q^2TC^2, which is BDM's pledge to provide the requisite Quality and Quantity of work, on Time, with Controlled Costs. Note the "requisite." It means that BDM always seeks to match solutions and systems against real-world yardsticks of practicability and affordability, with quality as a constant imperative. The concepts, principles, and processes known today as Total Quality Management (TQM) took root early at BDM, have been refined over years of practical application, and are applied today to all of BDM's efforts.

What Does BDM Do?

In its long history, BDM has undertaken assignments as diverse as probing and developing new energy alternatives and new solutions to waste management problems...providing research and analysis that underlies much present-day thinking about national security, arms control, and treaty verification . . . and helping automate factories and production lines to help American industry achieve greater competitive success. The work program typically spans 800 concurrent projects, large and small, defense and non-defense, long-term and short-term. Among BDM's activities and achievements are:

· Helping test virtually every weapon system that proved so successful in Operation Desert Storm.

· Developing and integrating airspace management and air traffic control systems in the U.S. and abroad; BDM systems can operate alone or as fully integrated components of the National Airspace System.

· Designing and integrating a huge Air Force logistics system that forecasts future needs for billions of dollars worth of spare parts and repairs.

· Automating warehouse and distribution operations and systems to provide clients with greater efficiency, responsiveness and economy.

· Helping design the "architecture" of future defense systems while also supporting defense analysis, planning, policy making, and program implementation.

· Performing innovative, cost-saving management and technical support for state government human resources departments and divisions, speeding the processing of public assistance benefits to needy citizens.

· Designing, integrating, and implementing an information system that will ultimately enable all 15,000+ public companies in the United States to file their financial reports electronically with the Securities and Exchange Commission.

Concurrent with these large-scale efforts are many smaller programs of research, analysis, and problem-solving. They involve such tools and techniques as computerized modeling and simulation and the translation of new scientific principles into practical methods and solutions focused on engineering, computer, and communications problems and requirements.

BDM *People and Their Culture*

People are paramount to BDM's success and achievement. Because the company does not manufacture products or systems, its most important resource and asset is the brainpower of BDM's exceptional staff. This staff is strong in today's most important sectors of technology, science, and systems.

Equally strong is BDM's corporate culture, an affirmative and nurturing blend of commitment and concern for people, for "doing things that count," and for ethics and honesty in all dealings. The people of BDM, and its leadership, place high value on corporate and individual citizenship. Profit-and-loss figures are only one barometer of performance. Satisfied clients and recognized industry leadership are others. Service and quality are basic. Perhaps a recent corporate advertising tagline puts BDM best in perspective:

Technology. Systems. Solutions. **People.**

Systems integration specialists scan a BDM Software Blueprint[SM] (which shows all the elements in a software system in interrelated, graphic form) at the company's McLean Computer Center.

Teleconference technology links BDM/McLean with other company locations (here, BDM/Albuquerque) for immediate interaction, feedback, and rapid problem solving.

BDM routinely trains clients and other users on systems the company develops. Here, a training session on the Electronic Data Gathering, Analysis and Retrieval (EDGAR) system which BDM is integrating for the Securities and Exchange Commission (SEC). EDGAR will ultimately serve over 15,000 public companies in the United States and the nation's investment community as well as the SEC.

COMPREHENSIVE TECHNOLOGIES INTERNATIONAL, INC.

Comprehensive Technologies International, Inc. (CTI) is a widely diversified high technology professional services and software products company. Headquartered in Chantilly, Virginia, CTI has over five hundred employees operating in nine offices across the country.

CTI was founded by Celestino M. Beltran, President and Chief Executive Officer, and Peter M. Theobald, Executive Vice President and Chief Operating Officer. After graduating from the Masters Program of the University of Southern California, Messrs. Beltran and Theobald began their professional careers in Los Angeles. In 1980, they chose metropolitan Washington D.C. as the headquarters for CTI because of the area's position as a leading governmental, commercial, and international marketplace. A third partner, James D. FitzHenry, joined CTI in 1985 and is the Senior Vice President of Systems Management and Engineering.

Since its inception, CTI has continually expanded its reach. CTI's current business areas focus on Systems Integration, Telecommunications/Networking Systems, and Management Systems and Engineering Support, in addition to the development and sale of electronic commerce solutions. CTI's customer-oriented products and professional services are provided to both U.S. government and commercial clients.

CTI has historically supported the U.S. Department of Defense and the defense industry. Support has been provided to major defense initiatives such as the Trident Submarine Program, the Cruise Missiles Program, and the Battleship Modernization and Reactivation Program. Support is also being provided to key programs in the Strategic Defense Initiative Organization, Office of Commercial Space Transportation, the Department of Energy, and the Drug Enforcement Administration.

In regard to CTI's electronic commerce technology, CTI is developing software products that integrate electronic data interchange (EDI), imaging, relational databases, CD-ROM audio visual systems, and networking into off-the-shelf business applications. CTI's first commercial product is CLAIMS EXPRESS™. CLAIMS EXPRESS™ is one of the most advanced software packages for the processing and editing of electronic medical claims for any insurance company capable of receiving an EDI transaction. CTI's future EDI products will help businesses increase their competitiveness by increasing productivity and reducing operational costs.

CTI has parlayed its diversity into great success. In 1990 and 1991, the company was selected for INC. magazine's "Top 500" list, which honors America's fastest growing private companies, achieving a high of sixteenth in 1990. Also, CTI's Celestino Beltran and Peter Theobald were recently named Ernst & Young's Washington D.C. area "Entrepreneurs of the Year, 1990." Additionally, *Hispanic' Business* magazine honored CTI for its dramatic growth. In

CTI's corporate headquarters are located outside metropolitan Washington, D.C., in Chantilly, Virginia.

Left to right are Peter M. Theobald, Executive Vice President/Chief Operating Officer and Co-founder; Celestino M. Beltram, President/Chief Executive Officer and Co-founder; and James D. FitzHenry, Senior Vice President.

1990, CTI was awarded the No.2 position on the list of the fastest growing Hispanic-owned companies in the nation. CTI has also been included in *Washington Technology*'s list of the "Mid-Atlan Tech Fast 50" for three consecutive years reaching the No.2 spot in 1990. The company and President Beltran have been featured in several articles which have recently appeared in publications such as the *Washington Post's* "Washington Business" and the *Hispanic Business* magazine. These tangible rewards are the result of CTI's long-term vision of becoming a diversified company with distinct competitive advantages in selected markets, achieved by emphasizing customer oriented high technology products and services.

CTI believes its competitive advantage in technological areas can only be achieved by focusing on developing and retaining highly motivated people. This vision of combining technology and quality people has enabled CTI to boldly launch new ventures and has earned an impeccable reputation as one of the country's top defense contractors. CTI believes successful businesses in the 1990s must dramatically increase efficiency and productivity. With automated systems and technology to integrate internal operations, CTI is convinced it has the people and the technology to be one of its industry's winners.

In the 1990s, CTI's corporate mission will be to enhance its reputation and market position as a leading professional services firm. This will be done by increasing competitive ability and continuing on the leading edge of innovation in technology and management systems. As part of its strategic direction, CTI will strengthen its position as a leader in the analysis, design, development, and implementation of electronic commerce software solutions for government and industry. To achieve these complementary objectives, CTI will continue to develop software products that integrate electronic data interchange, imaging, relational databases, and networking into off-the-shelf business applications. These software products will enhance traditional professional services with distinct competitive advantages and will allow CTI to leverage its technology advantage into other products and markets. To achieve this corporate synergistic relationship between and among its areas of specialization, CTI will continue to promote a positive corporate culture that thrives on technological change.

Since entry into the Department of Defense market, CTI has provided support to mission critical defense initiatives such as the Trident Program and the Strategic Defense Initiative Organization.

CTI has built its reputation for excellence through merging highly qualified professionals with state of the art technology.

CTI has received many local and national awards for technical excellence and outstanding business performance.

D Y N C O R P

DynCorp, an employee-owned company based in Reston, Virginia, is a world leader in professional and technical services. Its reputation for quality customer service dates back to 1946 when the company began as a small commercial air cargo and aviation firm. Steady growth and diversification followed, accompanied by maturing capabilities and a widening array of services.

Today, DynCorp employees work in such varied and diverse environments as military installations, commercial airports, biomedical research facilities, and computer data centers. And, its high-level performance is setting the standard in three distinct areas: Government Services, Applied Sciences, and Commercial Aviation Services.

DynCorp's Government Services Group is one of the nation's largest providers of professional and technical services to the Department of Defense. DynCorp provides aircraft maintenance; engineering, test and evaluation, facilities management; and computer and information services to U.S. and foreign armed forces.

DynCorp's Commercial Aviation Services (DynAir) Group leads the industry in aviation services, providing aircraft maintenance, modification and engineering, composite structures repair, and avionics, as well as total ground support and passenger services to foreign and domestic airlines, aircraft manufacturers, cargo carriers, and overnight delivery companies.

DynCorp Corporate Headquarters in Reston, Virginia.

The Applied Sciences Group—the biomedical, scientific, and technological arm of the company—serves government and private industry clients in such diverse areas as biomedical research, health and information technology, energy exploration, the environment, robotics, and artificial intelligence.

DynCorp was founded by a group of former World War II pilots. The company incorporated in 1946 under the name of California Eastern Airways, Inc. (CEA). CEA provided commercial air cargo and aviation services. In the 1950s, the company purchased Land-Air, Inc., a company that performed aircraft modifications and missile tests, and operated telemetry sys-

DynCorp engineers and technicians provide range operations control, communications, timing, and data collections support to Department of Defense and NASA missions.

tems at the White Sands Missile Range in New Mexico, the location of the first nuclear explosion and a facility still serviced by the company today.

The year 1961 began a period of rapid expansion for the company under the new name Dynalectron. Over the next twenty-five years, the company launched a growth and diversification program, acquiring companies engaged in electrical contracting, naval shipboard systems services, commercial telecommunications, construction, airline ground handling services, commercial aviation maintenance, modification, as well as fueling, cargo handling, helicopter repair, military logistics, and repair of electronic and electro mechanical components used in computers. The explosive growth and diversity of the company's operations prompted a name change to DynCorp in 1986. By 1987, the company's revenues had increased to $800 million, up from $60 million in 1969.

DynCorp provides total ground support including maintenance, ground handling, passenger services, and fueling to the airlines of the world.

The year 1988 brought perhaps the most revolutionary step in DynCorp's history—the transition from a publicly-owned company to a privately-held company and the establishment of an Employee Stock Ownership Plan (ESOP), under which DynCorp employees became employee-owners.

Following the successful implementation of the ESOP and the introduction of a company-wide Total Quality Management (TQM) System, DynCorp began a new phase of growth and diversification. In 1990, the company expanded into such highly professional and technological areas as biotechnology, energy, the environment, and advanced computer technology.

Today, DynCorp's 18,000 employee-owners work at 180 locations around the world, meeting rigid professional standards for every mission, task, and service they perform.

DynCorp is proud of the achievements of its company and proud of the teamwork that has built its international reputation. DynCorp's performance is rooted in a culture of customer satisfaction, experienced management, and dedicated employee-owners. Throughout its history, customers have chosen DynCorp for reliability, innovative know-how, competitive prices, on-time performance, and corporate responsibility.

DynCorp provides complete information technology services, including management of the world's only super computer facility dedicated to biomedical research.

E D S   C O R P O R A T I O N

EDS (Electonic Data Systems) is a proud member of the Fairfax County community. The corporation, which employs over 70,000 people in 30 countries, opened its East Coast headquarters in Herndon, Virginia, in 1988. The facility, located on 202 acres near Dulles International Airport, features a 382,000 square foot office building which helps to support the 3,000 Washington area employees. The Herndon location houses the Federal Government Group and the State Operations Division, major business units which are responsible for serving the information technology needs of our country's federal, state, and local governments. Groups serving EDS' commercial customers are also located in Fairfax County. The site includes one of EDS' 18 Information Processing Centers (IPCs). These facilities are linked by the company's worldwide communications network called EDS*NET.

EDS has a strong record of active community relations programs. The company believes in taking the community *within*—its people and its resources—and applying it to the community *without* to improve and enrich each other's lives. Through successful environmental, educational, and volunteer programs, as well as financial contributions and personal caring, EDS is working to support Fairfax County.

EDS has declared education as its number one community priority and has launched a multi-faceted program called Education Outreach. The goal is to impact the quality of education by demonstrating how information technology positively affects the learning process. Local institutions that EDS has formed partnerships with include Floris Elementary School, John Adams Elementary School, Roper Junior High School, Scott Montgomery Elementary School, Herndon High School, and South Lakes High School. EDS encourages learning outside of the classroom as well, through employee volunteer mentor programs that show the benefits of staying in school and offer children positive role models. EDS also joined the Fairfax County Public Schools Education Foundation as a board member. In addition, EDS lends support to the Summer Institute of the Business Institute for Educators (BIE), a partnership of businesses and educators working to promote ties between schools and corporations. The Summer Institute offers two-week summer sessions that give nearly three hundred educators and administrators a first-hand view of the corporate environment.

EDS employs over 70,000 people worldwide—3,000 in the Washington metropolitan area. EDS' eastern regional headquarters is located in Herndon, Virginia.

More than 1,000,000 students across North America have participated in the three Jason expeditions, sponsored by EDS and led by Dr. Robert Ballard. Courtesy of the National Geographic Society, Joseph H. Bailey, photographer.

Hundreds of EDS employees and their families volunteer their support for numerous area projects. These programs address various aspects of community life: education, recreational, and civic. EDS and forty-one area companies were able to raise over $173,000 during a 1991 "Bowl for Business" tournament designed to help the non-profit Junior Achievement program. Other worthwhile causes include the March of Dimes WalkAmerica and the Patriots Cup Challenge, an annual 8K race held to benefit the Association of Retarded Citizens. EDS officials serve on the boards of the Fairfax County Chamber of Commerce, the Dulles Area Transportation Association (DATA), and the Make-A-Wish Foundation of Greater Washington.

Another way in which the company helps the community is through charitable contributions. "Your gift touches home" best describes the need to support the 230 agencies within Fairfax County alone who rely upon the United Way. By becoming a donor, businesses ensure that needed human services will be available to solve personal problems as they arise. Through EDS' board membership and employee support, almost $300,000 has been raised for the Fairfax/Falls ChurchUnited Way Campaign over the past two years.

EDS also recognizes the Washington area as one of the most important centers of cultural activity in the country. Wolf Trap, located in the heart of Northern Virginia, is the only national park for the performing arts in North America. Since 1989, EDS has been a member of the Filene Circle.

To help the local environment, EDS has become an active participant in the Virginia Department of Transportation Adopt-A-Highway Program. Through this special initiative, volunteers have agreed to keep the two mile roadway surrounding the corporate property clear of litter. In addition to keeping the roads clean, the company also participates in a vigorous recycling program.

These local contributions are complemented by national programs that can be enjoyed by area residents. One example is the acclaimed JASON Project, which uses satellites and data links to transport hundreds of thousands of North American students to sites where scientists uncover historic discoveries. EDS is also a founder and contributor to the Smithsonian's Information Age exhibit at the National Museum of American History, one of the largest computer interactive displays ever produced. And, the *In Touch* program has brought friends, relatives, and veterans of the Vietnam War together through a computerized database, designed and maintained in conjunction with the Friends of Vietnam Veterans Memorial.

EDS firmly believes that businesses should help each other and the people in the community. Being a good neighbor and helping one another will benefit everyone's future. EDS looks forward to further expanding its positive relationship with the people of Fairfax County.

For the Smithsonian Institution's Information Age exhibition, EDS combined diverse technologies—including laser audio and video, robotics, and interactive visitor workstations—to guide visitors through the history of information technology.

EDS supports a wide range of civic, charitable and cultural endeavors. Here, more than 150 employees gather at the base of the Washington Monument to participate in a 15-mile walk in support of the March of Dimes' WalkAmerica program.

OGDEN ENVIRONMENTAL AND ENERGY SERVICES

Ogden Environmental and Energy Services is a full-service environmental company.

Ogden Environmental and Energy Services was formed in December of 1988. The firm, a wholly-owned subsidiary of the Ogden Corporation, is headquartered in Fairfax, Virginia. The Ogden Corporation is a *Fortune* 500 public company headquartered in New York City. Ogden Environmental and Energy Services has a network of over thirty offices and EPA-accredited laboratory facilities throughout the United States and in Bonn, Germany and Tokyo, Japan.

Ogden Environmental and Energy Services is a full-service professional and technical services firm providing a wide range of analytical, environmental, and energy consulting, engineering, and design services to commercial and industrial companies and governmental agencies. The company employs 1,200 professional engineers, scientists, and support personnel who are committed to providing quality, reliable engineering, and scientific consulting services.

The company's environmental services include contamination analysis and characterization, remedial investigation, engineering and design, data management, project design, and regulatory assistance to detect, evaluate, solve, and monitor environmental problems and related health and safety risks. The company's analytical laboratories support these services by providing integrated support for designing sound solutions. Sophisticated high-technology equipment and rigorous quality assurance practices have earned the laboratories certification from many states, the U.S. Navy, and the U.S. Environmental Protection Agency (EPA).

Ogden Environmental and Energy Services is exceptional in that it provides comprehensive consulting and engineering services in the environmental, infrastructure, and energy arenas. Over the past decade, environmental issues and the associated engineering and scientific aspects have become increasingly prominent in the eye of both the public and private sectors. Ogden Environmental and Energy Services has over twenty years of experience in providing solutions to environmental problems and is well positioned to support industry and government with complex environmental issues.

The firm provides remediation expertise to treat hazardous and solid wastes safely and cost-effectively, through a highly sought after waste disposal technology of the solidation and fixation of hazardous waste. Ogden Environmental and Energy Services is one of two companies nationwide which has been pre-qualified by the EPA to employ this process.

The Power Division of Ogden Environmental and Energy Services develops, operates, and maintains clean-energy producing facilities, employing the most advanced technology in both geothermal and hydroelectric power generation. The firm's focus is directed toward plants that produce electricity with minimum environmental impact.

Ogden Environmental and Energy Services applies a synergistic blend of technical and professional expertise and resources that result in a single source of professional services focused to address the environmental and energy problems of the 1990s. Ogden Environmental and Energy Service's successful track record commands attention, as it becomes a major player in the national and international environmental and energy services arenas.

Headquarters building for Ogden Environmental and Energy Services, Fairfax, Virginia.

JAMES MARTIN & COMPANY

A Comprehensive Approach Designed To Produce Systems Of Enduring Precision.

ames Martin & Company was formed in 1981 under the chairmanship of Dr. James Martin, the world's leading author and lecturer in Information Technology. The firm employs over 250 consultants worldwide, with eight international offices, and eight offices in North America. Headquarters for North American operations were established at Reston, Virginia in 1983.

James Martin & Company's corporate mission is to be the premier provider of advanced methods and techniques for building software solutions to meet the strategic information needs of progressive businesses. The Information Engineering Methodology (IEM), first developed by James Martin and Chief Technical Officer Ian Palmer, has evolved over the last ten years as the firm has applied this approach at over five hundred organizations around the world. Customers include *Fortune* 500 companies, federal and state governments, large financial institutions, and utilities.

The Information Engineering Methodology is a process by which information systems are developed that precisely support the objectives of the business enterprise. The IEM's logical, common sense progression of steps is rigid enough to ensure comprehensiveness and accuracy, yet flexible enough to model precisely the uniqueness and idiosyncrasies of the business. The IEM is tightly fitted to several leading Computer Aided Software Engineering (CASE) tools. These tools are employed extensively in the Methodology to speed system development and enhance system accessibility to the end-user.

James Martin & Company also provides instructor-led training and develops software to assist in the implementation of the IEM and selected CASE tools. These knowledge-based software products include on-line descriptions of the IEM such as IE-Expert, which received the ICP award for over $1,000,000 in sales. Other offerings include computer-based training modules which cover all of the essential techniques of analysis and design.

With convenient access to Dulles International Airport, the federal government, and a skilled pool of technical talent, Fairfax County has provided an excellent base for the company's growth as revenues have increased 80 percent per year since 1986. Led by John Wyatt, the Chairman and Chief Executive Officer of James Martin & Company North America, the firm aggressively pursues opportunities to protect our environment. In addition to a comprehensive recycling program, the company seeks replacements for less efficient operational practices through technologies such as electronic communications and teleconferencing.

Through their products and consulting services, James Martin & Company is committed to helping major businesses and governments exploit Information Engineering, which is now recognized worldwide as the most appropriate CASE methodology. James Martin & Company has proven that with its expertise and the IEM, corporations and governments are able to link information systems development with their business and its objectives, and through automation and better management, achieve higher levels of information systems productivity and quality.

Like the highly evloved nautilus shell, the IEM produces solutions that are each unique, each perfectly suited to its purpose.

JAMES MARTIN
& Co.

M A N D E X ,   I N C .

There is strength in unity. But if the success of Fairfax Defense contractor Mandex, Inc., is any indication, there is also strength in diversity.

When physicist Carl Brown, Chief Executive Officer, took the helm of the fledgling company in 1975 as its minority owner and only employee, he was determined to make it a top contender for government 8(a) contracts. Brown was not new to this business, having gained experience from firms such as GE, GRC, and SAIC.

Mandex Chief Executive Officer Carl Brown and President Mary Lou Patel.

Getting the first few jobs, however, was a genuine struggle. But Brown had prepared himself to meet the needs of those early proposals by surrounding himself with engineering and design professionals of countless specializations. The government began to take notice of Mandex's many capabilities. Whatever the task, Brown—and Mandex—found a way to meet it.

Sixteen years later, with sixteen offices and $14 million in annual billings, Mandex provides the full spectrum of high technology services to both public and private sectors, in areas as varied as telecommunications, defense systems, life cycle management, and training development—thanks largely to the numerous skills of its 160 employees, including training specialists, computer scientists, electrical and mechanical engineers and technicians, logistics specialists, and various physicists and fabricators.

It also has a woman president.

In 1988, when the firm graduated from 8(a) status to meet the challenges of the more competitive Small Disadvantaged Business (SDB) arena and the fully competitive arena, sound financial strategy had become the essential guidepost for future development.

Mary Lou Patel, hired in 1985 as Chief Financial Officer, had the necessary systems in place. Her previous eighteen years of financial expertise, DCAA experience, interaction with bankers, and development of corporate policies and finance and administration procedures had already made Mandex more profitable, to move the company through its most challenging transition. Today, as president, she shares the helm with Brown.

The two also share a vision of Mandex's future in the technological marketplace—one in which the firm will not only continue its leadership in the design, testing, evaluation, implementation, and maintenance of informational and mechanical systems for the government and corporations, but excel in new areas, as well. Given the cutbacks in defense spending, the company must again diversify. Plans are in the works for geographic information systems and further development of Mandex's expertise in training development, image processing, and computer-aided design.

Mandex prides itself on its business relationships, and Mandex management subscribes to the following corporate creed: Mandex believes in providing our customers with the highest quality products and services, produced in a creative and open environment built on quality people, technical excellence, and effective management through ethical practices.

By hiring and teaming with the best, Mandex will continue to prove that a company's real success relies on more than unity of effort among those involved.

It also relies on their diversity.

P R C

PRC is one of the largest and most diversified firms in the information systems and services industry. Founded in 1954, the company provides systems integration and technology-based systems and services to government and commercial clients worldwide.

Its success stems from having talented, innovative employees, strong technical expertise, and long-standing relationships with its customers.

PRC is a recognized leader in creating information systems, developing custom software, designing sophisticated data networks, and managing entire computer facilities. The firm ties these services together through systems integration—a comprehensive information management solution requiring a precise combination of hardware, software, and communica-

PRC's world headquarters in McLean, Virginia.

tions. The company's systems integration expertise is evidenced by such large, long-term projects as a $455 million contract with the U.S. Patent & Trademark Office and a $154 million job for the Navy's Engineering Data Management Information and Control System.

PRC's strategy is to apply its expertise in solving complex information systems and engineering problems to a number of specific, defined markets. The firm's thirty-eight years of experience in tackling difficult technical challenges for its customers have given PRC competency in five strategically important disciplines: Imaging—electronically scanning, storing, displaying, and managing massive amounts of paper documents; Open Systems Integration—designing and building computer systems that adapt to evolving technology; Telecommunications— connecting information and telecommunications systems in large and small networks; Technology Transfer—developing methods and practices to transfer the understanding of technology to other organizations; and Software Engineering— continually improving the development and maintenance of computer programs using management, engineering, scientific, and mathematical techniques.

PRC has more than seven thousand employees providing technology-oriented systems, services, and products to government and commercial customers.

In 1990, PRC was awarded multi-year government contracts of $65 million to design data communications networks for the U.S. Senate, and $76 million by the General Services Administration to provide computer support to federal agencies. PRC's expertise also extends to the commercial market, where it is the largest provider of computer-based services to the U.S. real estate industry and public safety agencies worldwide. In 1991, PRC launched a strategy to expand its commercial and international business.

PRC's future remains strong. PRC understands technology, its customers' industries, and its customers' need to be successful. With its unique perspective and a company philosophy of "Strength Through Understanding," PRC is a company with total commitment to delivering superior service.

S E M A ,   I N C.

James C. Smith, President and Chief Executive Officer, Providing Leadership and Vision.

Systems Engineering and Management Associates, Inc., (SEMA) provides people-oriented solutions to the complexities of the technical age in which we live. A multi-disciplined company, the firm offers high technology engineering services and automated data processing support. The firm specializes in eight engineering and specialty areas: Systems Engineering; Software Engineering; Technology Management; Communications Engineering; Information Systems Engineering; Project/Program Management; Product Assurance and Tests; and Computer Security.

Incorporated on December 24, 1985, and open for business on June 1, 1986, SEMA began with the vision and confidence of James C. Smith, the firm's founder and chief executive officer. When Smith retired as a lieutenant colonel from the U.S. Army in 1981, he joined the Aerospace Group of General Electric and held several management positions before leaving to start his own firm. Said Smith, "There were certainly trepidations in leaving the security of an excellent job in a prospering company, but I had a good feeling about becoming an entrepreneur."

The company had no revenue during the first ten months of operation, but soon after won its first three contracts (the third for $700,000). Since those humble days, the company has grown to over 240 employees, 22,000 square feet of office space, and $15 million in revenues. SEMA's client list now includes many impressive names, such as the Commander, Naval Reserve Force, the State Department, AMTRAK, Teledyne Brown Engineering, BDM International, the Department of Energy, the Department of Commerce, Federal Emergency Management Agency, Defense Medical Systems Support Center, Strategic Defense Initiative Organization, National Technology Transfer Center, Federal Laboratory Consortium, and General Electric.

SEMA has also received numerous awards in its short history, including the Defense Communications Agency's "Small Business Contractor of the year, 1989"; the Northern Virginia Business and Professional Association's "MENTOR of the Year, 1990"; the Fairfax County Chamber of Commerce's "New Business of the Year, 1990"; Black Enterprise magazine's "Top 100" Black-Owned Companies in the United States, June 1990—No. 95, and 1991—No. 71; Washington Technology magazine "Jump Start" Recognition, April 1990 and 1991; and sponsoring group of Merrill Lynch, Ernst & Young, INC. magazine, and the Washington Business Journal "Entrepreneur of the Year" for the Washington area, June 1991. SEMA's most recent recognition comes once again from Washington Technology, as a 1992 "Fast 50" member (SEMA was the seventh fastest growing company in the Washington area from 1987 to 1992).

This success firmly establishes SEMA's credentials as a high tech company, but its focus on people is what makes the company special. SEMA's community service, support of area entrepreneurs, and relations with employees and customers has established deep roots in the Fairfax area.

The Most Valuable Asset, Employees.

One of SEMA's most significant contributions is its support of the Greater Washington INROADS Program, which sponsors minority college students so they can gain work experience while earning a college education. SEMA sponsors students under the program and supplements their work experience and personal growth by hiring them during the summer and short breaks. SEMA also supports—through fund-raising and other activities—the Patriot's Foundation, which was formed to build a landmark on the National Mall to honor the five thousand black soldiers and sailors who fought in the American Revolution. In addition, the company contributes to the John Tyler Elementary School, allowing disadvantaged children to receive gifts during the Christmas holiday; the Hopkins House Association, which provides needed counselling and support services to senior citizens in the Alexandria, Virginia, community; The Women's Center, which provides needed support for families and women in the local community; and the Gum Springs Youth Association, which provides clothing, counselling, and support services to underprivileged children in the community.

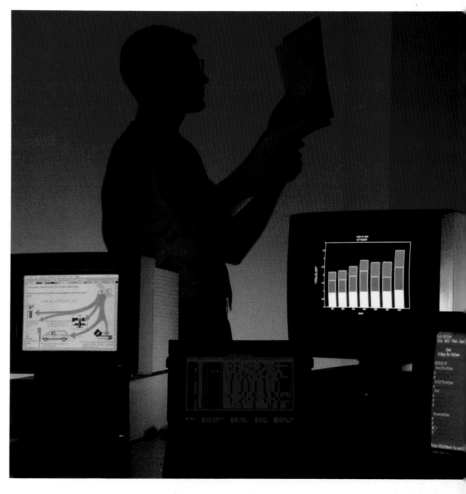

Developing Automated Management Systems.

Mr. Smith is also extremely involved in industry and community affiliations. He is a member of the Governor of Virginia's Task Force on "Workforce 2000" (now the Advisory Council, which was formed to improve the State of Virginia's educational system), the INROADS/ Greater Washington, Inc. Board of Directors, the George Washington University Northern Virginia Campus Advisory Board, and the Gunston Hall Board of Visitors. In addition, Mr. Smith serves as the Chair of the National Association of Black Procurement Professionals and as Co-chair of the One Nation Campaign for the Black Revolutionary Patriots Foundation.

SEMA, Inc.'s work relationships have also fostered a strong community standing. By providing counselling, temporary office space, and subcontracts—as well as by purchasing products and services—SEMA has helped support a long list of area entrepreneurs. SEMA also strives to build a team spirit among its employees and clients through an emphasis on constant communication and a variety of special events.

Looking forward to the year 2000, Smith expects SEMA, Inc., to become a $100 million company with several major regional and international locations. Smith is currently negotiating with markets in the United States and abroad, working to become partners with large technology-based firms and foreign governments that are searching for services such as automated social security systems. But even with SEMA's high tech expertise, the company's continued success will be the result of its emphasis on what matters most— people.

Applying Automated Tools to Improve Communications Systems.

USER TECHNOLOGY ASSOCIATES, INC.

U ser Technology Associates, Inc. (UTA) was founded by Yong K. Kim in 1985 as a dynamic and pragmatic solution to the problems and concerns faced by today's computer end-user.

The company presents an effective organizational approach to the needs of the ever-growing computer industry through the resources of six distinct technical divisions: Acquisition and Program Management, Information Resource Management, Engineering and Logistics, Systems Development and Operations, LAN and User Support, and Information Systems. UTA addresses its customers' automation needs with a unique "user-oriented" philosophy that combines state-of-the-art technical expertise with an ability to bridge the gap between technology and the user.

A systems engineer with 25 years of systems development and technical management experience with the U.S. Army, U.S. Navy, NASA, OMB/White House Computer Center, VA, NCI/NIH, Office of Education, and the Imperial Iranian Air Force and Navy, Mr. Kim started with nothing more than an innovative idea and infectious enthusiasm directed at improving the application and use of high technology among "low tech" users. He identified and focused on the need to integrate the user with the ever-advancing technology at his disposal; he single-handedly conceived and developed the *user technology* integration concept; he has worked tirelessly and steadfastly with UTA program managers, staff, and clients to

Mr. Yong K. Kim, *President and Chief Executive Officer.*

apply these basic concepts in varied programmatic environments; and he exercises a remarkable degree of direction and control over all client support through continuous feedback from clients, program managers, and field personnel, as well as an acute understanding and attention to client requirements. Taken together, Mr. Kim's UTA provides a unique and extremely successful approach to the delivery of technical support services.

The company further expanded the *user technology* concept by developing a *total user support* model. The model focuses on integration of the user and all currently available, proven technology. It emphasizes ergonomics, artificial intelligence/expert systems, relational database management systems (RDBMS), voice recognition and response, and LAN and WAN telecommunication.

The company's client base includes three Department of Defense branches and over 10 civilian agencies and commercial and international clients. Contracts with the departments of Education, Treasury, Agriculture, Labor, State, Interior, and Justice, and the General Services Administration, Defense Nuclear Agency, Army Corps of Engineers, Departments of the Army and Navy, Securities and Exchange Commission, Resolution Trust Corporation, and other organizations have helped to double UTA's revenues for the second consecutive year. In commercial operations, UTA has been solicited by several large corporations seeking a growing, leading edge, user-oriented technology firm with solid expertise in the user support arena. On the international front, Mr. Kim toured the Persian Gulf countries in early 1992 as a member of a U.S. Trade Mission sponsored by the Department of Commerce.

The UTA corporate headquarters is located in Arlington, Virginia. Other UTA offices are in Crystal City, Lorton, and Virginia Beach, Virginia; Denver, Colorado; and Camarillo, California. The company supports regional customer sites in Atlanta, Boston, Chicago, Dallas, Denver, New York, Philadelphia, Kansas City, and San Francisco. Beginning with only three employees in 1985, UTA now operates

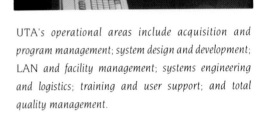

UTA's *operational areas include acquisition and program management; system design and development; LAN and facility management; systems engineering and logistics; training and user support; and total quality management.*

with a personnel base of over 250. Approximately 70 percent of the staff are located on-site at the various customer locations. The company received its nine year 8(a) certification from the Small Business Administration in 1987.

At UTA, no customer is ever looked upon as a onetime opportunity. It is hoped that every customer will enter into a durable and mutually beneficial relationship with the company. This is an objective which can be realized only by continuously reinforcing and justifying the very identity of the organization as set forth in the corporate name— User Technology Associates. UTA places the user in the forefront and dramatically emphasizes the overriding importance of the user to the success of any project.

Due to its rapid growth and innovative business philosophy, UTA has recently been the recipient of much media attention. UTA was No. 1 in *Washington Technology's* 1991 Fast 50 competition with a 13,500 percent growth rate. The Fast 50 recognizes the fastest growing companies in the Washington, D.C. metropolitan area. Keeping with its tradition of rapid growth, UTA was No. 8 in 1992, with a 4,000 percent growth rate. UTA was featured on the front page of the *Washington Times* business section in an article entitled "UTA Advances in High-Tech Field by Caring About Low-Tech Users," which addressed Mr. Kim's ideas on the *user technology* concept. UTA was also featured in the CBS television production "Success Stories," aired in September 1991, a program which focuses on innovative entrepreneurs and their successful businesses. With a business philosophy that influences all company activities and is constantly put into actual practice on all developmental projects, Mr. Kim's vision for the *user technology* concept should become a widely implemented reality by the year 2000.

Mr. Kim is a member of *Washington Technology* magazine's Fast 50 Council, a position which helps to keep UTA at the leading edge in this age of rapidly changing technology. Most importantly, he puts leadership and innovation back into the various user communities through vehicles such as the Small Business Council of the local chambers of commerce in Arlington and Fairfax counties in Virginia. In these roles he is a mentor to future business leaders and their growing companies.

Mr. Kim lives in Springfield, Virginia, in Fairfax County, with his wife of seventeen years, Meranda, and their three children, Kandis, Thad, and Anisha.

CHAPTER

Marketplace

Fairfax County is unparalleled in retail establishments, offering an impressive variety of choices for area residents and visitors.

Tysons Corner Center   160

Tysons Corner Center.

TYSONS CORNER CENTER

Tysons Corner Center has been a shopping tradition in Northern Virginia—and the Washington metropolitan area—for over two decades.

With more than 230 shops and five department stores, the selections at Tysons Corner Center represent a distinct style and an impressive mix of innovative retailers that is simply unequalled in the region. Gleaming brass accents on stainless steel, 44,000 square feet of skylights, and beautiful, lush greenery create a richness that complements the affluent Northern Virginia area.

Nordstrom, Bloomingdale's, Lord & Taylor, Hecht's, Woodward & Lothrop—but

With more than 230 stores, Tysons Corner Center is the largest shopping mall on the East Coast.

shopping isn't the only activity at Tysons Corner Center. The selection also includes thirty eateries and an 8-screen movie theater. Additionally, you can have your nails done, get a haircut, drop off your vacation film or your dry cleaning, or bring in your shoes for repair.

Located eleven miles west of the nation's capital, Tysons Corner Center serves as the cornerstone of an area which today has more than 20 million square feet of office space with 80,000 workers. This is more than the downtown areas of Baltimore, Cleveland, Milwaukee, or Cincinnati. In just a little more than two decades, Tysons Corner has become the largest downtown in Virginia—and Tysons Corner Center is at its heart.

Tysons Corner Center opened in 1968 as the Washington D.C., region's largest single-level mall and the area's first enclosed shopping center. It was was purchased in 1985 by The Lehndorff Group of Dallas who initiated what is believed to be the most extensive renovation and expansion of an existing mall in the country. Culminating in 1988, the two-year, $160 million transformation included the addition of 450,000 square feet of retail space and more than seventy-five new shops and restaurants.

Perhaps the most dramatic aspect of the renovation was the transformation of the mall's former delivery and storage area into the addition of a complete new level of shops and restaurants below the existing mall. The mall's exterior underwent a facelift too, from the vaulted roofline entranceways to the new parking terraces which have helped to increase the total number of parking spaces from six thousand to ten thousand.

In conjunction with the expansion, the East Coast's first Nordstrom store joined the center's three existing anchors—Bloomingdale's, Hecht's, and Woodward & Lothrop. Lord & Taylor opened in the spring of 1990. Today, Tysons Corner Center is the largest shopping mall in the Washington area and the ninth largest in the United States. The average shopper expenditure at Tysons Corner Center is $95.80, more than double the national average.

Tysons Corner Center's owner, The Lehndorff Group, is one of the nation's largest commercial real estate firms which, for itself and on behalf of its clients, owns and manages a portfolio of U.S. commercial real estate valued in excess of $3 billion. The firm's portfolio includes more than 20 million square feet of retail, office, and industrial property across the country.

The mall's former delivery and storage area was transformed into a complete new level of shops and restaurants in 1988.

Tysons Corner Center is among the top 1 percent grossing malls in the nation. Photographs by Angie Seckinger

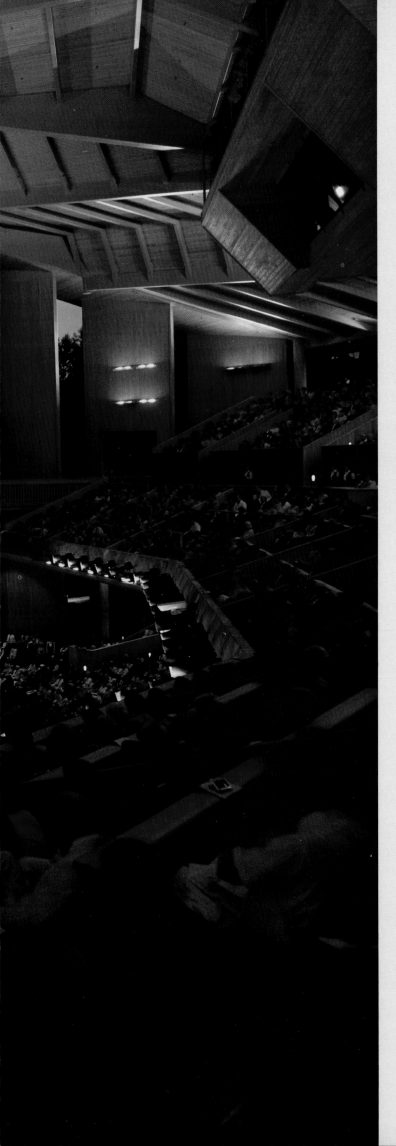

12

Building Fairfax County

Designing, developing, and managing property, Fairfax County's building and real estate community has ensured a progressive future.

MRJ, Inc.   164

West*Group   165

Scott-Long Construction, Inc.   166

A cultural outing to an old farm in the country may seem to be a contradiction in terms but it is an experience which has been enjoyed by millions of lovers of the arts since the Filene Center first opened at Wolf Trap Farm Park for the Performing Arts in July 1971. The amphitheater holds 3,786 seats inside. Courtesy of Dewberry & Davis

M R J, I N C.

MRJ, Inc., is an employee-owned science, engineering, and analysis company founded in 1978 and is located in Oakton near the interchange of Route 123 and Interstate 66. In the fourteen years of its existence, MRJ has grown from a few dozen employees to nearly three hundred and presently occupies a building with approximately 100,000 square feet. In 1990, MRJ became employee-owned through an ESOP program.

MRJ has had long and successful cooperative relationships with several universities including George Mason University in Fairfax, Virginia. In 1991, MRJ joined Fairfax County's "Adopt a School Program" and is working closely with Oakton Elementary School. MRJ has worked with the Virginia Center for Innovative Technology to provide supercomputing courses and technical seminars.

One of MRJ's key focuses is in Engineering Analysis covering two important areas: marine systems and spacecraft systems. In the marine systems area, MRJ specializes in ocean, marine, and systems engineering with strong capabilities in ASW/NAASW, SONAR systems, control/electrical systems, SIGINT, GIS, and oceanographic data collection. In the spacecraft systems area, MRJ specializes in precise pointing and tracking analysis, multiple flexible body dynamics, coupled structural/thermal controls analysis, power subsystems design, and subsystem modeling.

Another key focus is in military support. MRJ has a strong background in military projects, and many of its efforts paid large dividends in the successful Desert Storm operation. MRJ's specialties in this area include the Tactical Exploitation of National Systems Capabilities (TENCAP) with strong emphasis on theater and tactical C3I support, intelligence collection and management, simulation workstations, and target database manipulation tools and a strong effort in wargaming, training, and exercise support. In addition, MRJ is performing military applications of digital map data through Geographic Information Systems (GISs).

MRJ was the first commercial user of a Connection Machine™ supercomputer and is committed to remaining in the forefront of supercomputer technology. MRJ's expertise includes algorithm and application development using various parallel supercomputers, including Cray, DAP, NCube, and Transputers. MRJ has applied parallel supercomputing technology in the areas of image and signal processing and extremely large database storage and retrieval problems. MRJ has more recently developed a strong capability and reputation in the area of high performance workstations and computer networks. MRJ provides network design, integration, and operation for a variety of clients, performing Management Information Systems (MIS) and scientific analysis problems. This normally involves graphical user interfaces, object oriented programming, and commercial off-the-shelf (COTS) software integration.

MRJ has a highly educated, experienced, and talented technical staff. Approximately 50 percent have advanced degrees, many with multiple degrees, and a large number have PhDs ranging from physics to computer science to engineering. MRJ has built a strong reputation for solving complex problems for government and industry; and its remarkable growth, strength, and diversity are evidence of its commitment to quality work.

Processing Van.

Corporate headquarters, Oakton, Virginia.

W E S T * G R O U P

WEST*GROUP, a developer of superior office, industrial, retail, and residential environments, continues its longstanding commitment to enhance the quality of life in Fairfax County. Its officers and employees are involved in the community and serve as leaders in many civic, health, education, and arts organizations:

WEST*LYNCH Foundation * Northern Virginia Community College * Virginia Foundation for Independent Colleges * Tysons Transportation Association * Crestar Bank * McLean Orchestra * Washington Airports Task Force * McLean Citizens' Foundation * INOVA Health Systems * Fairfax Bar Association * Tysons Task Force * Fairfax County Chamber of Commerce * Fairfax Symphony * Boy Scout Troop 1966 * National Association of Industrial and Office Parks * Northern Virginia Building Industry Association * SOVRAN Bank * Claude Moore Colonial Farm * The Retired Officers Association * Committee for Dulles * Wolf Trap Foundation * Fairfax Hospital Association * Urban & Regional Information Systems Association * Oak View PTA * Potomac School * Waterview Plantation Homeowners' Association * Airports Association Council International * Marine Corps Executive Association * McLean Project for the Arts * Institute of Real Estate Management * Innisfree Village * New Start * Northern Virginia Press Club * Vienna Little League * Virginia Society of CPA's * Washington Air Cargo Association * Fairfax Business Recycling Task Force * Air & Space Heritage Council * Southern Financial * Center for Excellence in Education * Junior League of Northern Virginia * McLean Business & Professional Association * The Virginia College Fund * Greater Washington Research Center * Braddock Road Youth Basketball * Hospice of Northern Virginia * George Mason University Urban Systems Engineering Institute * NationsBank * Virginia Building Officials Association * School for Contemporary Education * Friends of the National Zoo * Northern Virginia Corporate Community Relations Council * Bell Atlantic Corporation * American Horticulture Society * Medical Care for Children Project * Woodlawn Foundation

We know the importance of being a good neighbor at WEST*GROUP.

*Freddie Mac headquarters in WEST*PARK: Winner of the National Association of Industrial and Office Parks (NAIOP) Awards for Best Corporate Build-to-Suit and Best Mid-Rise Office Building.*

Springfield Tower Shopping Center: Winner of a NAIOP Award for Best Rehabilitation of a Neighborhood Shopping Center.

SCOTT-LONG CONSTRUCTION, INC.

Since its founding in 1968, clients have come to Scott-Long Construction, Inc., when they needed someone a cut above to accomplish their building goals. The company, based in Fairfax County, is known for its ability to thrive on projects that require sensitivity to people as well as a high level of creativity to accomplish the end result. A good example is The Barns of Wolf Trap, which has become a landmark for the Washington, D.C., area.

One of the keys to Scott-Long's success is their tenacious dedication to being principle driven as opposed to market driven. They believe that to provide a quality building, on time, within budget is a given. The challenge comes in providing the product while maintaining an atmosphere supportive of Scott-Long's company beliefs: we care; we believe in the value of people; we believe in mutually profitable relationships; and we listen.

"Our first priority is people, not buildings," states Bruce Scott, the company's president and chief executive officer. "Hank and I both grew up here in Northern Virginia. We've raised our families in Fairfax and founded our businesses here. That makes the motivation to invest back into the community very high."

The company continues to win craftsmanship awards each year in a wide variety of categories—a testimony to the calibre of people who make up the company of Scott-Long and to their contribution of excellence in construction to Fairfax County.

The Barns of Wolf Trap: Two historical barns were brought down from New York state and reassembled piece by piece, then protected by an outer shell of new construction. They now house a performing arts theater.

Truro Episcopal Church: Through Scott-Long's creative approach to problem solving, Truro's congregation never missed a service during renovation. The work was awarded first place, Best Workmanship for Restoration and Renovation by the Associated Builders and Contractors—1984.

Scott-Long Construction, Inc., was founded in 1968 by Henry A. Long, left, and Bruce Scott, right.

APPENDIX

The Exceptional Design Awards Program

In November 1984, the Fairfax County Board of Supervisors established the Exceptional Design Awards program. Administered by the Office of Comprehensive Planning, it recognizes and grants awards for exceptional architectural and site designs in the county. The Design Jury includes representatives from the American Institute of Architects and the American Society of Landscape Architects, as well as from the History Commission, the Architectural Review Board, and the Chamber of Commerce.

Fairfax County Exceptional Design Awards Winners, 1985

Honor Awards

Times/Journal Company Headquarters
(Commercial, Office)
Dewberry & Davis

The Salvation Army Adult Rehabilitation Center
(Institutional)
Kamstra, Dickerson & Associates, Inc.

DMV Express Offices
(Institutional)
Dewberry & Davis

Concession/Restroom Complex
Occoquan Regional Park
(Recreational)
Donald, LeMay & Page

Merit Awards

Bromley Village
(Residential, single-family detached)
CPI Enterprises, Inc.

Howard House
(Residential, single-family detached)
Cross and Adreon Architects

South Lakes Village Center
(Commercial, retail)
Western Development Corp.

Bowman Green
(Commercial, office)
Beery, Rio & Associates

Building #1, Westwood Corporate Center
(Commercial, office)
Ward/Hall Associates, AIA

Building #1, Westwood Corporate Center
(Commercial, office)
The Henry A. Long Company

Kiddie Country Day Care II
(Institutional)
Abrash, Eddy & Eckhardt, Inc.

Westwood Baptist Church
(Institutional)
Lawrence Cook AIA & Associates

Citations

Waterside Garden Apartments
(Residential, multifamily)
Artery Organization, Inc.

Tysons Executive Plaza
(Commercial, office)
Clark, Tribble, Harris & Li Architects, P.A.

Farm Credit Administration
(Commercial, office)
Davis & Carter, P.C.

One Parkridge Center
(Industrial, research & development office)
ADD, Inc.

Benjamin Franklin Intermediate School
(Institutional)
Strang and Samaha, AIA

Burke Presbyterian Church
(Institutional)
Lawrence Cook AIA & Associates

Terraset Elementary School
(Institutional)
Davis & Carter, P.C.

Headquarters Addition for Northern Virginia
Regional Park Authority
(Recreational)
Lawrence Cook AIA & Associates

Fairfax County Exceptional Design Awards Winners, 1986

Honor Awards

Tyson McLean III
(Commercial, office)
Davis & Carter P.C.

Arboretum Maintenance Building
Meadowlark Gardens Regional Park
(Recreational)
Lawrence Cook Associates, P.C.

Merit Awards

An Evolutionary House
(Residential, single-family detached)
Robert Wilson Mobley, AIA, Architect

Virginia Power - Northern Division Headquarters
(Commercial, office)
Ward/Hall Associates, AIA

Parkridge Business Center, Phase II
(Commercial, office)
ADD, Inc.

Fairfax Unitarian Church
(Institutional)
Lawrence Cook Associates, P.C.

Lewinsville Day Health Care Center for Older
Adults
(Adaptive reuse)
Helbing Lipp, Ltd. - Architects-Engineers

GT Renaissance Centre
(Mixed use development)
Lewis/Wisnewski & Associates, Ltd

Fairfax County Exceptional Design Awards Winners, 1987

Honor Awards

Fair Lakes One in Fairfax
(Commercial, office)
Davis & Carter, P.C. and Hazel/Peterson Co., Inc.

Merit Awards

The McLean Bank, Herndon Branch
(Commercial, office)
Robert Wilson Mobley, AIA, Architect and the
McLean Bank

Campus Point in Reston
(Industrial, research & development office)
Davis & Carter, P.C. and Lee Sammis Associates,
Inc.

Pohick Regional Library in Burke
(Institutional)
Cross & Adreon, Architects and Fairfax County
Public Libraries

Fairfax Yacht Club in Lorton
(Recreational)
Karl E. Kohler Associates, Architects and Fairfax
Yacht Club Development Corp.

The Hutchison House-Lafayette Business Center in Chantilly
(Historical/adaptive reuse)
Adena Landry Patterson and Lee Sammis Associates, Inc.

Fairfax County Exceptional Design Awards Winners, 1988

Honor Award

One Skyline Tower in Bailey's Crossroads
(Commercial, office)
Weihe Partnership and the Charles E. Smith
Companies

Merit Awards

Stouffer Residence in Fairfax
(Residential, single-family detached)
Christian J. Lessard, AIA, and Mr. & Mrs. Spence
Stouffer

A River House in McLean
(Residential, single-family detached)
Robert Wilson Mobley, AIA

Tyson Dulles Plaza in McLean
(Commercial, office)
Weihe Partnership, the Alan I. Kay Companies,
the Milton Companies, and John G.
Georgelas & Sons

Honorable Mentions

Jonathan's Keepe in Reston
(Residential, multi-family)
Reg Narmour/the Architectural Group, P.A., P.C.
and the Oxford Development Corporation

7600 Leesburg Pike in Falls Church
(Commercial, office)
Weihe Partnership, the Beatty Management
Company, and the Wills Companies

Fairfax County Fire and Rescue Station #36 in
Herndon
(Institutional)
Strang & Samaha, AIA, and the Fairfax County
Department of Public Works

**Fairfax County Exceptional Design Awards
Winners, 1989**

Honor Awards

The Oaks Apartments, Fairfax
(Residential, multi-family)
Craycroft Architects of Dallas, Texas, and Hazel/
Peterson Companies of Fairfax, Virginia

Pond Office Building, Reston
(Commercial, office)
Stanmyre & Noel Architects of Reston, Virginia,
and Tetra Partnerships of Reston, Virginia

Merit Awards

Grey Gables - A Mail Order House in a New
Package, Great Falls
(Residential, single-family detached)
Robert Wilson Mobley, AIA of Great Falls, Vir-
ginia, and Harrison and Joan Wehner of
Great Falls, Virginia

A New Residence, McLean
(Residential, single-family detached)
Muse-Wiedeman Architects of Washington, D.C.

Fairview Park Marketing Center, Falls Church
(Commercial, office)
Bowie-Gridley Architects of Washington, D.C.
and Prentiss Properties Limited, Inc. of Falls
Church, Virginia

Central Park at Dulles Corner, Herndon
(Special amenity)
EDAW, Inc. of Alexandria, Virginia and Sequoia
Building Corporation of Herndon, Virginia

Fairview Park, Falls Church
(Mixed-use development)
Dewberry & Davis of Fairfax, Virginia, and Prentiss
Properties Limited, Inc. of Falls Church,
Virginia

Honorable Mention

Sully Station Community Center, Centreville
(Recreational)
Martin Organization of Philadelphia, Pennsylva-
nia, and Kettler & Scott, Inc. of Vienna,
Virginia

Chantilly Bible Church, Herndon
(Adaptive reuse)
William A. Klene Architects of Fairfax, Virginia,
and Chantilly Bible Church of Herndon,
Virginia

**Fairfax County Exceptional Design Awards
Winners, 1990**

Honor Awards

Fairfax Building, Tysons Corner
(Commercial, office)
HOK, P.C., of Washington, D.C., and West*Group,
Inc. of McLean, Virginia

The Old Schoolhouse, Great Falls
(Adaptive reuse)
Robert Wilson Mobley, AIA of Great Falls, Vir-
ginia, Great Falls Heritage, Inc. of Great
Falls, Virginia, and Fairfax County Park Au-
thority of Fairfax, Virginia

Merit Awards

Tysons Corner Shopping Center Expansion,
Tysons Corner
(Commercial, retail)
RTKL Virginia Corp-Architects of Dallas, Texas,
and Lehndorff Group of McLean, Virginia

Center for Innovative Technology, Herndon
(Institutional)
Arquitectonica International Corporation of
Coral Gables, Florida, Ward/Hall Associ-
ates, AIA of Fairfax, Virginia, and Innovative
Technology Authority of Herndon, Virginia

Westfields International Conference Center,
Westfields
(Conference center)
Perkins & Will of Washington, D.C., and Westcot
Limited Partnership of Fairfax, Virginia

Westfields Corporate Center, Westfields
(Streetscape)
LBA Limited of Fairfax, Virginia and Westfields
Corporate Center Associates of Westfields,
Virginia

Honorable Mention

Software A.G. of North America Headquarters,
Reston
(Commercial, office)
Stephenson & Good of Washington, D.C.,
Donnally, Donnally Associates of Bethesda,
Maryland, and Software A.G. of North
America of Reston, Virginia

Chantilly Country Club, Centreville
(Adaptive reuse)
Dewberry & Davis of Fairfax, Virginia, and
Chantilly National Golf and Country Club of
Centreville, Virginia

BIBLIOGRAPHY

Books

Alexander, Brian, ed. A History of the Faeirfax County
Park Authority. Fairfax , Virginia.: Division of
Historic Preservation, Fairfax County Park
Authority, Revised July 1982.
Dawson, Grace. No Little Plans: Fairfax County's
PLUS Program for Managing Growth. Washing-
ton, D.C.: The Urban Institute, 1977.
Discover Your Regional Parks: 30 Year Anniversary
Issue. Fairfax Station, Va.: Northern Virginia
Regional Park Authority, 1989.
The Fairfax County Planning Horizons: The Comprehen-
sive Plan for Fairfax County, Virginia. Draft.
Fairfax County Office of Comprehensive
Planning, 1991. Six volumes.
Garreau, Joel. Edge City: Life on the New Frontier.
New York: Doubleday, 1991.
Goodale, Thomas L., and Godbey, Godfrey. The
Evolution of Leisure: Historical and Philosophical
Perspectives. State College, Pa.: Venture Pub-
lications, Inc., 1988.
Growing Together: 35 Years of Excellence. Fairfax, Va:
Fairfax County Park Authority, 1986.
Hodgkinson, Harold L. Fairfax County: Its Educa-
tional System in Context. Washington, D.C.:
The American Council on Education, 1987.
Netherton, Nan. Clifton: Brigadoon in Virginia.
Clifton, Va.: Clifton Betterment Associa-
tion, 1980.
Netherton, Nan. Reston: A New Town in the Old
Dominion. Norfolk, Va.: The Donning Com-
pany, 1989.
Netherton, Nan, and Rose, Ruth Preston. Memo-
ries of Beautiful Burke, Virginia. Burke, Va.:
Burke Historical Society, 1988.

Netherton, Nan; Sweig, Donald; Artemel, Janice; Hickin, Patricia; and Reed, Patrick. *Fairfax County, Virginia: A History*. Fairfax, Va.: Fairfax County Board of Supervisors, 1978.

Netherton, Ross, and Netherton, Nan. *Fairfax County in Virginia: A Pictorial History*. Norfolk, Va.: The Donning Company, 1986.

Regardie's Report. *Fairfax County, VA: How the Travel Industry Affects the Local Economy*. Washington, D.C.: December, 1989.

Rust, Jeanne Johnson. *A History of the Town of Fairfax*. Washington, D.C.: Moore & Moore, 1960.

Schneider, Lottie Dyer. *Memories of Herndon, Virginia*. Marion, Va.: Privately published, 1962.

Steadman, Melvin Lee, Jr. *Falls Church: By Fence and Fireside*. Falls Church, Va.: Falls Church Public Library, 1964.

Stuntz, Connie Pendleton, and Stuntz, Mayo Sturdevant. *This Was Tysons Corner, Virginia Facts and Photos*. Vienna, Va.: Privately published, 1990.

Stuntz, Connie Pendleton, and Stuntz, Mayo Sturdevant. *This Was Vienna, Virginia Facts and Photos*. Vienna, Va.: Privately published, 1987.

Whitt, Jane Chapman. *Elephants and Quaker Guns: A History of Civil War and Circus Days*. New York: Vantage Press, 1966.

Wrenn, Tony P. *Falls Church, Va.*: Falls Church Historical Commission, 1972.

Periodicals

Annual Reports. Vienna, Va.: Fairfax County Chamber of Commerce, 1984-1990.

Annual Reports. Vienna, Va.: Fairfax County Economic Development Authority, 1980-1989.

Annual Report 1990. Fairfax Station, Va.: Northern Virginia Regional Park Authority, 1991.

Business Reports. Vienna, Va.: Fairfax County Economic Development Authority. Published periodically, various subjects, since 1981.

Classes, Etcetera. Fairfax, Va.: Fairfax County Recreation Department, quarterly since 1964.

Facts for Voters. League of Women Voters of the Fairfax Area, 1990. Annually.

Fairfax County Citizens Handbook. Fairfax, Va.: Office of Public Affairs, 1990.

Fairfax County Economic Development Authority. Information sheets. *Community Resources, Economic Overview, Educational Resources, Housing, Labor Market Profile, Population and Demographics, Quality of Life, Transportation*. Vienna, Va.: Fairfax County Economic Development Authority, 1985—.

Fairfax County Profile, 1990. Fairfax, Va.: Office of Research and Statistics, 1991.

Fairfax County, Virginia. Fairfax County Chamber of Commerce. Biennial since 1983.

The Fairfax Journal.

Fairfax Newsletter. Reston, Virginia. Biweekly since 1959.

The Golden Gazette. Fairfax, Va.: The Fairfax Area Agency on Aging. Monthly newsletter for senior adults.

Herrin, Sheryl L.; Kregel, Laura J.; and Smith,
Brad B. "Fairfax County." *New Dominion Magazine*, September 1989.

League of Women Voters for the Fairfax Area. *Bulletin*. Monthly newsletter with occasional issue papers.

Lisbeth, Robert L. "Fairfax County Post Office and Postmasters, 1774-1890." Historical Society of Fairfax, County, Va., Inc., *Yearbook*, 1977.

Parktakes. Fairfax, Va.: Fairfax County Park Authority. Quarterly, 1985—.

Partners in Education. Newsletter for the business and professional communities. Fairfax County Public Schools. Quarterly.

Scientific American. September 1980.

This Month: A Free Calendar of Events. Fairfax, Va.: Fairfax County Public Library, 1988—.

The Washington Post.

I N D E X

A

A.J. Dwoskin Associates, Inc., 66
Accotink, 17, 20
Adopt-A-School, 66
Advanced Technology, 42, 66
Aetna, 49
AFCEA, 56
air and water pollution, 37
Air France, 35
air passengers, 33
air show, 106
airlines, 33
Alexandria, 13, 14, 15, 16, 17, 22, 106
Alexandria, Barcroft & Washington (AB&W), 23
Alexandria Light & Power Company, 24
Alexandria, Loudoun & Hampshire Railroad, 15, 34
Alexandria Water Company, 30
Alexandria-Leesburg Turnpike (Route 7), 31
Alvin Ailey Dancers, 59
amenities, 33, 36, 50, 75
American Alliance for Health, Physical Education, 46
American College of Radiology, 56
American Council on Education, 66
American Heart Association, 73
American Institute of Architects, 92, 99
American Legion, 76
American Legion Bridge, 32
American Press Institute, 46
American Society of Landscape Architects, 92
Annandale, 68, 75
Annandale Festival of the Arts, 62
annexation suits, 34
Annual Valor Awards, 79
Aqueduct Bridge, 15
Arabian Data Systems, Inc., 63
archaeological resources, 54, 88, 90
Architectural Review Board (ARB), 90
Aries helicopter, 78
Arlington, 106
Artists United, 116

Arts in the Parks, 103
Association of Community College Trustees, 63
Astroturf, 104
AT&T, 28, 42, 43, 44, 61, 66, 112
Atlantic Research Corporation, 66
Automobile Club of America, 22
automobiles, 27
Awret, Azriel, 116, 117
Ax, Emanuel, 59
Ayr Hill, 74

B

Bailey's Crossroads, 38, 54, 62, 75
Baltimore & Ohio Railroad, 15
Barbe, Serge, 19
Barton, Clara, 16
Battle of Chantilly, 16
Battle of Manassas, 16
Barns of Wolf Trap, 113
Bay Ridge Riding Stables, 102
BDM International, Inc., 42, 51, 57, 61, 66, 112, 136, 137
Beckner, William C., 103
bedroom community, 38, 41, 95
Bell Atlantic (C&P), 28
Belote, Melissa, 104
bicentennial project, 88
"Black Jack", 77
Black Women United, 76
Bloomingdales, 42, 44
Blue Ribbon Committee, 38, 39, 51
Board of Supervisors, 22, 30, 31, 34, 37, 41, 45, 46, 50, 53, 55, 56, 57, 63, 72, 74, 84, 88, 90, 96, 103, 112
Boeing Computer Services, 42, 112, 116
Bohen, Dolores, 64
bomb threats, 77
bond referendum, 34, 91
Brentano's, 29
Brinckerhoff, Parsons, 50
British Airways, 35
Broadcast News, 73
Brookfield, John, 91
Brown, J. W., 19
Brown's Hardware, 19, 75
BTG, 56
Buchanan, James M., 61
Buckley Brothers, 73
Buckley Brothers Store, 89
Buddhist, 76
Bull Run Country Jamboree, 106
Bull Run Power Company, 24
Bull Run Regional Park, 107
Bull Run Stone Bridge, 83
Bull Run/Occoquan Regional Parks, 106
Bull Run/Occoquan River watershed, 104
Bulletin, 72
Burke, 20, 33, 73, 75
Burke Centre, 46, 73, 75, 76, 96, 104
Burke Centre Partnership, 96
Burke Lake, 102, 103
Burke; King's Park Library, 68
Burke's, 15
buses, 23
Business and Professional Women, 76
business investment, 38
Business/Industry Advisory Council (BIAC), 64, 67
Byrd, Harry, 22
Byrd Road Act, 21, 22

C

C&P Telephone Company, 20, 28, 62, 66, 112
C.J. Shepherdson, Sr., 46
Cabell's Mill, 83, 91
Callahan, Vincent F., Jr., 81
Cambodian language publications, 71
Cameron Run Regional Park, 110
Camp Russell Alger, 18
Cancer Society, 73
Cantone, Joseph, 61
Capital Beltway, 31, 32, 45, 46, 51
Capital Centre organization, 104
carpooling, 32
Carr, Edward R., 45
Carthage Foundation, 61
Catherine Filene Shouse Endowment Fund,
    113
Cecchi, Giuseppe, 75
Centec, 46
Center for Business and Government Services,
    62
Center for Innovative Technology, 60, 61
Central America, 74
Central Intelligence Agency, 36
Centreville, 14, 15, 54, 75, 84, 91
Centreville High School, 66
Centreville Historic District, 90
Chain Bridge, 15
Chain Bridge Road (Route 123), 31, 89
Chamber of Commerce's Tourism Committee,
    91
Chantilly, 17, 33, 75
Chantilly Bible Church, 92, 93
Charles E. Smith Company, 50
Charles G. Koth Charitable Foundation, 61
Charles P. Johnson & Associates, 93
Chesapeake & Ohio Canal Company, 15
"Chesapeake Bay Ordinance", 56
Christ Church, 17
Christian churches, 76
churches, 17, 45
citizens advisory committees, 79
Citizens Advisory Council, 79
Civil War, 16, 18, 27, 83, 90
Clarence Robinson Trust, 61
Classes, Etc., 72
Claude Moore Colonial Farm at Turkey Run, 83
Claude R. Lambe Charitable Foundation, 61
Clay, Edwin S., III, 69
Clerk of the Circuit Court, 88
Clifton, 15, 17, 19, 20, 34, 69, 73, 83, 89
Clifton Historical District, 73
Clifton Hotel, 19
Colchester, 14
Colvin Run, 102
Colvin Run Mill, 16, 83, 91
Colvin Run Miller's House, 83
commerce, 13, 15, 22, 25, 27
commercial services, 32
commercial space, 29
commercial-industrial development, 50
Committee of 100, 72
Committee to Study the Means of Encourag-
    ing Industrial Development, 38
communications, 27
"Communities of Excellence" Award, 54
Community Business Centers, 54
Community Cultural Center, 62
Community Development Block Grants, 74
community service programming, 62

community services, 73
commuter, 17, 23, 32
Comprehensive Plan, 54, 56, 91, 96
comprehensive planning process, 90, 92
Computer Sciences Corporation, 42, 66
Comsat Telesystems, 42
Concorde, 35
Conrad, Suzanne H. Paciulli, 62
conservation, 96
Continental Telephone, 28, 69
Control Data Corporation, 62
Coopers & Lybrand, 112
County Council of PTAs, 72
county court, 17
county executive form of government, 29
county government office complex, 49
county jail, 67
county manager form of government, 29
Countywide Plan, 37, 38
courthouse, 14
Creekman, Tod, 88
Crestar Bank, 112
crime rate, 33
Crime Solvers, 79
Cumbie, Stephen M., 61
Cunningham, Ann Pamela, 84

D

dairy, 17, 22, 93
dairy farming, 15, 22
Danforth Foundation, Inc., 61
Darrell Winslow, 110
Datatel, 56
David H. Koch Charitable Foundation, 61
Defense Systems Management College, 29
Department of Environmental Management,
    51
developers, 88
Dewberry, Sidney O., 34, 51, 81
Dewberry & Davis, 34, 49, 51, 52, 54, 93
DeWitt Army Community Hospital, 80
Digital Equipment Corporation, 66
District of Columbia, 16
Division of Historic Preservation, 91
Doag Indians, 106
Downs, Joseph P., 103
Downtown Heritage Preservation District, 74
Downtown Reston, 46
downzone, 50
Dr. George W. Johnson, 61
drainage problems, 37
Dranesville, 75
Dranesville Tavern, 91
Drewer, Milton L., Jr., 81
drought (1951-1954), 31
drug abuse centers, 67
Dulles Access Road, 31, 32, 46
Dulles Airport terminal, 83
Dulles Corner, 92
Dulles International Airport, 33, 35, 48, 74, 75,
    91, 102, 104
Dulles South Industrial Area, 49
Dulles Toll Road, 49
Dunn, Bernard J., 61
DuVal, Clive L., II, 81
Dyncorp, 66, 112

E

E Systems, 43
East Suburban Center, 49

economic development program, 38
Edsall's, 15
education, 22, 33, 59
Edward R. Carr Associates, 45
Eero Saarinen, 33
electric railway, 17, 22, 33
Electronic Data Systems, 66
Elizabeth Hartwell, 111
Emery, Li, 92
Emhart PRC and ATI, 112
Engineers and Surveyors Institute (ESI), 51
"English as a Second Language", 63
environmental issues, 33, 37, 73, 96
Ernst, Dr. Richard J., 62, 63
ethnic diversity, 71
ethnic population, 77
express bus service, 49
express buses, 32
expressways, 31
Extended Learning Institute (ELI), 62

F

Facts for Voters, 72
Fair Lakes, 49
Fair Lakes Office Building, 49
Fair Lakes Office Park, 56
Fair Lakes One, 48
Fair Oaks, 49, 53
Fair Oaks Hospital, 80, 81
Fair Oaks Mall, 50
Fair Oaks Shopping Center, 51
Fairfax, 20, 24, 28, 54, 73, 74, 76, 84, 106
Fairfax Choral Society, 112, 116
Fairfax City, 69, 74
Fairfax City Hall, 75
Fairfax County Chamber of Commerce, 22,
    23, 25, 30, 39, 61, 79, 84, 120, 121
Fairfax County Citizen-of-the-Year Cup, 73
Fairfax County Citizens Handbook, 71
Fairfax County Council of the Arts, 72, 112,
    113, 116
Fairfax County Court, 88
Fairfax County Cultural Association, 112
Fairfax County Economic Development
    Authority, 38, 41, 42, 49
Fairfax County Exceptional Design Awards
    Program, 51, 92, 93
Fairfax County Extension Service, 76
Fairfax County Family Night at the Filene
    Center, 72
Fairfax County Federation of Citizens Associa-
    tions, 28, 72, 84, 116
Fairfax County Fire and Rescue Department,
    79
Fairfax County government, 61, 116
Fairfax County Government and Information
    Center, 50, 69
Fairfax County Heritage Conservancy, 92
Fairfax County History Commission, 84
Fairfax County Park Authority, 16, 72, 91, 103,
    104
Fairfax County Park Authority (FCPA), 96
Fairfax County Parkway, 46, 49
Fairfax County Police Department, 76, 77
Fairfax County Public Library, 67, 116
Fairfax County Public Schools, 63, 72
Fairfax County Water Authority, 31, 45
Fairfax County Public Schools Education
    Foundation, 66
Fairfax County Court House, 14, 15, 17, 74, 83
Fairfax Fair, 72, 104

Fairfax Fair Corporate Board, 62
Fairfax Herald, 17, 19
Fairfax High School, 112
Fairfax Hospital, 80
Fairfax Hunt, 102
Fairfax Journal, 72
Fairfax Planning Horizons, 56, 96
Fairfax Square, 44
Fairfax Station, 15, 16, 75
Fairfax Symphony, 73, 103, 112
Fairfax Town Hall, 19
Fairfax/Falls Church Community Services
    Board, 74
Fairfax/Falls Church United Way, 72
Fairview Park, 51, 80, 88
Falls Church, 14, 17, 18, 19, 20, 22, 24, 28, 29,
    69, 73, 74, 75, 104, 106
Falls Church Volunteer Fire Company, 74
Falls Church Water Company, 30
farm produce, 18
Farmers' Markets, 76
farming, 15, 16
Farsi language publications, 71
Fauquier County, 20
Faxfair Corporation, 72
Federal Aviation Administration, 33
federal housing, 24
Federal Systems Group, 112
Fendi, 44
Fenwick, Senator Charles, 35
ferryboats, 17
Feuer, Dorothy Farnham, 112
Filene Center, 113
fingerprint analysis, 77
Finley Administration Building, 60
fire, 29
fire protection, 28
First American Bank, 112
First American Bank of Virginia, 61
First Virginia Bank, 33, 112, 116
Fiscal Policy Advisory Commission, 38, 45
fishing, 15
Flakne, Joseph T., 110
Fleary, Dingwall, 115
Florida Rock Industries, 46
Floris Vocational Agricultural High School, 22
foreign-born students, 63
"Forging the Future of Education in Fairfax
    County 2010," 67
Fort Belvoir, 29, 53, 54
Fort Hunt, 110
Fort Marcy, 83, 110
Foundation for Research in Economics and
    Education, 61
Founders Award, 81
"Fountain of Faith", 116, 117
Franconia Associates, 46
Franklin Farm, 97, 99
Fred M. Packard Center, 116
Fredericksburg, 55
Freedom Hill, 83, 91
Freeman, Anderson, 20
Freeman Store, 74
Friends Meeting House, 89
Friends of the Library, 69
Frozen Dairy Bar, 71
Frying Pan Park, 83, 102
Fulton, James and Mary, 80
Furman, Alan B., 61
Furman, Arthur F., 61
FYI, 71

G

Galleria, 44
Galway, James, 59
garden, 17
garden clubs, 76
Garfinkel's, 29
George and Carol Olmsted Foundation, 62
George Mason College, 35
George Mason Institute for Science and
    Technology, 60
George Mason Regional Library, 68
George Mason Square, 75
George Mason University, 35, 51, 59, 60, 61, 72,
    72, 104, 109
George Mason University Foundation, 61
George Mason's Center for the Arts, 59, 112,
    117
George Mason's School of Law, 59
George Washington, 15, 101
George Washington Memorial Parkway, 32, 110
George Washington Parke Custis, 15
Georgetown, 15, 17, 22
Georgetown Pike, 89
Giant Food Store, 76
Gibbs, Joe, 81
Gibson, Annetta Hyde, 61
Golden Gazette, The, 72
golf courses, 104
Goodale, Dr. Thomas L., 110
Goose Creek reservoir, 31
Government Technology, 56
Governor's Commission to Study Historic
    Preservation, 91
Grange, 17
Great Falls, 13, 15, 16, 18, 75, 84, 91
Great Falls Canal, 83
Great Falls National Park, 110
Great Hunting Creek, 18
Greater Reston Arts Center (GRACE), 116
Greater Vienna Chamber of Commerce, 74
Green Spring Farm, 91, 102
growth policy, 53, 57
Grupo Folklorica di Argentina, 114
GTE Business Communications, 46
GTE Telenet Communications, 42
Gucci, 44
Gulf Reston, 46, 74
Gulledge, Charles G., 41, 81
Gum Springs, 22, 75
Gundry, Mattie, 22
Gunn, Burwell, 39
Gunnell's Chapel, 89
Gunston Hall, 83, 84, 91
Gunston Hall Plantation, 110

H

H-L Mall Venture, 44
Harris Charitable Foundation, 61
Hazel, John T., Jr., 61, 66, 81
Hazel, Virginia E., 81
Hazel, William A., 61
Hazel/Peterson Companies, 48, 49, 75
Hazleton Laboratories, Inc., 42, 66
Health Department, 80
"Heart in Hand," 73, 89
Hecht Company, 42, 44, 51
Hekimian Laboratories, Inc., 66
helicopter, 79
Hemlock Overlook, 106, 109
Hemlock Overlook Regional Park, 107

Hermitage, 19
Hennessy, Gerald, 16
Henry G. Shirley Memorial Highway, 31
Heritage Resource Management Plan, 91
heritage resource preservation, 90
heritage resources, 91
Hermes, 44
Hermitage, 19
Herndon, 17, 20, 28, 54, 69, 73, 74, 83, 104
Herndon, Captain William Lewis, 74
Herndon High School Marching Band, 74
Herndon Historical Society, 74
Heron House, 75, 90
Herrity, John, 41, 50
Hickory Hill, 89
high technology, 42
high-density development, 32
high-tech economy, 53
high-tech industries, 49
highways, 23
Hindu language publications, 76
Hirst, Omer L., 61
Hispanic population, 53
Hispanic Institute for the Performing Arts, 114
historic district, 84, 89, 90
historic landmarks, 50
Historic Landmarks Preservation Commission,
    84
historic preservation, 83, 90, 91, 92
historic preservation programs, 89
historic resources, 54, 89
Historic Vienna, Inc., 74
history, 83, 89, 90, 92
History Commission, 88
Hodgkinson, Dr. Harold L., 66
Holland, Edwin T., 33
Homart Development Corporation, 44
Honeywell, 66
Hope Park Mill, 83
Hospice of Northern Virginia, 73
Hospital Corporation of America, 81
Hoyt, Homer, 30
Hudson, William, 112
human resources, 28
human rights, 73
human services, 81, 96
Humphreys Engineer Support Center, 29
Huntington Metro station, 53
Huntley Meadows, 101
Hyatt Regency Hotel, 47, 49
Hybla Valley, 101

I

I-495, 32
I-66, 30, 33
I-95, 31
IBM Corporation, 62, 66
Inc. Magazine, 56
Industrially zoned land, 95
infrastructure,
    27, 30, 31, 32, 33, 34, 49, 50, 56, 57
INOVA Health Systems, 80, 166
Interim Development Control Ordinance, 37
International Children's Festival,
    113, 114, 115
International Developers, Inc., 75
Irving Group, 66
Islamic mosques, 76

J

Jefferson Hospital, 80
Jewish synagogues, 76
John M. Olin Foundation, Inc., 61
Johnson, George W., 81
Johnson, Joanne, 81
Johnson, Mike, 88
Junior Symphony, 103
juvenile detention centers, 67

K

Karate classes, 101
Kass-Berger, Inc., 29, 33
Kennedy Center, 60, 112
Kettler & Scott, 93
Key Bridge, 15
"Kids 'n' Cops", 77
Kidwell Farm, 102
King's Park Library, 68
kiosk libraries, 68
Kiwanis, 76
Koo, Bobby, 116
Koons of Manassas, 66
KPMG Peat Marwick, 112

L

la cicogna, 44
labor-saving machinery, 25
Lafarge Corporation, 56
Lake Accotink, 102
Lake Anne, 75, 90
Lake Anne Village Center, 46, 47, 90
Lake Braddock, 97
Lake Fairfax, 102, 103
Lake Occoquan reservoir, 109
Lake View Plaza, 56
land development, 28, 34
land-use planning tools, 24
landfill, 31
Landmark Systems, 56
Langley Fork Historic District, 89
Langley Ordinary, 89
Langley Toll House, 89
Langston Hughes Intermediate, 65
Lawrence, David, 29
Lawrence, E. C., 103
League of Women Voters, 28
League of Women Voters of the Fairfax Area,
      72, 73, 116
Lee Highway, 19
Lee, Richard Bland, 84
Lee, Robert E., 101
Leesburg Pike (Route 7), 19, 31, 44, 46
Legato School, 84
Legislative Information Services (LIS), 68
leisure services, 96
leisure time, 71
Lerner Development Company, 44
Lerner, Theodore N., 44
Lewinsville, 17
Lewis, James T., 81
libraries, 28
Library of Congress, 61
Lilly Endowment, Inc., 61
Lin Emery, 92
Lincolnia, 75
Lions, 76
Little Falls, 13
local government, 73
"Long Bridge," 15

Longfellow Intermediate School, 63
Lord & Taylor, 42, 44, 51, 154
Loudoun, 106
Loudoun County, 45
Lucas Aerospace, 56
Lynch, Edwin, 61
Lynde & Harry Bradley Foundation, 61

M

Mackall House, 89
Macy's, 44, 45, 46
Manassas Gap Railroad, 15
manufacturing, 16, 17
Mark and Catherine Winkler Foundation, 61
Marriott Corporation, 54
Marriott Hotel, 44
Marsalis, Wynton, 60
Martha Washington Branch Library, 116
Martin Marietta Corporation, 66
Mary Washington, 18
Maryland and Virginia Milk Producers
      Association, 22
Mason magazine, 61
Mason District, 103
Mason District Park, 103
Mason Neck State Park, 110
Mason Neck Wildlife Refuge, 110
mass transit, 32
Massey Building, 34, 84
Massey, Carlton, 29
master plan, 30
Mathy, Sonny, 61
Matrek Division of MITRE, 42
Matrin Organization, 93
Matthews, Frank, 113
McCord, Robert E., 112
McDonalds Corporation, 103
McGrath, Bob, 115
McHugh, Francis Dodd, 29
McHugh Master Plan, 29, 30, 36, 37
MCI, 28
McKee, Herbert, 62
McLean, 75, 76, 104
McLean Community Fire Association, 28
McMahon, Toni, 115
Meadowlark Gardens, 106, 109
Meadowlark Gardens Regional Park, 108
media centers, 48
Media General Cable, 61, 62, 66, 69
Medianet, 69
Meloy Laboratories, 42
Melpar Division of E Systems, 42, 43
Merrifield, 17, 54
Merrill Lynch, 44
Merton Church, 20
Mess, Walter L., 106
Metro, 30, 32, 33, 55
Metropolitan Area Transit Authority (WMATA),
      32
Mid-Atlantic Coca-Cola, 66
Military personnel, 54
Miller's House, 91
Milles, Carl, 116, 117
milling, 17
mills, 16
Mitre Corporation, 61
Mobil Corporation, 41, 42, 50, 56, 61,
      62, 80, 116
Mobil Foundation, Inc., 61, 112
Mobile Intensive Care Units, 80
Mohasco Corporation, 49, 56

Montgomery Ward, 46
Moody's Investors Service, 34
Moore, Audrey, 50
moratorium, 37
Morton's, 44
"Mount Murtagh," 31
Mount Vernon,
      14, 18, 22, 76, 83, 84, 91, 101
Mount Vernon area, 68
Mount Vernon Hospital, 80, 166
Mount Vernon Ladies' Association of the
      Union, 84
Mount Vernon Recreation Center, 100
Movement for Children, 101
Mueller, Judith, 81
municipal bond market, 34

N

National Aeronautics and Space Administra-
      tion (NASA), 46
National Archives, 61
National Association for the Advancement of
      Colored People (NAACP), 116
National Endowment for the Arts, 116
National Gold Medal award, 103
National Health Laboratories, 42
National Institutes of Health, 61
National Marie Y. Martin Chief Executive
      Officer award, 63
National Memorial Park, 116, 117
National Merit Semi-finalists, 63
National Park Service, 72
National Recreation and Park Association, 110
National Register of Historic Places, 46, 89
National Society of Colonial Dames, 84, 110
National Trust for Historic Preservation,
      84, 99
Native American archaeological sites, 90
nature centers, 102
Navy Elementary School, 81
NEC America, 66
Neighborhood Watch, 77, 79
Network of Entrepreneurial Women, 76
New Town, 46, 83
"New Town" concept, 32
Newington, 32
newspapers, 72
Nickum, Wayne, 73
Nieman Marcus, 44, 45, 154
Nordstrom, 42, 44, 154
Norfolk Southern, 55, 74, 89
Northern Virginia Building Industries Associa-
      tion, 116
Northern Virginia Chapter of the Associated
      Builders and Contractors, 50
Northern Virginia Community Appearance
      Alliance, 51, 92
Northern Virginia Community College,
      35, 62, 116
Northern Virginia Community College
      Educational Foundation, 62, 66
Northern Virginia Community Foundation, 81
Northern Virginia Graduate Center, 61
Northern Virginia Institute, 61
Northern Virginia Model Railroaders, 74
Northern Virginia Regional Park Authority,
      91, 104, 107
Northern Virginia Theater Alliance, 113
Northern Virginia Youth Orchestra, 112

Northern Virginia Youth Symphony Association, 116
Norton, Bob, 88
nursing homes, 67

O

Oak Marr, 101
Oak Marr Recreation Center, 100
Occoquan, 14
Occoquan Basin, 50
Occoquan Brick Kiln, 83
Occoquan Reservoir, 104, 106
Occoquan River, 13, 18, 29, 50, 79
Office of Comprehensive Planning, 84, 92
Office of Public Affairs, 71
"Old Potomac Path," 15
Omer L. Hirst-Adelard Brault Expressway, 46
O'Neal, William, 116
open space, 50
Optimists, 76
Orange & Alexandria Railroad, 15, 16
Orbital Services, 56
Orkney Springs, 112
Otis, Harrison G., 19
Outdoor Recreation Study Commission, 84

P

Packard, Fred, 91
park, 91
Park Authorities Act, 96
park resources, 54
parking, 29
parks, 45
Parktakes, 72, 103
Partners in Education, 72
Patowmack Canal, 15
Patriot Center at George Mason University, 104
Patrons of Husbandry, 17
"Pause for Planning", 38
Penney's, 46, 51
Perlman, Itzhak, 59, 60
Pfohl, Dr. James Christian, 113
Philip Arnow Foundation, 116
physical facilities, 27
Piatti, Primi, 44
Piedmont Milk and Produce Association, 17
planned development, 93
"planned development communities," 36
Planned Land Use System (PLUS), 37, 56
planning, 28, 36
planning and zoning, 36
Planning Commission, 30
planning process, 89, 91
Planning Research Corporation (PRC), 42, 61, 62, 147
planning studies, 84
Pohick Bay, 105
Pohick Bay Regional Park, 111
Pohick Church, 17, 83
Pohick Regional Library, 68
police, 28
Police helicopters, 76
police protection, 29
Policy Advisory Commission, 39
Pope-Leighey House, 83, 84
population, 14, 15, 16, 17, 18, 20, 25, 28, 30, 32, 33, 63, 71, 74
Potomac, 15, 18, 55
Potomac Canal, 84

Potomac Fruit Growers Association, 17
Potomac River, 13, 15, 31
power, 33
Powhatan chiefdom, 106
Prince William County, 13, 20, 45
Proctor & Gamble Company, 61
"proffer system," 50
Prohibition, 21
property taxes, 38
property values, 32
Providence, 14, 101
Providence Recreation Center, 100
PTAs, 76
public education, 21
public facilities, 36, 96
public health department, 20
public health service, 29
public improvements, 55
Public Safety Communications Center, 76
public schools, 73
public works projects, 25
Publications, 72
Pulsecom Division, 42

Q

Quakers, 15
Quintron, 56

R

Racame, Flight Nurse Nancy, R.N., 78
railroad, 15, 17, 89
railroad bridges, 15
railroads, 16, 20, 22, 23
Ramos, Anita, 102
rapid transit rail, 49
Ravensworth, 15
real estate agencies, 18
records, 88
Recreation programs, 96
recreation resources, 54
Redevelopment, 56
Redskin Park, 104
regional shopping mall, 29, 33
Reilly, Philip, 39
residential development, 95
residential subdivisions, 29
residential taxpayers, 38
Resource Management Districts, 56
Reston, 17, 25, 32, 34, 36, 37, 46, 47, 53, 56, 69, 73, 74, 75, 76, 77, 83, 90, 104, 113
Reston Chorale, 113
Reston Community Center Theatre, 113
Reston Community Players, 113
Reston Land Corporation, 46, 74, 75
Reston Land Corporation's population, 75
Reston Town Center, 47
Reston Triathlon, 75
Restonians, 75
Reston's Lake Anne Village Center, 90
Reston's Town Center, 46
retail business, 27, 33
retail development, 42
rezoning, 29
Richmond, 55
Richmond, Fredericksburg & Potomac Railroad, 45
Riverbend Park, 102
road building, 22
roads, 13, 15, 17, 18, 20, 21, 22, 24
Robinson, Charles, 91

"rolling roads", 13, 14
Rose Hill, 75
Rotary, 76
Route 1, 54
Route 1 Corridor, 53
Route 28, 49
Route 50, 51
Routing Technology Systems, 56
RTKL Associates, 47, 50
Rural Electrification Administration, 24

S

Saks Fifth Avenue, 44, 45
Sallie Mae, 66
Sandy Run, 106
Sandy Run Regional Park, 95, 109
Sarah Scaife Foundation, Inc., 61
Satellite Business Systems, 42
Schneider's store, 20
school bus fleet, 63
school foundations, 66
school transportation, 22
schools, 17, 18, 21, 22, 28, 29, 45, 88
scientific farming, 17
sculpture, 116
Sears Roebuck, 51
Seminary, 15
senior citizens, 67
sense of community, 72
Seven Corners, 27, 29, 33
Seven Corners Market, 27
sewage, 24
sewage treatment facilities, 31
sewer, 29, 33, 45
sewer moratorium, 36
sewer system, 30
Sherwood Regional Library, 68
Shirley, Henry,, 23
Shirley Memorial Highway, 29
shopping centers, 45
Shouse, Jouette, 112, 113
Sideburn, 15
Sikh, 76
Simon, Robert E., Jr., 32, 46
Sky Courier, 46
Skyline Center, 38
slums, 33
Smith Richardson Foundation, 61
Smithsonian Institution, 61
soccer fields, 105
Software AG, 56
solid waste, 31
Sony Corporation, 66
South Run, 101
Southern Railway, 45
Sovran Bank, 112
space station program, 46
Spanish language publications, 71
Spanish-American War, 18
Sperry Corporation, 42
Sperry Systems, 46
Spillane, Dr. Robert R., 64
Spring Hill, 101
Springfield, 15, 32, 33, 45, 46, 53, 54, 75, 76
Springfield Art Guild, 116
Springfield Bypass, 46
Springfield Mall, 46, 76
Springfield/Newington area, 49
Sprint, 28

Spyrison, Joe, 88
St. Mary's Church, 16, 83
Standard & Poor, 34
Starr Foundation, 61
state and national awards, 84
steam trains, 17
steamboats, 15, 18
storm sewers, 28
strip development, 37
Strong Foundation, 66
Student Union I, 60
subdivisions, 24
"suburban bedroom" satellite, 29
Sully Plantation, 83, 84, 91, 103
Sully Station, 93
Sully Station Community Center, 92
Sunset Hills, 25, 34
swimming, 104
Swing, James, 19
Systems Center, Inc., 66

T

T.G. Bauer Associates, 56
TABS the robot, 78
Tandem Computer Corporation, 42, 46
Task Force on Comprehensive Planning and
    Land Use, 37
Tautron Corporation, 66
Taux Indians, 106
tax rate, 33
tax structure, 38
Telecommunications Center, 62
telephone, 20, 28
Terra Centre, 75
Terraset Elementary School, 65, 75
Thomas Jefferson High School, 64
Thomas Jefferson High School for Science and
    Technology, 51, 64, 116
Thompson, Dr. William Dove, 96
Thornton Station, 17
Tiffany & Company, 44
tobacco, 13, 14, 15
"Today is Tomorrow", 116
toll lanes, 46
Toups, John M., 81
Tourism, 44
townhouse, 36
traffic congestion, 37, 49
trail systems, 91
transportation, 18, 57
transportation facilities, 31
transportation management association, 49
transportation planning, 32
triathlon, 75
trolley, 17, 18, 20, 22, 23
TRW, 42, 49, 66, 112, 116
TRW Federal Systems, 49, 116
TRW Foundation, 61
turnpikes, 15
Tycon Tower, 44
Tysons Corner,
    14, 31, 32, 33, 42, 44, 45, 50, 53, 75
Tysons Corner Center, 42, 43, 44, 45
Tysons Corner I, 43
Tysons II, 44, 45

U

U.S. Corps of Engineers, 62
U.S. Department of Education, 62
U.S. Olympic Trials, 109

Udall, Stewart, 84
Unisys, 112
United Community Ministries, 72
United States Fish and Wildlife Service, 110,
    111
United States Geological Survey, 37, 46
University of Virginia's Division of Continuing
    Education, 61
Upton Hill Regional Park, 111

V

VA Limited Partnership, 61
van pools, 49
Vanguard Research, 56
Vernon K. Krieble Foundation, 61
Versar, Inc., 66
Vesper Island, 102
Veterans of Foreign Wars, 76
Vienna, 17, 20, 24, 28, 45, 68, 69, 73, 74, 76, 83,
    104
Vienna Choir Boys, 59
Vietnamese, 53, 71
"Virginia Byway", 89
Virginia Chamber Orchestra, 116
Virginia Commission for the Arts, 116
Virginia Community College System, 63
Virginia Concrete, 46
Virginia Department of Highways, 22
Virginia Department of Transportation, 49
Virginia Electric & Power Company, 24
Virginia Polytechnic Institute and
    State University, 61
Virginia Power, 62, 66
Virginia Public Service, 24
Viva! Vienna!, 74
Voluntary Action Center, 73
Volunteer fire departments, 79
volunteer firefighters, 76
Volunteerism, 73
volunteers, 81, 88, 103
Vuitton, Louis, 44
Vulcan Materials Company, 46

W

W&OD Railroad, 22
W&OD Trail, 106
Wakefield Chapel, 91
Walney, 91
Walter Mitty, 102
Warner Cable, 69
Warner-Amex Communications, 69
Washington, 17, 18, 20, 22, 23, 25
Washington & Arlington Railway Company, 17
Washington & Old Dominion Railroad,
    18, 24, 34, 74, 91
Washington & Old Dominion Railroad
    Regional Park, 74, 108, 109
Washington & Old Dominion Trail, 91
Washington & Virginia (W&V)—"The Arnold
    Line", 23
Washington Airports Task Force, 61
Washington, Alexandria & Mt. Vernon Railway
    Company, 17
Washington, Arlington & Falls Church Railway
    Company, 17
Washington Dulles International Airport, 55
Washington Gas Light Company, 47
Washington Metropolitan Area Transit
    Authority, 52
Washington Plaza, 90

Washington Post, 116
Washington Redskins, 104
waste disposal, 33
water, 29, 33, 45
water resources, 50
Weekly Agenda, 72
West Falls Church Metro, 30, 49
West Potomac High School, 95
West Springfield, 46
West*Group, 62, 112, 159
Westfields International Conference Center, 48
Westinghouse Airbrake Company, 43
wetland wildfowl refuges, 54
Wheelchair Race of Champions, 109
Wiehle, 20
Wilder, L. Douglas, 66, 81
wildfowl refuge, 102
William & Flora Hewlett Foundation, 61
William A. Hazel, Inc., 112
William A. Klene Architects, 93
Williams, Earle C., 51, 57, 61, 62, 81
Williams, Vern S., 63
Wolf, Congressman Frank, 39
Wolf Trap Farm, 112
Wolf Trap Farm Park for the Performing Arts,
    72, 110, 113
Wolf Trap Foundation, 72, 115
"Woman on a Hammock", 117
women, 21
Women's Center, 81
women's clubs, 76
Woodlawn, 83, 84
Woodlawn Plantation, 53, 84, 91
Woodrow Wilson Bridge, 32
Woodward & Lothrop, 29, 33, 42, 44, 51
Woolworth's, 29
workforce, 27, 28
World War I, 54
Wren, James, 17
Wright, Frank Lloyd, 84
Wygal, Fred, 113

X

Xerox Corporation, 61

Y

Yo Yo Ma, 60

Z

zoning, 84
zoning moratorium, 30
zoning ordinances, 36
zoning process, 84
Zonta, 76

ABOUT THE AUTHORS

Courtesy of the photographer, Rick Netherton

Ross and Nan Netherton moved to Fairfax County in 1951 and since that time have researched, recorded, and interpreted local and regional history. Their collaboration began in the 1960s with research on Fairfax County landmarks. In 1978, Nan directed and contributed to writing an 800-page history of Fairfax County. As historian in the county's Office of Comprehensive Planning, she headed its first inventory of historic buildings and started its photo archive. Meanwhile, Ross found time to work with national professional groups on historic and architectural preservation. Locally, the Nethertons serve as advisors to history commissions in Fairfax County and the City of Falls Church.

They are coauthors of pictorial histories of *Fairfax County* (1986) and *Arlington County* (1987), and in 1989 Nan was author of *Reston: New Town in the Old Dominion*, all published by Donning. She also is author or coauthor of histories of Burke and Clifton, Virginia, the Reston Players, the Fairfax County Public Library, the Mount Eagle estate, and Theodore Roosevelt Island. She has degrees from the University of Chicago and George Mason University. Ross, with degrees from the universities of Chicago, Michigan, and Wisconsin, has written widely on historic preservation law. Both are past presidents of the Northern Virginia Association of Historians.